LIMER

GAME OF MY LIFE

with David Byrne

HERO BOOKS

HEROBOOKS

PUBLISHED BY HERO BOOKS
LUCAN
CO. DUBLIN
IRELAND

Hero Books is an imprint of Umbrella Publishing
First Published 2023

Copyright © David Byrne 2023
All rights reserved

Without limiting the rights under copyright reserved above, no part of this publication may be reproduced, stored in or introduced into a retrieval system, or transmitted in any form or by any means (electronic, mechanical, photocopying, recording or otherwise) without the prior written permission of the publisher of this book.

ISBN 9781910827680

A CIP record for this book is available from the British Library

Cover design and formatting: jessica@viitaladesign.com
Photographs: Sportsfile and Limerick Leader

★ DEDICATION ★

To those who have gone before us who have missed this epic
Limerick hurling journey,
my grandfathers Vincent Byrne and Billy Higgins
my grandmother Bernie
my uncle Eamon
my cousin Tina

To the legendary Vivian Cobbe who kindly told his story in
this book, but sadly passed away before publication

To all those who have worn the famous green and white,
and to Limerick supporters all over the world

★ CONTENTS ★

VIVIAN COBBE 9

MOSSIE DOWLING 17

ÉAMONN GRIMES 25

PAT HARTIGAN 32

TOM RYAN 42

ÉAMONN CREGAN 49

DAVID PUNCH 59

JIMMY CARROLL 67

PAULINE McCARTHY 75

GER HEGARTY 85

CIARÁN CAREY 91

MIKE HOULIHAN 100

PADDY KELLY 106

JOE QUAID 115

GARY KIRBY 123

BRIAN FINN 132

MARK FOLEY 139

TJ RYAN 146

MARK KEANE 153

OLLIE MORAN 160

NIALL MORAN 168

ANDREW O'SHAUGHNESSY 175

BRIAN BEGLEY 181

STEPHEN LUCEY 187

DAMIEN REALE 193

DAMIEN QUIGLEY 201

GRAEME MULCAHY 208

MIKE CASEY 215

DAN MORRISSEY 222

SEÁN FINN 230

★ ACKNOWLEDGEMENTS ★

WALKING UP THE steps of Croke Park on August 19, 2018, I, like the tens of thousands of Limerick supporters in GAA headquarters on that historic day, never in a million years thought what was about to unfold before our eyes was ever possible, never mind the years ahead and the unimaginable success that followed.

I am too young to fully remember the heartbreak of 1994 and '96, but old enough to remember the stories, and the many years of the pain thereafter, about those two mid-90 All-Ireland final defeats, and old enough to hold the memory of Limerick going almost 10 years – having won just two Munster Championship games in the decade – before the epic trilogy against Tipperary in 2007.

For that reason, it was really, *really* special to be able to tell and share these 30 legends' stories; a journey through the ages, of many years of ups, and unfortunately many years of downs, in a hurling county waiting and waiting to be unleashed.

The Limerick players, past and present, are the stars and heroes of this book. Their generosity, time, modesty, honest insight, and great humour, is something for which I'll be forever grateful. The 30 legends gave me their time over the past year or so, and I was really blown away by the response. It was a pleasure to meet with them and to be able to share their stories.

The fact that nine of these 30 legends chose a club match as their most memorable game really brings home what the GAA is all about – the parish and your local community.

I am genuinely humbled and privileged to have been given the opportunity to write this book. This is not only a story of our beloved game of hurling, but a story of resilience, a trait I find most endearing amongst Limerick people.

Thanks to Liam Hayes and Hero Books for again putting their faith in me. The ever-growing *Game of My Life* series is a fantastic way to remember the great GAA days for each county and I am honoured to get the call for a second time (after working with so many legendary Kerry footballers in the past).

Thanks to all the people who helped me track down our Limerick heroes. From the great contacts I've made throughout the years, to the club secretaries and PROs, the GAA community when it comes to doing something like this, really is special.

A special thanks to my amazing parents, Mike and Teresa, who gave me the platform and support from an early age to go on and do what I love doing now. They have been behind me every step of the way.

My thanks to my wonderful colleagues at *Kerry's Eye* who not only gave me the opportunity to work with a fantastic local paper but have supported me throughout this brilliant journey of putting together both *Kerry Game of My Life* and *Limerick Game of My Life*.

Thanks too to the great team at the *Limerick Leader*, especially former sports editor Donn O'Sullivan, who gave me a 'break' freelancing in 2016; along with current sports editor Colm Kinsella, who it is a pleasure to work with. It has been, and still is, a real privilege to report on county, Munster, and All-Ireland matches.

For me it is poignant that this book is out the same year as the 50th year anniversary of that famous All-Ireland win in 1973. Growing up, I remember my grandfather Vincent, or Vinnie as we'd more affectionately call him, talk with such pride about '73 and I'd often wonder if he'd ever see another Limerick All-Ireland win in his lifetime. He didn't. He died a young man of 66, in 2002.

And that's why 2018 was extra special for me. I am not religious or spiritual, but looking into the sea of green that day, and seeing what it meant to thousands of other Limerick supporters, it felt like he was there with us that day. It was a strange feeling, but one I'll never forget. The fact he is mentioned in this book, not once but twice, is very, *very* special to me.

What happened that day in Dublin is a wonderful memory from a historic day that will forever remain in Limerick people's minds and in our hearts forever more.

Long may this journey continue.

To the fantastic Limerick supporters… I hope you enjoy this book and great memories from eight different decades as much as I enjoyed putting it together.

Luimneach Abú.

David Byrne
September 2023

VIVIAN COBBE

LIMERICK 4-5 WATERFORD 3-5
Munster SHC Semi-Final
Cork Athletic Grounds
MAY 22, 1955

Vivian Cobbe (front row, second from left) got his senior career with Limerick off to a blistering start by hitting 2-3 on his debut

★ **LIMERICK:** P Cunneen; D Broderick, P Enright, J Keogh; E Noonan, D Kelly, Jack Quaid; M McInerney (0-1), Jim Quaid; A Raleigh, T Casey (1-0), **V Cobbe (2-3)**; P O'Malley (capt), E O'Malley, J Fitzgibbon (0-1). **Sub:** M Fitzgibbon (1-0) for Raleigh.

★ **WATERFORD:** J Murphy; N O'Connor, A Flynn, J Barron; M Queally, P Grimes (1-2), S Hayden; S Conlon, K O'Connor; M Flannelly (capt), T Cunningham, M Óg Morrissey (1-0); S Power (1-1), M Healy (0-2), C Ware. **Subs:** T Cheasty for M Healy, M Healy for T Cheasty, T Cheasty for Conlon.

★ GAME OF MY LIFE ★

THE ACTION

IT WAS A case of David vs Goliath in Cork when Limerick, for years the Cinderella of Munster senior hurling, ousted the far more fancied Waterford team, creating one of the biggest upsets in the provincial competition for many years. The game provided some exciting exchanges between two evenly-matched sides, and at no time was the scoring tally more than three points between the contestants, before 21-year-old left half-forward Vivian Cobbe turned the tide for Limerick at a vital stage of the game after Waterford had led by a point at the interval.

A product of Limerick CBS, Cobbe came into prominence when he won a Junior All-Ireland medal with the county in 1954. A year later, he made a glorious entry into senior championship fare, scoring 2-3 on his senior debut in the Cork Athletic Grounds on a glorious day on Leeside. By reason of his small stature, he favoured the policy of looking for the loose ball, tactics which he turned to great dividends, as any time he got possession an uninspired Waterford defence was always in trouble.

Cobbe's personal tally was a goal and a point in the first-half, and an early goal and two points in the second-half. Highlighting the St Patrick's clubman's impressive display was the headline in the following day's *Irish Independent* which said, *Cobbe brought about Limerick revival*. And that it sure did!

Despite Cobbe soloing his way through the defence for a smashing goal from 20 yards out Cobbe and Limerick trailed 2-2 to 2-1 at the break. Waterford went further ahead after the restart with a goal from Martin Óg Morrissey, but Limerick, boosted by the lively Cobbe, had other ideas. The 21-year-old Limerick forward notched a goal – his second – and two points in quick succession to give the Treaty men the lead once again.

A hectic second-half ended in a three-point win for Mick Mackey's charges. Limerick went on to surprise Clare to win the 1955 Munster Championship in the Gaelic Grounds – a day that will go down in the annals of Limerick hurling as one of the most glorious. The team, labelled 'Mackey's Greyhounds' after their legendary trainer Mick Mackey, were subsequently beaten by eventual champions Wexford in the All-Ireland semi-final.

★★★★★

> 66

THE MUNSTER SEMI-FINAL stands out for me… My first game really! We had won the Junior All-Ireland the previous year and a few of us got onto the senior team in 1955.

It was my first senior game for Limerick and I scored 2-3. That was the first round for us and we won the Munster final afterwards.

Clare had beaten Cork and Tipperary in the first round and the semi-finals, and we had beaten Waterford who were the weakest team in Munster. Clare were odds-on favourites and we beat them. We were seen as complete underdogs. It was a complete surprise… to us as well as everybody else. The final was a scorching Sunday in July.

It was a lovely feeling to be called up to the senior squad. As I said, it was my first game. I had played a Thomond Feis game before that, but I was picked for the championship then along with three or four others from the junior team. The Quaids were on it and all those lads.

Everyone called us Mackey's Greyhounds. Limerick hadn't won the Munster Championship for 15 years at that stage, since Mick Mackey's playing days.

They didn't win another then until 1973 – the year they won the All-Ireland.

They won a couple of Munsters after that but didn't win the All-Ireland again until recently. The current team are a great team. They are just marvellous! They are just lovely guys.

I was born in Laois… in Portarlington. My father moved down to Limerick when he got a job in the Board of Works, and we all moved down in 1942. I was eight at the time. We lived up in Mulgrave Street for 10 years, and that's probably where I got the interest in St Patrick's. They were the county champions in 1950 just before I started playing with them, but they haven't won it since.

And we never won it… we were beaten in three or four finals. But we had good teams!

There was no hurling in the family before me. My brothers played after. They played with Limerick as well. I picked up hurling in school. It all started in CBS there on Sexton Street. It was known for hurling in those days… but we never won the Harty Cup, of course! Éamonn Cregan and those lads came on a few years later in the school… in the 60s. That's where it all started… I picked up a hurley in CBS and then off I went down to St Patrick's.

It was a great feeling then to go on and play with Limerick. You'd be delighted at the time, but it only lasted four years. Of that time, it is that semi-final in 1955 that really stands out for me. But the final then was a complete satisfying sensation… nobody expected it, no more than we did.

There was no build-up to that game against Waterford in Cork. We just went down in cars. There were a few thousand there – that's all there was.

I remember my first goal that day. It was a mess in the square – there must have been 10 lads inside in the square and I just managed to tip it in. The other goal was a 21-yard drive. I got it from far out. It was a lovely feeling.

The game has changed so much now. We enjoyed it, but then you see all they are getting now with all these trips and everything… we got none of those. I like telling people that when I was playing, we managed to get a trip to Thurles, and that was about it… and twice to Croke Park.

There is a sense of pride having played with that team though because people keep bringing it up, but I suppose my name is unusual in the first place, so that's why people remember it.

My daughter is a physio in the hospital and there are auld fellas my age coming in and when she mentions her name, they ask her, 'Oh do you know your man?' They remember me because they saw me playing. They'd all be in their eighties like myself.

It's nice that they remember me.

I do remember scoring the goals against Waterford, but after that I don't remember much. It is more or less a blur. After that game in Cork we were inside in a hotel getting a meal – the usual stuff – and the waiter came over to me and he says, 'There is a fella on the phone. He wants to talk to you'. It was a reporter. He had never heard of me before. He wanted to know a bit about me. He was doing a story for the newspaper. That was a nice feeling. You don't expect those things.

I had expected to play the game, have a meal, and just go home. It ended up in the paper.

There are only a few of that 1955 team still alive. We met quite a few times down through the years. The Clare and the Limerick teams met at the 40th anniversary of us winning that game. Clare were in the Munster final that year. That was in 1995.

We had a meal in a hotel in Thurles. Both teams were brought to Thurles and put up in the best seats and brought onto the pitch. It was a great time. Everybody knew Mick Mackey back then. He was a great character. He was an ordinary guy, but good fun. He was always cracking jokes with the taxi drivers and that type of thing… good old times!

We had won the Junior All-Ireland in London in 1954.

We won the Munster Championship in Limerick, and then we got to the semi-final against Antrim in Croke Park. The final was played in London against London, and we beat them.

We got a huge reception when we came home because they hadn't won an All-Ireland for years… for 14 years or something like that!

The crowds were gathered around the train station and then they brought us in around the town. It was like the way All-Ireland celebrations are now. If we hadn't done well and won it that year, I probably wouldn't have got into the senior team the following year.

That was the start of it! It was all junior hurlers from the junior clubs in Limerick. It was my first year playing senior with St Patrick's so that's why I was eligible for junior. You had to be playing junior or be a senior playing in his first year. That's how I came into it.

I've some fond memories of playing with St Patrick's. They are a great auld club. I got a photograph taken with Gearóid Hegarty when the club gave us a presentation. He is a huge man compared to me; a lovely guy! That day, he came down to the field to get the presentation… and the same night all the underage – the under 6s, 7s, and 8s – were up training and Gearóid arrived in his car, got out of the car and took out a hurley, and went onto the field with the kids for about half an hour. He left us waiting, but, of course, we didn't mind! He was out coaching them. He was out on the field that day at seven o'clock at night playing with the kids, showing them what to do. You get hundreds of young kids down there on a Friday night now, both girls and boys. There was none of that in my time.

It is tough for gaelic games in the city. There is no gaelic games in the city, really. You've a few clubs, but they are all playing rugby. You go into town during the winter and the red Munster flags are up everywhere. They'll put the green and white flags up then when Limerick are playing in June and July, but once the rugby season starts again, the red ones are up. It is tough to compete with that. All the city kids end up playing rugby. That's why there are no real great teams in the city at the moment, with the exception of Na Piarsaigh. They are out on their own out there. I really greatly admire what Na Piarsaigh have done out there.

It is great to see what this Limerick team are doing now, what they do for the city and county is just amazing. And it is lovely to watch them! They play lovely hurling. Players these days are more skilful and their passing of the ball is just something else!

Looking back at my time, I found you'd never get a pass of the ball. Most guys were out for their own score to get their name in the paper.

I was always told in school by Brother Forrestall that what I had to do was to get loose, because I was small. But I found that, in inter-county in particular, when I was getting loose, I was getting no passes and the crowd were shouting at me, 'Why don't you mark your man?'

My policy was to get loose and get scores, but I couldn't if I wasn't getting the passes.

Brother Forrestall had me in second class in school. I met him years afterwards; the old All-Ireland hurlers had a get together up in Artane and he was up there at the time. I had a great chat with him. That was in the 70s.

When I picked on the senior Limerick panel, I got a letter from the county board. It said to let them know if I couldn't play. I was on the sub-panel in the previous year; in the autumn of '54, but I didn't make the team until the following year.

As Pat O'Reilly says to me one day, 'Don't you worry, your time will come in the summer'. That's back when we were playing the matches in the winter. And he was right! My time came! Pat was the chairman of the county board at the time. Before and after every match you used to get a letter from the county board.

It was great to get the first one… very proud!

My dad, Paddy used to follow the football in Laois. It was all football in Laois in those times.

I'd say it was a very proud moment for my father when I got to play with Limerick. He wouldn't say much but you could see it in his face. My mother, father, and Liam Moloney – he is dead now – used always meet at the matches together, even if we'd be playing Claughaun. Liam played with Claughaun but they'd always be together. And they'd have great craic, all of them.

It was great to win the Munster in '55, but of course we thought we were going to win the All-Ireland then! Wexford brought us down to earth very quickly. They were a great team.

I played for a few years and then I was dropped, and that was it. I was too small, basically. A lot of people were saying that at the time.

Ah, they were probably right in a way, but shortly after that I got married and I just played with St Patrick's after that. The way it was at the time, there were about 10 selectors on the county team and all most of those guys were interested in was getting someone from their own club in the team. That's what you were up against. That was a big problem in Limerick for years. I could see it coming. Everyone that was there had a man pushing for them. I didn't have anyone. St Patrick's never had a selector so I knew it was coming. I could see the writing on the wall.

We had some great days with the club. We were beaten in four senior county finals. Claughaun had a good team back then, we had a good team, and Treaty Sarsfields were good at that stage. Sarsfields won three senior county championships in-a-row from 1951. They beat us in the final in '52.

There were three good teams in the city at the time, and at one stage the city teams beat a pick of the county teams. But there was that rivalry between them, and it wasn't good. I knew it wasn't good. A lot of people from the county didn't want city people on the team. I knew that at the time, but we carried on. Eventually the young fellas in the city saw that and they didn't play – they gave up hurling! They started playing rugby or soccer, and the city teams went downhill. And they are still down! It is hard to get back from that.

Back when I was playing, we had three good senior teams, and Old Christians came along later. They took most of the players out of CBS, and that didn't do the rest of us any good either. We suffered from it anyway! That was a long time ago now, way back, so it is tough seeing the way the city teams are now because there is no sign of a city team coming up playing senior, apart from Na Piarsaigh.

The 1950s were good times. We had good teams, and good county teams as well. The county lads on the Limerick team were good friends. It was not so much the county lads on the team, but more so some of the supporters that created a city versus rural divide. I remember many a time after we were beaten in the Munster Championship; there were three or four city fellas on the county team, and we'd go out against a country team in the county championships with our clubs the following Sunday and we'd be slagged off from the sideline, just because we were from the city. That didn't help either.

The young lads could see that too. It was just a rivalry with the city.

They even had a law made… at the time the country clubs had a majority on the county board. Every club had to have a delegate, and they brought in a law at one stage declaring that the Gaelic Grounds was a home ground for all the city teams. There was a stage where we never got a match in the city.

When you think of all those barriers, it was great to have gone on and played with Limerick. There was nothing at all wrong with the country players, they were all good hurlers and good lads; the Quaids, and Donie Broderick from Dromcollogher who was a great friend of mine… all lovely lads! I liked the hurling when we played it.

It was a nice feeling that day against Waterford, that despite all those barriers I was able to go on and score 2-3 in a Munster semi-final. There were some good lads on that team. You had Liam Ryan, one of the Ryans from Cappamore, and you'd a good few lads from Kilmallock too; they were very good hurlers. We all got on very well together.

It was just great to go on and win that Munster title together in 1955.

I remember coming back into the Imperial Hotel in Limerick for a meal after the Clare match, and I cycled home on my bike after that. There were no mad celebrations. We didn't even meet afterwards. We just went in for a meal, had our meal, and just came home. There were no receptions or anything like that. We didn't expect to win it, I suppose! It wasn't a done thing in those days. We just got on with it. They felt we were going to win the All-Ireland and they said they'd wait to celebrate then. That's the way it was back then. I never got another chance to win Munster. We were beaten in the final in '56. We threw that one away. Christy Ring beat us that day.

99

MOSSIE DOWLING

LIMERICK 1-11 DUBLIN 2-9
National League
Croke Park
FEBRUARY 18, 1968

Mossie Dowling beats Kilkenny goalkeeper Noel Skehan in the 1973 All-Ireland final (including from left, Fan Larkin, Phil Cullen and Nicky Orr of Kilkenny, Ned Rea of Limerick and Pat Henderson of Kilkenny)

★ **LIMERICK:** J Hogan; J McDonagh, J Alliss, M Hoolan; T O'Brien (0-2), T Bluett, T Ryan; B Hartigan, S Quaid (1-1); É Grimes, **M Dowling**, É Cregan (0-4); L Hogan, L Grimes (0-1), B Savage (0-2). **Subs:** PJ Keane (0-1) for L Hogan, M Flaherty for Bluett.

★ **DUBLIN:** M Behan; N Doolan, F Moyles, C Brennan; W Markey, P Maycock, E McGrath; D Foley (0-1), B Cooney; B Galvin (0-2), E Davey (0-1), H Dalton (0-1); F Whelan (1-0), E Flynn (0-2), N Kinsella (1-2). **Sub:** A Boothman for Dalton.

17

★ GAME OF MY LIFE ★

THE ACTION

LIMERICK'S INTEREST IN the 1968 National League ended at the hands of Dublin – a single point in a cold, but dry, Sunday afternoon in Croke Park. Limerick came into this penultimate Division 1B clash with The Dubs, having drawn at home to Cork in their opening league game before suffering a heavy defeat to nearest neighbours Clare in Ennis back in November. This game was like a firework at Halloween, slow to get going but making quite the bang right at the end. In truth, Dublin, who showed vastly improved form since their five-point loss to Cork two weeks' previously, had so much control of the game but let at least four golden goal scoring opportunities go abegging.

The 1967 Leinster semi-finalists led by a point at the interval – 1-4 to 0-6 – with Eoghan Ruadh clubman Fran Whelan raising the green flag in the first-half.

Limerick equalised with a superb point directly from a '70' from Tony O'Brien immediately after the restart, but Noel Kinsella slammed home Dublin's second goal to open up a three-point lead.

As the Limerick midfield struggled to get a foothold on Des Foley in midfield, Dublin took control of the game and slotted over some vital scores. Limerick goalkeeper Jim Hogan, full-back Jim Allis, and right half-back Tony O'Brien were all impressive in defence however, allowing the visitors to come back into the game, boosted by an improved second-half performance from Bernie Hartigan, who battled hard in midfield, and the decision to push Séamus Quaid further up the field.

The lively Éamonn Cregan threatened in attack, but the Claughaun star was left regretting not going for goal when he twice sent the ball over the bar as the momentum started to swing in Limerick's favour. Goals were there for the taking, but Limerick's late comeback proved to be too little too late as Dublin held out.

In a poor league campaign, Limerick ultimately went on to lose 3-7 to 1-5 against Galway in their final group game, finishing bottom of the Division 1B table with just one draw to show from four games. The Shannonsiders' poor form continued into the championship as a five-point defeat to Cork in Thurles Sportsfield saw Limerick crash out of a heavily contested Munster SHC in the first round.

★★★★★

>

IT IS A league match that stands out for me – it was the first time I played in Croke Park. That is the biggest game for me!

It was my first time playing in Croke Park and the same night, my grandmother died. She died at five o'clock in the morning… before the game! We were up all night. She had been dying for about a week-and-a-half… she was 96 and she just decided it was time to go.

They all said to me, 'You will have to go to the match, she'd want you to be there'. But I don't think she was ever that interested because where she came from in West Limerick, hurling wouldn't be a big thing.

They all packed me off on the train anyway. The memorable thing about that was, there were four of us from Kilmallock in the Limerick panel – Bernie Savage, Mick Healan, Mike Flaherty, and myself. We got off then above at Heuston Station, and there was no such thing even as a car to Croke Park… we had to walk to Croke Park with the gear up on our backs.

That was our first introduction to it.

I had a small drop of whiskey before I left to settle the nerves! I was on Dessie Foley… we got into a bit of an altercation anyway! I pulled on a high ball and he got six stitches out of it. He used to always play football with Dublin, as well as hurling, and had a twin brother playing. They were two hard men!

I missed my grandmother's wake during that day. She was in the house during the day and when I came home, she was gone. That always sticks in my mind, that game – that was the big one! That was in February in 1968. The league started earlier on in those days – we used to have the league before Christmas.

Everyone's dream is to play in Croke Park. I had it in my head that day heading up to Croke Park that I hadn't slept. I hadn't slept for a couple of nights because my grandmother was progressively getting worse. I don't remember too much about the game itself – it was so long ago – but I do remember Foley was trying to bully me, and I decided that he wasn't going to.

I wouldn't normally be like that… I was awfully quiet altogether.

The same year, we were going down in the car to play Clare in Ennis and we were just coming to Shannon when a plane passed over. One of the selectors from

Kilmallock, Mick Leahy, said, 'See that plane, we'll be on that plane going to New York for the League final'. We had been going well in the league.

Next thing, the car broke down. We had to get out and thumb a lift to Ennis. One of the boys says back to Mick then, 'Go to New York?... We can't even get to Ennis, never mind go to New York!'

We had played a couple of matches and we were doing well in the league at that stage. Back then if you won your 'home' league final you played New York in New York in the final. We must have been doing well in the league to be thinking about going to New York. But we were lucky to get to Ennis first!

That league campaign then led on to me being part of the Limerick team that went on to win the All-Ireland in 1973.

I was dropped after 1968 but I came back on the panel again in 1970. Winning an All-Ireland was just massive because I was only after getting married the year before. It was huge. The Munster final was really special because it was so long since we had won a Munster final in Limerick. It made it even more special the fact it was Tipp we beat, in their own backyard.

It was great that year. Not only did we win the All-Ireland, but I captained Kilmallock to win the county title which was just a step below winning the All-Ireland, because it was a massive thing.

We hadn't played well the year before, and the year before that, and I more or less dragged them by the bootlaces.

The boys would be training and they would get tired and say they had enough of it, but I f***ed them all out of it one night... the trainer and everything, and I said, 'Ye either want to do it or I'm going home'.

So, the trainer said, 'If you think you can do better than me, I'm going'.

I said, 'Fine,' so I broke their hearts! They decided then that maybe there was something there worth training hard for. I called back to the trainer, Willie O'Brien, one night and I said to Willie, 'Come in and see what I am doing'.

I said, 'I want you to take over'. Willie came in one night and he kind of sneaked in and he was looking. He called me afterwards and said, 'I want to train them again. We'll win a county'.

I didn't want to train the team at all, but I wanted to show Willie what could be done. I told him he was too soft. He was giving the boys a way out constantly. Fellas would say they were sick or they were tired or they were after pulling something. I didn't care what muscle they were after pulling, they were training regardless.

Willie said to me, 'By Jaysus, if you thought you were tough, wait until you see what I'm going to do'. He broke their hearts and they were all saying, 'Oh Jesus, we want Dowling back again, he's not as hard as you!' To me that was a great honour as well, to be captain that year.

I don't know if it has happened since, but at the time Mick Mackey and myself were the only two in Limerick who won an All-Ireland and also captained their club team to win a county in the same year. If you look back on a lot of teams, it hasn't been done.

The train stopped at Birdhill on the way home after winning the All-Ireland final. That was something very special. It took hours to come into Limerick from Birdhill, because we were going at a snail's pace. We came across an old woman with sods of turf up on her pitch-fork. The sods were lighting, and she was running after the bus. That is something that will always stick in my head. I can still see her running down the road after us.

I was working that time out in Shannon. We were in the building trade. I was a carpenter. I'd be collected here in Kilmallock or I'd drive every second week. You'd leave here at 7am to go to work and you'd be working until 6pm. I'd pass out the Gaelic Grounds to come home to Kilmallock to change, before going back into Limerick again. You often wouldn't get home until 11 o'clock at night, and you still had to be in Shannon at 8am the next morning.

You grew up to play with Limerick and try to get in the team.

I'd be training in the middle of the winter. I remember one night I was training and it was snowing. I was out running on the road and this woman knocked on the door when we were living up town. My father came out. She said, 'Mick, do you know your young fella is running up the road up to Ballingaddy towards Kilfinane, and it's snowing?'

'Do you know he's out?'

'He can do what he likes,' says the father.

She thought I'd gone mad! But I thought it was a great night to be out training. That was the kind of dedication you had. But it wasn't really dedication at all because I loved training. The worse the weather, the more I liked being out in it. It could be p***ing raining and I'd say to the younger brother... 'Come on, we'll go up to the hurling field', and he'd say, 'Sure it's raining!'

'Sure, we'll only get wet,' I'd say to him. 'Nothing else is going to happen!'.

Before Mickey Cregan took over Limerick, Joe McGrath was there! Joe was before his time in a sense of the things he was doing. Joe was so fit he would lead the training on his own... out in front. Whereas a lot of the boys... I won't name them, but they are from Patrickswell... they would be dodging training constantly.

Them times, inside in the Gaelic Grounds, there was only one spotlight, so there were three dark corners. Now and then you'd see a fella coming out of the corner, skipping around trying to join the back of the group. Mickey had trained under Joe, so he knew the dark corners so nobody was allowed in that corner. The training was 10 times tougher with Mickey in a sense that it was army training. I loved training so I didn't mind how hard it got. I'd even train at home during the nights we weren't going into the Gaelic Grounds to be fit for the training. They are saying now, that the players these days are doing six or seven nights. We were doing that. If you wanted to be the top of your game you had to.

It had been 33 years since Limerick had won the All-Ireland when we won in 1973, and it took them 45 years to win it again. That's ridiculous, when you look at it. I don't think you'll ever again get a bunch of players like the group that are there now because of the dedication.

People would be saying that we were dedicated, the team that won it in 1973, but I don't think we were a patch on the current team.

But saying that, we were all working physical jobs so we were naturally fit. You were either a farmer, or you were working on the buildings. There were very few fellas in what we would call 'soft jobs'. We had natural strength, but nowadays they seem to go to gyms to build up that strength. Fellas weren't as big as they are now, but saying that they said our team was a very big and strong team.

There is huge pride, even talking about it now.

First of all, I was the first man in Kilmallock to win the All-Ireland. That was a big thing. They had won minor and junior in Kilmallock alright, which is a great achievement, but the senior was the big one. I thought it was the dream, and you'd be saying, 'Will the dream ever come true?' When it came, it was surreal. But then you'd be hoping it would last. It just comes so fast and it goes so fast, you hardly get time to think about it or enjoy it.

The hurling field was more or less at the back of our house growing up.

We were on the street and the hurling field was alongside us, only within 30 or 40 yards of us, so it was a case that you would have spent your whole time in the hurling field. We lived on a corner at the back of the pitch. We were within a strike of a ball of the field the whole time, and if we weren't in the field, we were out on the side of the road playing hurling against the wall.

When I was a young fella there were no walls around the ground like there is now. I remember my father giving them a hand to build the wall. It is proper ground there now. There was only a kind of a ditch, and bushes, around it when I was growing up.

There were a couple of great hurlers in Kilmallock at that time. You'd a fella called Mick Galvin. Mick was a fabulous, stylish hurler, something like Paddy Kelly. He went to England early though because there was no work here. He went to Birmingham and ended up playing hurling with Warwickshire.

There was a man called Vincy Cusack… you looked up to Vincy, but poor auld Vincy died when he was only 32. The day he died, there was a Munster final on. I came out from the house. Cork and Tipp were playing in Limerick. Vincy was walking across the road. There was a shop across the road, and he said, 'I'll see you in a minute, Mossie'. He'd had a hard night the night before and he was saying he must buy a bottle of lemonade. He was walking across the road, he was after drinking the lemonade, and he fell straight into my arms… dead as a doornail!

I went into the father and I said, 'I must get a chair and put Vincy onto it'.

'What's wrong?' says the father.

'He's dead,' I said.

'He couldn't be dead'.

I said, 'He is.'

There was a doctor about 100 yards down, Micky O'Connor. He'd bad legs on him and he sat into his Volkswagen and he drove up. 'Ah', he says. 'You called the wrong man'. It was the undertaker I should have called. I f**ked him out of it anyway.

He gave him an injection, but he was dead… in those days there was no such thing as doing mouth-to-mouth or anything like that. I was in my 20s at the time… 23 or 24! That was a huge shock in Kilmallock at the time. Vincy was a fabulous hurler. We'd a great club team at that time. I'd say there were no stars in it… we were all more or less even. There were some fellas as good, if not better, than I was that should have been on the county team. They were hard done by, a lot of them. Your face fits or it doesn't, and thankfully my face fitted.

At that time, we went 18 or 19 matches in-a-row with Kilmallock without being beaten… five or six years in-a-row without being beaten.

You'd never look back at the games you were expected to win, but the losses felt like such a big deal. I often read books there about other fellas and it is the games that they lost that stand out… they never talk about the wins. It is the losses that bug the brain!

We won the juvenile county final in 1962 – that was the start of it! We won the minor then in 1964 against Knockaderry. In 1967 then, we got to the under-21 final against Patrickswell, and we had seven or eight of the under-21 team on the senior team when we beat South Liberties in the county final that year. You are really going into the big time almost straight away. I had only turned 21 then and I started playing senior with Limerick and then I captained the team in 1966 so I thought all my stars had aligned. And then the following year, I got to play in Croke Park.

"

ÉAMONN GRIMES

SOUTH LIBERTIES 2-13 CLAUGHAUN 6-6
Limerick SHC Final
Gaelic Grounds, Limerick
DECEMBER 12, 1971

Éamonn Grimes and the Limerick team that defeated Kilkenny in the 1973 All-Ireland final

★ **SOUTH LIBERTIES:** J O'Connell; J Grimes, P Hartigan, B O'Riordan; M Grimes, W Shanahan, M Butler; **É Grimes (1-9)**, S Hartigan; T Ryan (0-1), L Grimes (0-1), M Shanahan; E Dooley (1-1), W O'Donoghue (0-1), D O'Sullivan. **Sub:** M Lundon for Ryan.

★ **CLAUGHAUN:** J Hogan; B O'Gorman, M Savage, S O'Connor; S McAuley, É Cregan (0-1), C Cregan; M Graham, D Sheehan (0-1); B Galligan, M Cregan (capt) (1-0), R Prendergast (1-0); A Dunworth (3-3), M Tynan, L Moloney (1-1).

THE ACTION

OUTHURLED FOR ALL but the closing eight minutes, cool, calm, and collective Claughaun smashed home two late goals to secure their ninth county senior hurling championship title in front of a huge crowd at the Gaelic Grounds.

South Liberties, who were in search of their first Limerick SHC title in 81 years, were the pacesetters and controlled the game for just over 50 minutes before being stung by two quick-fire goals that left them on the wrong side of the scoreboard when it mattered the most.

Not too often is the Man of the Match left collecting a runners-up medal, but Liberties, and the brilliant Éamonn Grimes, were left wondering just what could have been and what more they have to do to win the championship for the first time since 1890.

Once Claughaun edged ahead eight minutes from time, they were in never in a position to be caught and the city side showed their experience and class to hold out. With nine minutes remaining, the men in the famous green and gold were clinging tenaciously to a single point lead that should have, and could have, been a lot more. Despite the narrowest of leads, even the most optimistic of Claughaun supporters felt it was only a matter of time before Liberties would pull away again, given the fact they were hurling so well.

Claughaun, boosted by an unbelievable display of hurling by Andy Dunworth, normally a goalkeeper, had other ideas and with a shocking suddenness the floating Liberties bubble burst.

Having previously scored three goals in the first half with Dunworth twice finding the net from 21-yard frees, along with Michael Cregan, Claughaun went in front, 4-5 to 1-12, with eight minutes left on the clock. Micky Graham gained possession in midfield before passing it off to Ralph Prendergast, who popped in a great goal past John O'Connell to ensure Claughaun were back in business. With just five minutes to go, Liam Moloney scored Claughaun's fifth goal to put the city side four points ahead, 5-5 to 1-13.

Liberties' star Éamonn Grimes showed his class to burst past several Claughaun defenders before blasting into the net. This was to be Liberties' last score, however, and with the title already as good as Claughaun's, Dunworth got in for another goal with what was the last play of the game.

★★★★★

> 66

WE WERE IN four or five Eastern junior finals up to 1966, and then they decided in 1967 that we'd go Senior. We were beaten by Kilmallock in a county final replay. We had a good team back then. We won four county championships between that and the early 80s. It is a defeat that I remember the most!

That was the 1971 county final against Claughaun. We were beaten, but sometimes a game goes your way… and it did for me that day! We were just beaten by Claughaun but the following year then, we won the championship when we beat Patrickswell in the final.

As a result of that, I got the opportunity to captain Limerick and from an inter-county player's point of view, the following year, 1973, is memorable. It was 40 years prior to that the last time Limerick won the All-Ireland. What it brought to Limerick hurling, and Limerick people in general, was a new lease of life.

That loss in '71 gave us motivation to drive on the following year… absolutely, it did! We had a fine team…we had a great club team! Everything that followed might not have happened if it wasn't for '71… including me captaining Limerick to win that All-Ireland in '73. At the time the club could nominate someone to captain Limerick the following year.

There are days when you're playing and no matter what you do, it will never go right for you, but on that occasion in 1971 no matter what I did, whether it was left or right, the ball seemed to be dropping. I felt extremely gratified after the match that I played well. We lost that day, but it wasn't a mixed feeling because it definitely felt like it was the start of something. And it was… because we won four county championships after that. We knew we had the nucleus of a good team. We didn't have a big panel, but we had a brilliant panel. We'd fellas who'd stick their leg in, where you shouldn't even stick a hurley in.

I wouldn't have been the eldest in that team in 1971. I was playing with a few guys that were a good bit older and they relished the idea of even being in a senior county final for a second time, because we were there in 1967, and beaten, and four years later we were beaten in the final by Claughaun. The following year we went on to win the first of our senior championships, in 1972. There was a huge crowd in the Gaelic Ground that day in 1972.

We had a huge following at that time. Like any country clubs at the time, we had a watering hole in town that we'd go to after each game. At that time, it was John Joe O'Dea's. It was packed to capacity that evening after that game!

Still to this day, everyone on that team is one unit. We often meet. We were very close at that time. But you must remember, it was 51 years ago... jobs were scarce at that time! People didn't have the transport and the money that they have now to go to wherever they wanted. That situation was, for us at that time anyway, you go above to Maloney's field... and you cycled there; you didn't have a car. Some people did have a car the older they got, but we weren't too long out of school. The social aspect of life back then was the field, but now you have a different social side of it because people have jobs now, they have money, and they can travel and do their own thing.

I am not saying teams today aren't as close, they are in a different way, but now they can go different ways and go to different places. Before, we had a choice of one or two places, and those one or two places, apart from the hurling field, were Spellacy's Pub, or Willie Connells' and Keane's. That was it! A good few of them were fond of an auld jar!

Vincent Byrne was involved with us back then. He was a fantastic singer – Brendan Bowyer was his idol. When we used to go back over to Caherconlish, we used to call to a pub called Riordan's after all the matches and the sing-songs that we used to have were just something else. You'd go nearly to hear that as much as you'd go to see a match. It was a great occasion. All the parish used to converge on that one pub on the day. It was a real community event!

After 1971, we got to four finals and we won four, and we were beaten twice in Munster club finals, by Mount Sion of Waterford in one and Glen Rovers from Cork in another. So, we hadn't just gone and won a county final, we had gone that little bit further of almost winning Munster which would have been great.

But I don't think we can have any complaints, we had a great, great few years! We won it in 1972, '76, '78, and '81. Mike Lundon had gone to Galway and he came back to us. Myself and my three brothers were playing; you had the three Dooleys, Johnny, Eamon, and Willie. There were seven of us out of just two families, so that's how close that team was.

We had little, but we had everything! Hurling was our life.

There was a neighbour of ours at that time, Michael Ryan… coming into spring we used to go around to the rivers and the lakes and cut out hurleys from the ash out of the rivers. The best hurley came when the ash was coming out of a river because when it came out it went one way and there was a complete turn on the boss. What we used to do then was throw them up on the haybarn, cut them to the length and throw them up on the hay until April or May. We would then take them into a sawmill in Thomondgate to get them cut for the summer.

Every Christmas, every mother that was involved in the making of the hurleys made sure that 'Danno' and whiskey bottles were held. They were never thrown out because we used to break the bottle and use it as a spokeshave. Different times!

I was captain of Limerick in 1973, but it could have been any one of the three of us, however. It could have been Joe McKenna, Pat Hartigan, or myself. The fact I was captain of South Liberties in 1972 when we won the county meant they put my name forward. I can't forget 1973! I remember going up on the train and we were so privileged… the Mayor of Limerick, Michael Lipper, drove the train. We stayed out in the Crofton Airport Hotel.

That Saturday night – the night before the game – in order to do something, myself, Bernie Hartigan, Pat Hartigan, and Jim Hogan… we walked into O'Connell Street because the Liam MacCarthy Cup was on display in Clerys. We hadn't seen the cup. None of us had seen the cup… we weren't old enough to have seen it in Limerick. We walked in and we had a look at the cup and we went back out to the hotel and slept. We never physically saw it until we were inside in Clerys. Just to be in the presence of it was amazing.

I remember the following morning the bus left without me. We had gone to Mass and came back and had the breakfast. We had been up early that morning, so I decided to go back up to the hotel room for a rest. The next thing, the bus had gone 200 yards from the hotel when somebody said, 'Where is Éamonn Grimes?'

After it all, I met Mick Mackey, and he presented me with a replica of the cup, which I still have. It was marvellous.

Even though we were just three or four miles out from the city, we were rural. Everything that had to be done at that time, had to be done with a bicycle. Very few people locally had a car. Times have changed, but the one thing that's constant is the club. In the last few years, we haven't had the success that we'd hoped to have had, but we are staying together and there is a huge bond there. We lost Janesboro to Old Christians – it used to be part of the parish, but the parish itself is still great. There is a fierce spirit there.

Growing up, there was Ryan's field above at the bridge in Ballysheedy. That was the only place that people from Ballysheedy and Roxborough used to meet. We had the Coughlans, the Walshes, and the Shaughnessys. They used to come down across Brendan McMahon's field, and McManus' field, down to Ryan's and that's where we'd play a bit of hurling. We used to have a bit of craic at the bridge. If it was a good evening we'd have a bit of a sing-song. A real country life.

It was great to be able to go on and play hurling with my brothers, Mike, Lar, and Joe. It was mighty. It was absolutely brilliant. On the field itself, you always knew you had somebody else to back you up. Not that the rest of them wouldn't, but it was nice to know you'd your own flesh and blood there.

To win the All-Ireland in 1973 as captain was a huge honour.

How we played at all the following year, I don't know, because we visited every huckster shop, every school, and every pub… you name it. I went all over the place, and luckily enough I wasn't drinking at the time. I joined a drink's company as a sales rep and I spent 35 years at it, which was grand.

1973 was massive for my mam and dad, as well. They were in the stand behind me when I got the cup. They talked about it for many years afterwards. It was probably the thrill of their lifetime too, apart from when they got married.

Then you had people calling… the amount of post and people calling themselves, sure the kettle was always boiling. Mam was always baking cakes. She loved it. Then it just wore out after the year, but it was great.

If I meet people on the streets now and they mention 1973, it makes me feel young. When Limerick won the All-Ireland in 2018, they brought out the souvenir car number plates. They brought out 1973 ones then… and the amount of ones that I've got to sign was just amazing. It was like old times again! And I'm still doing it.

We were waiting 33 years to win an All-Ireland in '73 and they were waiting 45 years when they won it in 2018. It was very similar. It is an amazing situation, be it at club level or at county level; the winning of an All-Ireland is better than a doctor's visit for a lot of people, especially at a later stage in life. I know that people got 10 or 15 years younger after Limerick won the All-Ireland. Life was brought back into the place.

When we came back the following day in '73, first of all we'd a reception out in Castleconnell, and then we got on the open Guinness truck and saw the turf fires coming in before getting out below in Arthur's Quay where there was a stage set up. I'd say people didn't get home. I know that there was no sleep in our house anyway that night.

I remember we brought the cup back to Spellacy's bar in Ballysheedy. Spellacy's were to the point, insofar as if you got 10 or 15 minutes after closing hours, that would be as much you'd get. It was nearly 11pm by the time we got out of where we were inside in town, between all the hullabaloo and anything… and sure that was closing time.

Chief Superintendent Patrick Spillane, a Kerry man who'd be related to the Spillanes who played with Kerry, told Cormac Hurley, a guard, to go and supervise 'because it is going to be busy out there'. He went out by himself, and he didn't even take the squad car.

He came out of the car. We hadn't arrived yet, but there was a crowd there. Everyone was being told to get out.

I remember him saying to me, 'That woman got very excited, and I was only waiting to have a pint myself. I tried to convince her that I was after being sent out there to just control, because we knew they were going to have a crowd'.

They saw the guard and wanted the pub emptied straightaway.

Cormac Hurley to this day still remembers that Monday night when we came back with the cup.

Vincent Byrne and Michael Ryan had the place green and white, and green and gold, all the way up to our home place in Ballysheedy. That sing-song that night was something else.

The following morning – the Tuesday – my mother got up and she walked over 11 bodies to get into the kitchen. She woke my sister Nora.

'How am I going to feed all these people? I don't have enough rashers, sausages, or eggs to feed everyone.'

99

PAT HARTIGAN

SOUTH LIBERTIES 4-8 PATRICKSWELL 1-5
Limerick SHC Final
Gaelic Grounds, Limerick
DECEMBER 10, 1972

Pat Hartigan being introduced, with the Limerick team of 1973, at half-time during the Munster Championship game between Limerick and Cork at the Gaelic Grounds in 2023

★ **SOUTH LIBERTIES:** M Lundon; J Grimes, **P Hartigan**, S Hartigan; M Grimes, W Shanahan, M Butler (0-1); É Grimes (0-3), T Ryan (0-2); L Grimes, J McKenna (1-2), M Shanahan (1-0); E Dooley (1-0), D O'Sullivan, W O'Donoghue (1-0).

★ **PATRICKSWELL:** J Shields; PJ O'Grady, T Quaide, B Nolan; Phil Bennis, T O'Brien, T Bennis; R Bennis (1-4), L Enright; F Nolan, S Foley, L Foley (0-1); C Jeffers, L Mann, Peter Bennis.

THE ACTION

THE FAMINE WAS finally over as South Liberties, appearing in their third final in five years, secured their first Limerick SHC title in 82 years in impressive fashion seeing of a fancied Patrickswell side that included Limerick stars such as brothers Phil and Richie Bennis, Seán Foley, Leonard Enright, and Frankie Nolan.

A gale-force wind blew with rigorous force from the windswept Woodcock Hill bringing with showers of rain, hail, and even sleet that made this county final a real test of stamina, determination, and a fight for who was to finally get their hands on that coveted John Daly Cup. The game was won and lost in the opening half, when the Ballysheedy men played with the aid of the elements into the city end.

Although Richie Bennis had opened the scoring for the 'Well as early as the first minute, Liberties were soon up and running, opening up a substantial lead knowing they'd be facing into the teeth of the howling gale in the second-half. They opened their goal-scoring when Joe McKenna, an inter-county star with Offaly at the time before his transfer to Limerick a year later, lobbed a shot from 40 yards into the back of the Patrickswell net in the fifth minute.

The goal that put them in the ascendancy for county glory, however, was created by none other than Éamonn Grimes who tore through the 'Well defence before setting up Mike Shanahan for a great goal. Points from Grimes and two beautiful long range scores from McKenna put Liberties seven points in front – 2-4 to 0-3 – midway through the half, a lead that was extended to a mammoth 12 points by half-time, with Walter 'Wally' O'Donoghue getting in on the goal scoring action with a dazzling shot to the net in the 18th minute.

There was no way back for Patrickswell, wind or no howling gale.

Pat Hartigan was once again monarch of all he surveyed on the fringe of the square with a flawless display of fielding and lengthy clearances from the towering full-back from Drombanna. And when the chairman of the Limerick County Board, Rory Kiely, presented the cup to the winning captain Éamonn Grimes amidst great excitement, there wasn't a dry eye in the large Liberties contingent.

★★★★★

>

FROM 1960 ONWARDS, I used to go watch South Liberties play junior hurling, and we could never get over the line. We were beaten by Boher in a couple of Eastern junior hurling finals. It just sort of felt like that South Liberties weren't destined to win, and that hung over me for many, *many* years.

But then the county board introduced the divisional championship at senior level in 1971. And here was an opportunity to wipe away all the junior matches that we lost, that we should have won but we didn't win.

We got to the Eastern final and we played Fedamore. Fedamore were arch rivals, inter-married into many of the Liberties' people and vice-versa. Both teams had a sporting hatred for each other. I've a lot of good friends in Fedamore, and there are a lot of Fedamore people who have good friends in Liberties, but it was just a 'sporting' dislike.

There was a huge build up to that match. In the previous year, 1970, we played Fedamore in the county championship, and they beat us. It was a very, very sad day for us because we lost Johnny Dooley. Johnny got sick; he died subsequently on the Thursday after the match.

The next year, it was a chance to make up for all the lost times. We had a fantastic team because we had the Grimes brothers, Tom Ryan, and all the great players that came through at Liberties at that time.

I remember, we were togging out in O'Riordan's pub in Caherconlish. They had a stable or a garage at the end of the house, and we went in there to tog out as was part of the custom at the time. Mikey Butler's milk truck took us up to the field… all of us piled up on the back of the truck. The crowd was so big going up to that match that we were stopped at Lynch's Cross, as you turn up to Caherconlish's field, and from there on it was people 10 deep going up to the match because everybody could see this as being a new stage of Liberties' hurling.

The Fedamore people arrived out onto the field… no sign of Liberties, we weren't even in the dressing-room. And word got out that Liberties were afraid of Fedamore and we weren't going to show up.

We arrived into the field anyway on the back of Mikey Butler's truck… it maybe took 20 minutes to get from Lynch's Cross up to the pitch with the crowds.

We went out and we hurled one of our great games. All the old Fedamore players were there… the Gleesons, the Burtons, the Clohessys… they were all part of that Fedamore team.

And we'd the young lads like Grimes, McKenna, Denis O'Sullivan… and all the younger lads came of age. Particularly from my point of view, I probably had one of my better games. And that's what stands out. To be part of a South Liberties team and to be so much part of the win stays with me forever! The celebrations went wild for whatever length of time.

We then played a county quarter-final, then a semi-final, and we played Claughaun in the final which we subsequently lost.

It was a wet day, 12th of December… the pitch was a mud bath, we couldn't do a lot. They got a couple of soft goals, and they beat us by five points. Éamonn Grimes was outstanding that day. But then we came back and played in the East final the following year. We were beating Pallasgreen in the Eastern final.

I remember the game was in the balance. Mikey Butler was playing on John Condon and a ball broke in behind him. Condon was practically clear in front of goal. I was in his way of course, but he would have had a decent shot at a goal, or at least a point, and what did Mikey Butler do?

He took off his cap – he used to wear a cap – and threw it ahead of himself. The ball landed on the cap and John Condon wasn't able to rise it. He wasn't able to get the ball into his hands. By the time he eventually did, we had him swarmed, took the ball off him, and Liberties won the East final by a point.

What that was telling me was that now Liberties are starting to win, starting to get the breaks, starting to make the luck turn for themselves.

We then ended up going into the county final against Patrickswell.

In 1971, after the game, we all walked back down. There was no coming back down in Mikey Butler's truck so we walked down in our boots and with our jerseys still on us. It took us a lifetime to come down from Caherconlish's pitch to Riordan's pub, and we went back into the old garage that we togged out in.

Paddy Shanahan was a great believer in rhubarb.

We all used to have sticks of rhubarb going out to the match because it keeps you chewing, it keeps your mouth moist. At that time, if they saw you taking a sip of water before a match, they'd tell you to spit it out, that it was going to KILL you! Now, you can't get enough of it into you.

We weren't drinking water, but Paddy said keep the rhubarb in your mouth, it will moisten it. 'I'll bring some up to the field and ye can have some more at half-time,' he says.

I remember coming back into the dressing-room, and the place was full of water. It was a warm day, and there were 25 fellas inside in the room. There were full barrels of water there for washing your face, and fellas were throwing off their jerseys and throwing the water up on their bare bodies.

That was the showers we had back then. The place was just a massive pool of water... and rhubarb everywhere!

Patrickswell had won their first Senior Championship in 1965, and they won again in '66. We were in the county final in '67 but didn't win it... and Patrickswell won again in '69 and '70.

It was a desperate, *desperate* wet for the final in 1972... and a windy day. Patrickswell had never been beaten in a county final. They'd only been senior since 1965 but they'd played in four of them, and won four, so the odds were very much against us.

Rumour has it that Patrickswell got the forecast that day from the Met Office in Shannon. They were way ahead of us. They were told that there was going to be a storm and it was going to rise about 3pm. They said they would play against whatever bit of wind was there, and they'd have the storm behind them in the second-half. We got the advantage of the wind in the first-half, got a big lead up against them, and the storm never came at half-time. South Liberties went and won that county championship very well. We won it substantially.

To beat Patrickswell in a county final... when they had the likes of the Bennis brothers, Seán Foley, Frankie Nolan, the Careys... all great players. For South Liberties to beat them in that county final, it says it all!

Two things often come up about the county final. It was so wet that we changed our jerseys at half-time. We had only one set of jerseys and the jerseys that we had in the second-half were like the Kerry jersey. People often ask, 'Where did you get that set of jerseys?'

I thought they were from Cappamore, but somebody said to me subsequently that they came from a team called Camogue Rovers. They supplied us with a set of jerseys. And when the photograph was taken after the match, I was sitting inside in the photograph, and what had I on me? Only a green and white Limerick jersey. For years fellas would ask me, 'Why were you wearing a Limerick jersey?'

I'd laugh it off and say, 'It was the only jersey I could get to fit me'. But they'd say to me, 'But you didn't play in the match in a green and white jersey?'.

I'd say, 'I don't think I did'. What happened was that Limerick were playing Wexford in the National Football League after our match. I was on the Limerick team for the football and having been selected I didn't want to not play.

I put the green jersey on me and on my way out into the field Liberties were still on the field celebrating, and I jumped into the photograph with the Limerick jersey on me. To this day, an awful lot of people don't know that story.

I ended up playing two games that day. I actually played three games in one day back in 1968. I played intermediate hurling with Limerick, I played junior football with Limerick and, that evening, we played St Patrick's in a tournament in the Gaelic Grounds.

And they talk about player welfare today!

To make matters worse, I went dancing in Dromkeen after that and got up for work the following morning at eight o'clock.

I remember we were leading by four goals.

My brother Seamus was crying…'I think we have it!' And I said to him, 'We never have this thing until the whistle goes! ... even though the game was up.

People were on the line. I was afraid that if they came onto the pitch, the match would be called off…and we'd have to go through all of this again.

And then when the whistle went, it wasn't euphoric…it was RELIEF! It wasn't a question of jumping up and down and doing handstands. It was a question of saying, 'Thank God it's over. Thank God we got it. Thank God we have something to shout about!'

It was a relief more than any emotion. I am a non-drinker. I would go to the pub and celebrate, but I always felt there was another match. I couldn't kind of let down the guard and say I don't care if I never won another match. You still want to get back on the horse again the following day and to start producing the matches that might help Liberties or Limerick win further.

Would I say it was euphoric? No, it wasn't euphoric for me personally.

If it was euphoric, I wouldn't have togged off and put on a Limerick jersey and got up and played football."

What I really enjoyed about that final in 1972 was that we conceded no goal from play. I was playing full-back. My brother Seamus was corner-back, and then you'd the likes of Ben O'Riordan, Joe Grimes, and Mikey Grimes… you were playing for fellas who would just absolutely die for you. I always felt I hurled well with South Liberties because of the back-up I had and the back-up that everybody else had with each other. You couldn't measure it.

You could play any match with Limerick and you played with Patrickswell fellas, Doon men, or Cappamore men, but it was only when you came into South Liberties that you never had to put your back to the wall. You could stand out in the middle of the field and you knew there is a guy front, centre, back, left, and right… all there to work with you, defend you, and to help you.

That was 1972. You are looking at 51 years ago. At that time, we were talking about the fact South Liberties hadn't won a county championship for 82 years. We are now almost 43 years back into that cycle again. It was only a moment, yet all of those guys who are still in the land of the living are all still great friends.

Denis O'Sullivan was a light guy, but he'd put his head on a block to save a goal, or to create a goal, for South Liberties. That epitomised what South Liberties stood for, and we all fed off of that.

The All-Ireland win in 1973 was also very important, and I think the best game I ever played for Limerick was the 1974 Munster final against Clare. That stands out in my mind a lot because the rivalry between Limerick and Clare is infectious, it is so strong. I was working in Clare at the time because I was travelling for Ranks Flour and my territory was County Clare.

Every town and every shop that I went into, I always met wonderful people. Clare is a fantastic county with wonderful people. They have a feel for the GAA and a love for the GAA.

The thought that I'd ever win a senior county championship with South Liberties went beyond my wildest expectations. I never thought it was possible.

Then when we won one, it was sort of a release. But we didn't think there was a bigger picture there, an All-Ireland club final, or a Munster Club Championship, or more county championships… we'd arrived at our goal.

At the time, the Munster Club Championship was in its infancy, and we probably didn't give it the attention that it deserves. It had only started in 1964. Now, it is a huge tournament. At the time, it was a bit of craic for us to get to go and play hurling somewhere new. We didn't get the maximum out of it because we had crossed the Rubicon.

We hit our peak mentally.

That county championship win in 1972 gave the Liberties lads on the Limerick team the belief to go on and win the All-Ireland in 1973.

I was very lucky to win an All-Ireland Colleges and a Harty Cup with CBS when Éamonn Grimes was captain. Then when we came to the South Liberties team in '72 Éamonn Grimes was captain, and we won again.

While I would have probably been considered vice-captain of the Limerick team in 1973, under no circumstances would I even consider putting my hand up for the captaincy against Éamonn Grimes. He was the man that led me to where I was, and he was the man to lead us forward.

There wasn't a better captain in the history of the GAA! Éamonn Grimes would stand up in a dressing and he would say what he was going to do and how he was going to do it, and you knew it was going to be done.

Éamonn Grimes was the catalyst. And behind it all then, we had JP McManus. You look at JP and see the multiple horses that he has in training. He knows how they are trained, he knows what it takes to win with them. He gives plenty of advice to whoever he has training them, and gives them his opinion.

He did the same with Liberties. He did the same when we were hurling with Limerick. His in-put to Liberties and Limerick before 2018 was unheralded. He was the youngest ever chairman of Liberties.

The only disappointment was that we weren't smart enough, or bright enough, or sharp enough, that we could align ourselves more to JP on the basis of realising what his talent was all about. He has a unique talent. He might say a few words before a match going out and it would only resonate with you when you go home in the car… *JP said that before the match. I see now what he meant'*.

He knew what it took, he knew how to manage it, he knew how to achieve, and we were blessed to have JP as chairman. We were blessed to have him in the club, and we were blessed to have Grimes as captain, and we were blessed to have great men who bought into both. It was only when we started to open our eyes, did we see what needed to be done. It happened really under JP's stewardship as chairman. He opened up a whole new world of thinking… a sense of belief.

A sense of belief to all of us. Those of us that understood JP more than most bought into it and we carried it through. Even to this day… you look at Limerick at the moment, and you can see JP's hand all over it.

That same hand was all over South Liberties.

The legacy of Liberties stands forever because if you look at the races, the green and gold jersey is flying on JP's horses. That's what stirs my heart.

The following year we went on and won the All-Ireland with Limerick. I probably had a very different approach to a lot of hurling people, myself personally, because of not socialising as much in the pubs, even though I'd go to the pubs and sing a song, or we'd have a laugh and a joke and we'd reminisce on the game.

I always felt there was another game on the horizon. You're only as good as your last good match. If your standards dropped, you would come under pressure. If not from people around you, you'd come under pressure from yourself because you'd know your standard when you play well and you'd wonder, 'Why didn't I produce that standard the next time?'

When I won that county championship in 1972, I was 22 years of age. I was playing full-back from 1970 and '71… I mean it was *Hell's Kitchen* with every club and county at that time because everything fell in there, and you had to mind yourself… you had to mind the ball, you had to mind the goalkeeper… and you had to take care of the fella you were on. It was multi-tasking… and then trying to hurl as well.

It was a very demanding position. I used to have to be very conscious. All you needed was a guy to put up his hurley, get a stick to the ball, and it could be in the net. That's why I talk about the '72 county final… Patrickswell got no goal from play. I give myself credit for a lot of that because all the ball was channelling into the square. It was a heavy sliotar, a wet day, and the ball was travelling.

It was coming in.

It wasn't as if fellas were hitting them from 30 or 40 yards out and it was going 20 yards over the bar. Fellas hit them from 40 yards out now and it's gone over the back wall. Fellas hit it from 40 years back in our time, it was going to be inside in your hands inside in the square or there would be a tussle around the square. That was the nature of the game back then.

I remember at that time when I was travelling with Ranks, and subsequently when I went to Grassland Fertilizers, at lunchtime I used to step into Cusack Park in Ennis. I'd go in front of the goal and stand in around the 14-yard line and I'd visualise balls coming from different sides of the field into me, even though I'd be on my own, and I wouldn't even have a hurley and I'd have my suit on.

I'd also go to Thurles if I was in Tipperary. I'd go into Semple Stadium. I'd do the same thing. I'd stand 14 yards out… watch the ball coming in, see how I would deal with it, see where I was in position, and where the goals were behind me.

I think it was a simple strategy, a simple exercise, and it was very helpful because I was able to be proactive rather than reactive in games.

I used to form a vision memory of these matches.
Limerick won the All-Ireland 1940 and won it in 2018… that's 78 years, and there is just one All-Ireland in between… when we won it in 1973.

Limerick, with there being such few counties capable of winning an All-Ireland, should never have been in a position where they won only one All-Ireland in the space of 78 years. That to me is the legacy that Limerick hurling had to carry from 1940 to 2018, and thank God we have a group of guys now who don't know what it is to lose. And as long they continue with the belief they have, the set-up they have, the management they have, the group of guys they have who are smart, sharp, intelligent lads and have no egos, and are well-trained with everybody doing the right thing for the right reason, I think we are blessed.

And while we have five All-Irelands in six years, if you break that down over 80 years it is still only an All-Ireland every 12 years for Limerick. If you break it down in that context, it is a poor return. We need these guys to improve the averages and they are doing a fantastic job of it.

The game has moved on now. The game that is being played now is a totally different game, nowhere remotely near what we played in 1973, whereas our game in '73 had a relationship with the game in 1940. Now, hurling is a science. We weren't far removed from that '40 team in '73, but we are completely removed from the current team because of their ability and their advancement.

"

TOM RYAN

LIMERICK 6-7 TIPPERARY 2-18
Munster SHC Final
Semple Stadium, Thurles
JULY 29, 1973

Tom Ryan still believes that Limerick had the players to dominate the game throughout the 70s

★ **LIMERICK:** S Horgan; W Moore, P Hartigan, J O'Brien; P Bennis, J O'Donnell, S Foley; É Grimes (capt.), R Bennis (1-5); L O'Donoghue (0-1), M Dowling (1-0), B Hartigan; F Nolan (2-1), É Rea, É Cregan (2-0). **Subs: T Ryan** for O'Donnell.

★ **TIPPERARY:** T Murphy; J Fogarty, J Kelly, J Gleeson; J Crampton, T O'Connor, J Gaynor, S Hogan (0-2), PJ Ryan; F Loughnane (2-10), M Roche, Noel O'Dwyer (0-1); J Flanagan (0-1), Roger Ryan, M Keating (0-4). **Subs:** J Ryan for Crampton, D Ryan for J Ryan

THE ACTION

AS TEMPERATURES SOARED to 25 degrees, Limerick heated things up on the pitch as the Treaty County scored six goals to win their first Munster final in 18 years, the first since 'Mackey's Greyhounds' days, but their victory was sealed by Richie Bennis' storied and controversial late '70'.

The midfield marshal from Patrickswell was met by the watchful eye of Tipperary's Michael 'Babs' Keating before scoring one of the most celebrated winning points in hurling history as Limerick snatched victory with the last puck of a thrill-packed game.

In a reverse of 1971, when Limerick had led by four points in Fitzgerald Stadium at half-time, it was Tipp who held the same lead – 2-9 to 3-2 – after the home side dominated the second quarter, before two second-half goals from Éamonn Cregan (two) and Frankie Nolan turned the game on its head. Nolan, Mossie Dowling, and Bennis had netted for Limerick in the opening half.

Just five minutes from time, Francis Loughnane had given Tipp the lead with a wonderful point. Two quick-fire Bennis frees had Limerick ahead once again, before the sides were level when John Flanagan flashed over a great point with just under two minutes to go.

Boosted by an enthusiastic support in Thurles, the Shannonsiders mounted a last-ditch attack, and with the seconds ticking away they forced a '70', an award hotly disputed by the Tipperary defenders. Bennis made no mistake and sent the sliotar straight between the Tipperary posts.

As the white flag went up and the final whistle was immediately sounded, Bennis could not hold back his excitement and the 'Well native, cool and calm just seconds before, jumped into the air before being pulled to the ground by Seán Foley during dramatic celebrations in front of the massive crowd of 41,700 in Semple Stadium.

Tipp players, who felt the ball had gone wide, turned to the umpire in protest, but Limerick didn't care – they were in their first All-Ireland semi-final since 1955.

★★★★★

> 99

THE GAME THAT stands out straightaway with regards to my playing career with Limerick would be the 1973 Munster final against Tipperary in Thurles.

That was the day that we won by a point, and there was that controversial free by Richie Bennis; there was a big dispute about whether it was wide or not because it was so high up in the air. There was no such thing as 'Hawkeye' at that time.

I played with Limerick for 10 years, on and off.

It was a totally different era, but you still had very, very good teams. Limerick weren't making the breakthrough and were always getting short-changed a bit; we were there and thereabouts, but we just couldn't make the breakthrough.

It came down to the wire in '73 in Thurles.

Tipp took over in the first-half. I remember it was a very, very strong Tipp team… you had Noel O'Dwyer playing with Tipp at that time. You had Babs Keating. Babs was huge at that time. He was a tremendous player, both hurling and football, but as a hurler he was just out of this world. They had all their big players.

But so did Limerick… we had Éamonn Cregan, we had Richie and Phil, and the Hartigans… we were coming! We had been trying hard.

At the time, there was no backdoor… every match was a final!

You didn't get any chance to put any kind of a system in place where you got an easy draw if you got beaten or anything like that, things that happen these days which I think ruined it… I'm not a backdoor man anyway!

Championship hurling for me is on the day, and when you lose, that's it!

We were being hammered in the first-half, but changes were made at half-time. The team was reshuffled a bit, and the second half was *power hurling* all the way.

That was a breakthrough match for us. The next game in that series was against London. That was a real banana skin in Ennis, and we were lucky there. We got through that game… that's all I'll say about that, because we just got through it, we didn't shine.

Then we went up to Croke Park for the All-Ireland final and we met a Kilkenny team that were short a couple of players, but on the day that particular Limerick team were able to overcome the boys from Kilkenny by playing well on the day!

It had been 34 years since Limerick won the All-Ireland before that. It was an awfully long time, and you'd wonder… you could ask yourself the question, *'Why was that?'*

'Why did Limerick, being such a hurling county, take so long to win it?'

Limerick is a serious hurling county!

We were definitely behind in the coaching stakes, playing the likes of Kilkenny and Cork and all them… they had great coaches. We hadn't. We were struggling a bit in that department. I believe that kept Limerick down for a long, *long* time. The tradition is there, the infrastructure is there, the crowds were there, but you really needed someone to get it by the throat and say, 'Look, this is what we are going to do'.

We were nearly happy to just be beaten by a point at the time. I was on the scene for 10 years and I could see well what was happening. I could see there were serious differences between the clubs. You had South Liberties who were very strong at the time, and Claughaun and Patrickswell were big. You definitely had inter-club rivalry… serious stuff that wasn't conducive to winning anything.

I was in the middle of it all and I saw where our frailties were, and I knew we were lacking at the time. We spent too much energy celebrating in 1973. We should have won again the next year. We'd a team that was nearly better in '74.

Then Cork started to come on the scene. You always needed to be pushing ahead and you needed to have a bit of vision, which we hadn't. We hadn't it on the sideline, and we hadn't it at board level… we hadn't it anywhere. It was like a ship at sea with no captain. If it kept going, well and good. There was no plan in place or no regime in place to maintain what we had already done… and to build on that. We didn't do that.

With the players we had at the time, we should have won a lot more. Individually, the players were brilliant. I played with them all. I played against the best hurlers in the country, and we'd some of the best hurlers in the country. We'd players such as Richie Bennis. Richie was it… no more about it. He was the king… goal-scorer supreme, and free-taker supreme. He had everything. He was a workhorse as well.

And then you'd Éamonn Grimes, the two Hartigans, and the two Cregans, Mickey and Éamonn. You'd also the likes of 'Ned' Rea, God rest his soul, who was a great battler as well, along with the likes of Frankie Nolan and Jim O'Brien. You had a very, very good team. You had a mixture of everything there. You had size, and you had physicality in the Hartigans… and they could hurl.

But despite all that, the one thing we hadn't was a leader. You need a leader.

I had several meetings when the management came to me. They were looking to meet to see what they could do. I was only a player, fighting for my place in the team. The manager would come and say, 'This player won't talk to me'… and the player might be the captain. The captain wouldn't be talking to the manager. I mean that wouldn't be a good way of trying to win anything… and these fellas were All Stars. Their names were written up in gold.

It went from bad to worse then.

I don't know who came up with the idea, but we had an open discussion amongst the players and the management inside in the Shannon Arms Hotel. We were all called together. I said to myself coming out of there, *This is over. The show is over!*

Fellas were complaining that the training was too hard… this kind of thing. If they were there now, there isn't a hope they would be able for it. Training at the time was very, *very* basic. A lot of fellas had the All-Ireland medal in their pocket, and they lost the hunger.

It was a marvellous feeling to be part of an All-Ireland winning team in 1973.

It was a marvellous time to be involved with the team, and to play a part in it. Saying that, we got a Kilkenny who had three of their best players not available. It might not have been magnificent when you consider that, but it was a win. At that particular time and in that particular era in the 70s, or in any era for that matter, it was always hard to win an All-Ireland…and it is still hard to win an All-Ireland.

It was definitely great to be involved. It was great to see the team progressing and to see the Liam MacCarthy Cup coming to Limerick. It was great to be able to play a part in that, however big or small, because it isn't a one-man team at all or a one-man effort… everyone contributes. That's the way I wanted a team to be – every team member, every squad member, and every member of the panel recognised, no matter how small a part they played. You can play half an hour and you can contribute just as much as someone who played all of the matches.

That is one thing that always annoyed me, and I wrote about it in my column in the *Daily Mail;* when Henry Shefflin retired, the talk was that he won 10 All-Ireland medals on the field. Was he on his own? There was all this nonsense about him winning 10 medals as if he'd done it on his own. He was playing on a *team*. Does that mean that the man next to you or the sub that is waiting to come in, maybe to pull the game out of the fire, isn't as important?

I'd always be a team person. It is all about the squad. That's one thing I always did when I was with Limerick as manager. The first night we ever met after picking the first squad I ever did with Limerick, we sat in the middle of the Gaelic Grounds… 34 of us out on the field. There was no one in the dressing-room. I sat them down. It wasn't easy putting that squad together.

I told them my feelings, how I think, and I said, 'Look, there are 34 of us here. There will be nobody here guaranteed anything. Everyone here is of equal importance.

'I won't be contacting anybody about the team. The team will be picked, and it will be called out here Tuesday night. I won't be ringing anyone telling them they are on or they are off.'

My whole theory is, every member of that panel has a part to play, and they have to be confident that they *know* they have a part to play. It is about explaining, and it is about confidence and giving fellas the inside track; that you are not just there in order to make up the numbers.

I learnt a lot through observation, through my own training that I did myself, and through management of people. We tried everything. Long before all this psychology and all that sort of thing came into being, we were doing that.

It was marvellous then to get to manage Limerick to Munster titles, and to contest two All-Ireland finals. It was a tremendous, unbelievable time, because we had come out of the doldrums.

You can't compare it to now because every match we played was a final. There was no back door. That suited me. I never wanted a backdoor. I milk 80 cows here. On a Sunday morning I milked my cows here, I'd be collected then by Charlie Hanley who did all the work really – he was the man who put the whole show together.

There was terrible sadness about losing in 1994, and it was terrible then what happened in '96, but the thing about it was that it is a sport. I always looked at it as a sport. I also looked at it as knockout championship hurling. We won one of the best leagues that was played in 40 years in 1997. We got to play it during the summer.

All of the time I was building, trying to build something. I went to every club in the county, I didn't care where they were. I grabbed fellas, got players, and coached them.

That's the secret of our success, and it was success because we had come out of the doldrums and we won two Munster Championships, we played in three finals, and we were in two All-Ireland finals.

People can analyse the two All-Irelands anyway they like, but we didn't play well in either, whether it was the occasion or whatever it was… the first one against Offaly, I have no regrets about that; we lost our game plan and our pattern, and everything went out the window; we forgot about it in the last five minutes and we started to change the game. It was gone from us then.

I have terrible regrets about 1996. I believe we were done out of it in '96. Refereeing decisions in '96 were diabolical decisions. If it happened today the match would be replayed. Brian Tobin's goal that was disallowed was a *shocking* decision. It was never questioned because the boys from Wexford were up and coming, and everybody wanted them to win as well.

I wasn't happy with the Munster final against Clare in 1995. I felt in that game and the All-Ireland against Wexford in '96 that we didn't get fair play in either of those games. But that's okay, we'll live with that.

That Clare match in '96 was unbelievable. You could compare it to my most memorable game as a player – that Tipp game in 1973. It had everything. I'll never forget Ciarán Carey's point in the 75th minute in unbelievable sunshine and heat. The quality of that score and the way the team responded to being five points down with not much time remaining; and your man on the whistle was about to blow but he couldn't blow it for a draw because Carey was in motion… just unbelievable.

Then we met Tipperary in the Munster final…10 points down at half-time. Then what happened was like poetry in motion. After a brilliant performance from Tipp in the first-half, we then came back and clawed back point by point by point. Tipp went ahead by two points again, and to come back and draw that game has to be one of the finest performances.

You had Limerick back contesting everything, and contesting and winning finals.

99

ÉAMONN CREGAN

LIMERICK 1-21　KILKENNY 1-14
All-Ireland SHC Final
Croke Park
SEPTEMBER 2, 1973

Mick Crotty of Kilkenny has his shot blocked by Éamonn Cregan and Pat Hartigan of Limerick during the All Ireland final in 1973

★ **LIMERICK:** S Horgan; W Moore, P Hartigan, J O'Brien; P Bennis, **É Cregan**, S Foley; R Bennis (0-10), É Grimes (capt.) (0-4); B Hartigan (0-1), M Dowling (1-1), L O'Donoghue; F Nolan (0-2), E Rea (0-2), J McKenna (0-1). **Subs:** T Ryan for B Hartigan.

★ **KILKENNY:** N Skehan; P Larkin, N Orr, P Cullen; P Lawlor, P Henderson, B Cody; F Cummins, L O'Brien (0-2); C Dunne (0-7), P Delaney (capt.) (1-1), P Broderick; M Crotty (0-3), J Lynch, M Brennan (0-1). **Subs:** K Purcell for Broderick, W Harte for Cummins, J Kinsella for Lynch.

★ GAME OF MY LIFE ★

THE ACTION

AN HISTORIC GAME that continues to be talked about in Limerick even to this day will long live in the memory of the share of the 59,009 crowd that had made the long journey from Shannonside to Jones' Road to witness the lifting of the Liam MacCarthy Cup for the first time since 1940.

Ahead of the game, Eddie Keher was ruled out for Kilkenny because of a broken collar-bone. Limerick saw their chance and made a masterful selectorial decision. With Keher out and Kieran Purcell sidelined because of appendicitis, Pat Delaney would take up the mantle as Kilkenny's chief scorer.

Delaney was an exceptional half-forward who was far too quick for most defenders. Instead of using a defender to mark him, the Limerick selectors moved Éamonn Cregan from the forwards back to centre-back where he was charged with the task of nullifying the Kilkenny marksman.

Delaney, in spite of Cregan doing an excellent man-marking job, scored the opening goal of the game to give Kilkenny the lead. Twice Limerick fell behind in the opening half and twice they fought back. At one stage they trailed by 1-5 to 0-3, however they held Kilkenny scoreless for two nine-minute spells in the first-half. At the half-time whistle Limerick were very much on top and left the pitch leading by 0-12 to 1-7.

Despite levelling the scores five minutes after the restart, and going ahead a minute later, Kilkenny could only watch on as Limerick secured the match-winning score less than 10 minutes into the second-half. A puck-out from Kilkenny 'keeper Noel Skehan was quickly sent back in his direction by Liam O'Donoghue. Skehan saved the shot but Mossie Dowling and 'Ned' Rea were waiting for the rebound.

Dowling became the Limerick hero as he turned the sliotar past Skehan and into the net. Kilkenny were held scoreless for 23 minutes during the half, while Limerick went on a point-scoring spree for the final quarter. Midfield marshal Richie Bennis finished the game with 10 points to his name as Limerick claimed their seventh All-Ireland crown.

★★★★★

> 66

WHEN I THINK back to when we played hurling in the People's Park growing up, we had no clubs at the time, and we just played hurling for the love of it. There would be Sam Brown, Michael Curtain, Joe Donnellan, my brother Michael, Anthony Reddin, Pat Twomey… these are all guys that used to play hurling with us in the People's Park because we were all from the inner-city.

Dermot Kelly then would have been the reason a trial match was held in Claughaun. Claughaun were a city club… I didn't even know who they were, but they announced that they were holding a trial in order to get players in. When Claughaun was formed, players on their underage teams were from Ballinacurra Weston, Prospect, St Patrick's Road, and Garryowen. They came from all over because of that particular trial match.

We came from the city so we were now playing with Claughaun and people didn't know where we were from. That's where we started and from thereon, Claughaun would have been myself and my brother, Michael's club.

We were a cosmopolitan group of young people who wanted to play hurling.

I was only 11 years of age playing in the trial game, playing against lads aged 15 and 16 so they put me in goals. The reason I was put in goals was because I was too small and I was the last one picked. As long as I was playing, I didn't mind.

I started off playing in goals then for Claughaun and I won a county championship medal in 1957 with the club when I was 12 years of age. We had a great team… and it all came from that practice match, that trial match above in the field. It is amazing how things happen. I still have an old photograph of the lads.

Limerick city in those days was a small town… a very small town. You played on the street. My mother owned Hanratty's Hotel. We lived in the hotel on Glentworth Street. There was a lane going in there, and out the back there were garages up along. That's where Michael and myself played… and we just hurled morning, noon, and night.

The only time we couldn't hurl was if it was raining or somebody decided to wash their car and water came down the middle of the lane. Michael would be up in one of the goals and we'd be playing 10 goals in… and we just hurled, and hurled, and *hurled*… and that's all we were doing. My father had played with Limerick in the 1930s and that's where we got our love for the game.

The hotel is still there today, but we sold it in 1957 and we moved out to Castletroy, but we still played with Claughaun, because Claughaun were a townie club. Monaleen had no underage team at that particular time, so we stayed playing with Claughaun.

My brother Michael became a physical trainer in the army. He did a PE course in the army. Army training in those days was totally different… they were the only ones doing PE. He retired in 1972 having dislocated his collar-bone against Clare in that famous 1972 match in Ennis.

He decided to give it up and concentrate on the physical side, so he took over from Joe McGrath with Limerick. He brought in a regime of training… we never saw anything like it in our lives. His theory was very simple. 'We are not as good as Kilkenny, but we can be fitter than Kilkenny'. He concentrated on the fitness side of it and Dick Stokes and Jackie Power concentrated on the hurling side. Both Dick and Jackie had won All-Irelands in the 1940s, which was a bonus for Limerick in the sense that it was a move to get somebody in that knew a lot about hurling and had been through the mill of winning an All-Ireland.

These were two men who had been through the mill and were looked up to. We needed somebody positive like that.

With Mikey's training it was unbelievable. This was the 70s… in those days people didn't train. They trained for two weeks… two weeks training prior to a match.

I was first picked on the Limerick panel in 1964. I played my first championship match in 1965 against Waterford. In October of '64, I'd played against Dublin in the league in Dublin. The following year the panel was picked and I went out to training in the Gaelic Grounds. Jim Quaid was the trainer. There were only four Limerick players there… FOUR!

That just tells you the standard of inter-county training in Limerick. We never even trained for the 1963 minor final. We never trained for the '66 under-21 final. We couldn't get Brian Cobbe on to the team because the selectors didn't want him on it. Eventually, he did come and we played in the Munster final in '66 and

Brian scored two goals and a point. This is the man the selectors didn't want.

In 1963, we had 13 selectors. The politics of it was unbelievable.

We were beaten in the All-Ireland minor final in '63. In one sense, it was a blessing in disguise because we had a lot of former Harty Cup fellas playing. The following year in April we got to the All-Ireland Colleges final and won that against St Peter's College of Wexford.

When Brother Burke came on the scene in '66 we trained properly for the first time.

The training then was animal in 1973.

We basically started with six laps of the field. The Gaelic Grounds is 100 yards wide by 190. We did six laps, but we had to do it to time. You had 55 seconds to get around, and if you dropped to 59 seconds you had to pick it up the next time. Everything was timed.

This was a new regime from Michael… typical army stuff. We did that and then we went into an hour and a half of hurling training. You can imagine what it was like… we had backs and forwards. You'd be bateing your head off these fellas, and you'd be getting lashed by Éamonn Rea and you'd be getting lashed by Pat Hartigan. The intensity was unbelievable.

We just barely won the early matches. We beat Clare by three or four points, struggled over them. Then we met Tipperary in the Munster final… and this famous, I call it, 'moving goal posts'. It was Ballinspittle all over again… Richie's point.

The match was the usual nip and tuck, and then came the '70'. Richie stood up to take the '70'… I remember 'Babs' Keating and Mick Roche roaring at him to put him off. Richie was as cool as a breeze, stood, rose the ball, and stuck it over the ball. The score counted and we won, though one of the umpires got a lovely lash of a fist into the jaw putting up the flag for a point. That was unbelievable really because we scored six goals that day, but we only scored seven points. It was easier to score goals than points.

We were then on a high and we met London in the All-Ireland semi-final in Ennis. I was hitting a ball for goals and I got a late tackle. The ball was gone and next thing this body came through the air and it hit me on the chest. I was turned. My right shoulder went back, my left shoulder went forward, and my left knee stayed in the ground.

I got up to move and I couldn't move. I had an unbelievable pain. I was taken off. In those days… injuries… hamstrings…we didn't know what a hamstring was. We knew it was something got to do with a pig.

Physiotherapy and all that sort of thing was at a very low ebb in Limerick. Eventually, I was sent out to John St George outside in the Regional Hospital. John was a physiotherapist. Unusually for a physiotherapist, he was blind. He'd lost his sight quite a number of years prior to that. I went out twice a week to get treated. It was three weeks to the All-Ireland final. He was treating me, but he never told me what was wrong with me… NEVER! And I hadn't a clue. I never asked. I said, 'Will I be alright?'.

'Ah, you will,' he said. He is massaging it, and he is doing heat treatment… everything like that. Eventually, he said, 'Éamonn'… remember now John is blind. He is at my feet and he says, 'I've never seen feet as bad as yours'.

I said, 'What do you mean?' He says, 'You've dreadful feet', which I have, I am paying for it now.

Then he said, 'You're okay to go'. I went back training. I thought I was flying it. I was ready to rock and roll. Dick Stokes and Jackie Power asked me if I would play at centre-back. My first question to them was, 'What about Jim O'Brien?' They said they'd talk to Jim. That was my first thought because if I was going centre-back then Jim wasn't playing. It just struck a raw nerve with me.

Then it transpired that Jim had an injury. I said, 'Okay'.

What people didn't know was that I was being moved from corner-forward to centre-back. It was like Barry Nash being transferred from the forwards to left corner-back. I was looking at the selectors saying, 'What are they doing putting Barry back in the corner?' Now, look at him. It is phenomenal what Barry has done.

I was back centre-back. I knew that Kilkenny always did their research work on the teams that they played against. The move of me back to centre-back must have put them off balance in the sense of, 'Why is that move taking place?'

People thought it was a mad move but I had played all my hurling at centre-back with Claughaun, and I don't think Kilkenny knew about that. Knowing that I was playing centre-back I watched the Leinster final two or three times and I had seen the way Pat Delaney played, and I adapted my tactics accordingly.

We were inside in the dressing-room before the All-Ireland final and I said I better go up to the loo now before we go out. I went into the toilet and Éamonn Grimes and Declan Moylan were inside. I looked up and there was a window inside in the dressing-room under the Cusack Stand. I could see JP McManus' head coming in the window. Éamonn was saying, 'Come on, come on, come on…'.

You could never get into the dressing-rooms in the Cusack Stand back then. The officials would run you… and there was JP coming in.

He eventually got in and Declan took him out into the dressing-room. The lads got ready then to go out. They were going out as I was still in the toilet.

We were told, 'Expect an almighty roar when you appear on the field'. The team went out, they heard the roar… and I'm still inside in the dressing-room. I arrived out and the roar was gone.

Next thing, the match progressed and the ball dropped down…and we did the usual things. I caught a ball and I went forward with it, and I slipped and I heard a click in my knee… same knee was the one that was being treated.

Carol, who is John St George's wife, went pale and she said, 'Éamonn is after falling'. Like a ghost he lost his colour because he knew what I had.

What had actually happened was, he had been treating me for cartilage trouble and instead of the cartilage coming out, it popped back in. I got up and I ran after the ball. The cartilage went back in, and if it hadn't gone back in, I wouldn't have lasted the game.

Nobody knew about it, except John St George who knew I was being treated. Only for John I'd never have got through it. I wrote to him recently thanking him for the efforts he put into it… because he did, he worked very hard.

I knew I was fine. I was able to play on which when you think about it, it's uncanny what happened.

To get that All-Ireland win then was an unbelievable feeling.

Our fitness levels on that particular day worked. We stopped training for the All-Ireland final in '73 ten days prior to it. I said to Michael, 'Why are we stopping?'

'We need to recover,' he said. The 10 days that were there allowed us to recover our strength.

We got on the train, the train pulled out, up to Dublin, we got on the bus, the bus pulled out, and we got to the Regency Hotel. The following year was the exact opposite. The train pulled out… but the train had to be brought back.

The county secretary had left a load of money in the boot of his car. Secondly, the county chairman hadn't turned up at the station and one of the players who was with him wasn't there either. The train was stopping at Limerick Junction and they got on there. We arrived in Dublin and we got on the bus. The bus broke down. We then went to the Green Isle hotel which is on the main dual carriageway into Dublin.

All we could hear at night was the noise of the cars. Everything that possibly could have happened, *happened*, plus the fact that we didn't train properly for the final the second year in 1974. We had reached the mountain and we weren't willing to go up the ladder again. It was very hard to get motivated, yet still we led by 10 points, but things developed then after that that left us down.

Unfortunately, we never recovered.

That All-Ireland final in 1973… I remember Hartigan played and he had two teeth missing in the front. He had the helmet on and he roars… four minutes to go and I am out centre-back. We were seven or eight points up and he roars… 'Cregan,' he says. 'We've them beaten'.

I turned around and I told him, 'There are four minutes left in this game, now concentrate'.

Next thing, a high ball comes in and he goes up into the air and he grabs the ball in the air, he shrugs off the shoulders… and he drives the ball down the field. It was great that it happened and it was a positive thing that he caught it and drove it down the field, but if he had dropped it, we would have been in serious trouble.

We won it, and the rest is history!

Forty-five years of famine then after that.

Knowing where I'd come from, and the obstacles we faced, it was an unbelievable feeling walking up the steps of Croke Park to get my hands on the Liam MacCarthy Cup. My father had died the previous year, in August of 1972.

I remember we stopped in Castleconnell train station on the way down. We got off the train there, and we got on the bus.

I'll always remember, Bernie Hartigan was standing beside me. A great guy. We came in the Dublin Road… it was unbelievable. We were at the back of the bus and we'd look out and there would be four lanes of traffic for miles back, right behind us. We were going slowly along the road towards Annacotty. There were people behind us and people in front of us that we'd be meeting all the way into town, until we got to the square beside the Hunt Museum.

We passed my house and Mick Herbet came up to us. He was on the bus with us at the time. 'God,' he says. 'You are very calm'. Bernie is generally calm, but I was thinking about my father as he had just died the previous year. He wasn't there. My mother was inside and they came out.

I still get emotional about it even to this day.

She came out and everything he wanted we had. Bernie was there beside me and we were just taking it all in. I've never experienced anything like it, except in 2018 when Limerick won the All-Ireland again.

Everybody gets emotional about that because all we wanted was for Limerick to win, and we were held back, and held back… for 45 years.

We had come up the hard way.

When you think about the '73 team, I was 28. I had played four league finals, I played in a Munster final, and I played in an Oireachtas final. We had all come through the ranks having been beaten… being close, but being beaten.

In 1966, Éamonn Rea was corner-back on the Limerick team. He was on the '73 team. He never thought at that stage that he'd be back on it, but himself and Jim O'Donnell used to come down from Dublin twice a week to train. There was something about that particular team, that they weren't going to lose. The hunger was there.

We were so fit. Remember now, we were playing 80-minute matches, and we were as strong at the end of 80 minutes above in Croke Park in '73 as we were in the middle of the game.

But then we lost the final in 1974, we lost the Munster final in '75, and we lost the Munster final in '76… and then two years gone in 1977 and '78. Then in '79 we were back in the Munster final and Pat Hartigan's injury happens. I was on him the night he was training. He was fidgety because Mike Barron was beginning to play well at full-back and there were talks that Pat might be moved out to centre-back.

In training that night, he wanted to prove he was good enough. We were playing 12-a-side – imagine playing 12-a-side outside in the Gaelic Grounds with that space.

I remember it well. Noel Dromgoole was in charge and he told me to stay inside at full-forward. I stayed inside. Pat drifted out. I can see it to this day. The ball broke in front of the Mackey Stand, out to the side of the pitch, and 'Bomber' Carroll was coming one way and Pat was coming the other way.

The hurleys came down. The ball shot up. The ball came up and the ridge of the sliotar hit Pat in the eye. The chances of that happening were so slim. He ended up losing 80% of his sight in one eye. I remember him hitting the ground. The ground shook. It was a terrible ordeal.

Then there was the waiting around to see if he would be available for the Munster final. We could have easily solved the problem by saying Pat wasn't available and if he ended up being available it was a bonus, and if he was not available, we would have already been acclimatised to it.

Then going down to the Munster final in '79 we were stranded a mile and a half from the grounds. At half past two we were still in cars. The guards had to put everybody into the car park on the way in from Holycross. Eight of the players were stranded; Tommy Quaid, Éamonn Grimes, Joe Grimes, all of those guys. We were all stranded in cars and we never got into Hayes' Hotel where we were supposed to be at one o'clock. We were still outside in cars at half past two and the match on at half three.

Pa O'Brien was driving the car. He called a guard and he said, 'Garda, I have players here to play in the Munster final and we are stuck outside here'. The guard said, 'Hold on a minute', and he pulled us out and we drove in.

We could only go so far because of the traffic. We had to take our gear and run the last mile of it.

This was the preparation we had for a Munster final.

99

DAVID PUNCH

PATRICKSWELL 3-7 KILLEEDY 0-7
Limerick SHC Final
Gaelic Grounds, Limerick
NOVEMBER 13, 1977

Winning the Limerick senior hurling title in 1977 was the start of a glorious era for David Punch (pictured on football duty with the club front row, centre) and Patrickswell, when they claimed 12 of the club's 20 titles

★ **PATRICKSWELL:** J Murphy; T O'Brien, J O'Brien, E Kelleher; P Foley, Phil Bennis, Dominic Punch; S Foley (0-1), T Murray; L Foley, R Bennis (0-3), **David Punch (capt) (0-1)**; J Lynch, Peter Bennis (2-2), F Nolan (1-0). **Sub:** Tom Bennis for Dominic Punch.

★ **KILLEEDY:** P Meehan; K McGrath, B O'Sullivan, B Mullane; J Mulcahy, P Fitzmaurice, PJ Cronin; M Scanlan, C Herbert; M Fitzmaurice (0-1), W Fitzmaurice (0-1), T Mulcahy; J Forde, D O'Flynn (0-3), M Shields (0-1). **Subs:** Denis O'Connor (0-1) for M Fitzmaurice, W Cronin for Forde.

★ GAME OF MY LIFE ★

THE ACTION

PATRICKSWELL WON THE Limerick senior hurling championship for the fifth time since 1965 when they beat Killeedy in the final at the Gaelic Grounds.

Four minutes before the interval, Peter Bennis got a goal for Patrickswell which put them 1-5 to 0-4 in the lead at the interval and two second-half goals by Peter Bennis and Frankie Nolan ensured that the championship would return to the 'Well.

Brothers predominated on both sides. For Patrickswell, the Foleys, the Punches and the Bennis' were outstanding and nobody could have done more for Killeedy than Limerick star Paudie Fitzmaurice, and his brothers Willie and Michael.

In a lovely passing of time, when Patrickswell won their first county senior title 12 years previously, a young toddler named David Punch, with boyhood dreams and ambitions of one day wearing the famous blue and gold, was their mascot. Fast forward to 1977, Punch, now a fearless and striking teenager with exciting, potentially inter-county level, talents achieved his ambition, captaining his club to county success on the hallowed ground of the Gaelic Grounds.

This hurling fairytale came to its finale when the lively Punch collected the coveted John Daly Cup. After a free-flowing and exciting opening half, the 83rd staging of the Limerick SHC final fizzled out, but that didn't matter to the large crowd that had made the short journey from Patrickswell.

Showing their superiority on the day, Patrickswell started slow and could only manage an interval lead of 1-5 to 0-4, despite the aid of a strong wind in the first-half with a Peter Bennis goal three minutes from the break really separating the sides.

An attack by the 'Well nine minutes into the final half hour decided the destiny of the trophy. Joe Lynch gained possession, tore down the right wing, and when tackled, passed to Peter Bennis who shot to the roof of the net for his, and the 'Well's, second goal of the afternoon.

★★★★★

"

WE HAD WON the county title in 1965, '66, '69, and '70, but then there was a gap... and we hadn't won it for seven years in Patrickswell.

And we won it 1977. We won it again in '78, and then we did three in-a-row in 1982, '83, and '84. What was unique about 1977 though was there was a gap of seven years, having been beaten in the final by Kilmallock in 1974 and '75. We won three under-21 county titles in-a-row in 1975, '76, and '77, and about eight-to-10 of that team – at least half the team – started with the seniors in 1977.

So, to win it in 1977 was HUGE! It was huge for the 'Well. That was the start of our run in the 70s, 80s, and 90s when we won 12 of the club's 20 county titles from 1977 to the end of the 90s.

With the build-up to the All-Ireland in 2018, not having won it since 1973 with Limerick... that group had no association with '73.

That happened. That was history. That was back then.

They were all about, 'This is us now'.

We do know Limerick hadn't won it since '73, but that was not a burden on them whatsoever. They were in the here and now. That's what they were looking at. It was the same in Patrickswell. We had our era. There is no doubt about it, Cian Lynch, Diarmaid Byrnes and Aaron Gillane knew we had success in the past, but it is about the here and now.

You are not going to win it because you won it 40 years ago. When we were winning, none of those lads were even born. Did we inspire them? I would have to say no. They probably read about it, but that was it. They created and achieved what they did themselves. A lot of the Limerick current success started with the academy outside in the University of Limerick. Joe McKenna was involved in it, and Gerry McManus – JP's brother – was involved with it.

They were part of the first group that set up that academy. Limerick hurling is where it is now because of that.

That was the benchmark.

But of course, success created that tradition in Patrickswell. the 'Well is associated with hurling. Since the 1960s there has been great, *great* players playing with the club and Limerick in each decade.

I was involved with the Limerick under-21s when they won the three All-Irelands in-a-row. We made one rule at the start. 'We don't care where they are from'. If you are from a well-known club, it doesn't mean that you are going to get a chance. If you are good enough, you will make the panel.

And that's what happened.

It brings me back to my time playing with Limerick in the 80s when Noel Dromgoole, who we used to call 'The Drummer', was in charge. A great character. They saw players that could do a job, not because they were from a certain club.

Players from a couple of clubs from West Limerick who wouldn't have been big hurling clubs or been successful clubs got a chance. It was the *players*. He saw the potential in the players.

We were all part of the Limerick panel. You weren't on the Limerick panel because you were from Patrickswell; you were on it because you were picked by the management, not because you were from a certain club.

Look at John Flanagan – Seamus' father – for example. Feohanagh-Castlemahon wouldn't have been a big club. They were junior. John Flanagan was one of the back-bone of the team, the reason we won the Munster final below in Thurles in 1980. It is incredible.

I think it was blended by the management. It wasn't blended because you came from a certain club or a not so well-known club or a not so well known traditional hurling club. There were great characters there as well.

They were the days you could smoke inside in the dressing-rooms or have a fag at half-time. It didn't make a difference.

It was such a different time.

Take John Flanagan as an example again. John Flanagan probably didn't even need to train because he was up milking cows, walking, and running, doing physical work seven days a week.

There was no dietician in those days. You weren't getting an App on your phone telling you to keep an eye on your hydration, that you needed to drink half a litre of water.

Now you have dieticians, and you've psychology. It is all part of the behind the scenes now. When we got to the All-Ireland final in 1980, we didn't even have a V-neck jumper to say we were from Limerick. We got boots, togs, and socks… but you wore your own clothes. That was what it was like back then.

But fair play to them, everything they get today… more luck to them. It is well deserved.

A game that stands out for me in a Limerick jersey is the 1980 Munster final. It was Limerick's first time beating Cork in a Munster hurling final in 40 years, since 1940.

That's why that game was so significant. It was a couple of tough years. We had several defeats in the previous few years and were straight out of the championship. That was the format back then. You had one chance and that was it. Your next game would have been the start of the league in the middle of October. That's the way it was.

That game is important because of what it meant to Limerick. I have an abiding memory of being in Hayes' Hotel after the match, and down at the end of the ballroom there was this curtain.

The curtain was pulled across.

We were getting fed in behind the curtain. The bar was down at the end and when the meal was over, I remember the place was packed with Limerick supporters. I'll never forget this one particular man… I didn't know his name or anything. He came up and he was actually crying and congratulating me. He had never seen Limerick win in a Munster final against Cork. That post-match memory has always stuck in my mind.

It probably meant more to them than to us on the day because he probably had 30 or 40 years of not seeing Limerick win a Munster final against Cork. That was a few hours post-match and we probably didn't realise what the win meant, but as the week went on, we realised what was achieved by Limerick that day.

There is always a sense of relief for yourself, but you know it's for Limerick… the celebration is for the county, not for you – it's not a personal thing. To me that man summarises what it really meant to the people. You are just one of the 30 lucky people to be representing Limerick, and we were the lucky 15 to start.

We had lost to Cork earlier that year in a league final replay, but we didn't know we'd meet them again in the championship. We played Clare in the semi-final. It is certainly an era that you look back on with huge pride that you were a part of. It is probably no different than it is now, but it is just a totally, *totally* different GAA. The organisation, the structures, what you have on social media, the sponsorship, the exposure… *totally different.*

You had one chance then… that was it.

I remember a good bit about the game itself. We travelled that time by taxis. There were different guys who would collect guys in say the likes of Croom. Jimmy Carroll would have been collected in the south of the county in Hospital/Herbertstown along with the lads from Garryspillane. So, you'd have the Carrolls from Garryspillane and Jimmy himself in one car.

We used to be collected by a man called Tommy Casey. The 'Well fellas used to always be collected by Tommy. He was an incredible character, just unbelievable. He drove Mick Mackey back in the 1930s and 40s, that's how far back he'd been doing it.

He never drank, never smoked in his life, but an incredible character. He'd bring us all the way down to matches. We wouldn't be gone past Newport, and you'd hear Pa Foley saying, 'Are we there yet? Are we there yet?'

He was the worst traveller ever in a car.

Tommy always went by Newport to go to Thurles. He'd nearly know everyone. He'd always say, 'So-and-so lives across the field there'.

'See that fella there, he was related to him'. The stories Casey would tell… you could just sit down all day and listen to Tommy Casey.

And then you'd have Pa Foley moaning, 'Are we there yet? Are we there?'.

Good times.

But I don't know if we had friendships back then because the following two weeks, we could be meeting each other in a club game and flaking each other on the field with hurleys because it was a different game of hurling back then.

It was shoulder to shoulder and hurleys were broken pretty periodically during matches. It is only years later when you meet up, do you create those friendships with players you played with.

There is going to be a celebration this year in 2023 of the 1973 All-Ireland winning team 50 years after. That is going to be absolutely fantastic. When it comes to fellas you went to school with back in the 70s and you meet up today and say, 'Well, how's things?' and you are talking about what you are doing now, invariably you'll end up going down memory.

'Do you remember this day? Do you remember that time?

'Do you remember we went here?'

It is the memories from the past that are brilliant.

That day against Cork, it was a very hot day. Thurles was packed.

We weren't expected to win because Cork were the dominant team in Munster. They had won four All-Irelands in the 70s.

I got a dubious point that day which I know was wide. Joe McKenna went in and remonstrated with the umpire and the umpire called in the referee. The referee went in and it was given as a point. I'll hold my hand up and say I believe it was wide. Thanks to Joe McKenna, we got the point.

We ended up winning by four.

I can remember we went slightly ahead and Seánie O'Leary got a ball, turned around and pulled, and it came back off the butt of the post. We got breaks.

Would you believe it? I was in Fuerteventura recently and I was watching Limerick and Tipp in the league semi-final. I was in this pub called the Step Inn, and there wasn't two or three people in the bar. I decided I was going to go up and watch the match anyway. There was one guy in the bar.

'Hello. How are you? Where are you from?'

Obviously, we both knew we were Irish anyway. I said, 'What county?'

And he says Cork.

I said Limerick.

I asked him what club and he said Blackrock.

I said, the Well, Patrickswell.

He looked at me and I looked at him.

He said Timmy Murphy.

I said David Punch.

Timmy was in goals in the 1980 Munster final. I never came across the man until then. We got talking then. Poor Timmy was the guy who watched the ball come in before it bounced off his stomach and Éamonn Cregan flicked it into the net.

We got breaks like that. We got goals at crucial times. We got a few lucky breaks. If Timmy Murphy never dropped the ball, Éamonn would have never got the goal. Éamonn Cregan was unique. Very few guys had the talent he had. He could play anywhere.

He even played in goals at one stage. With Limerick he played forward, corner-forward, centre-back in 1973, and corner-forward again in 1980. He was just a talent.

There was just emotion when the final whistle went against Cork in 1980. The sense of pride and relief comes after, but there and then it is just the whole emotion, the fact that you've won a Munster final and it is Cork. It is the emotion more than anything that I remember.

It was unique then. We were straight into an All-Ireland final against Galway. You look back and say maybe we were unlucky it happened that way because every second year the Munster winners and the Leinster winners went straight into the final.

We hadn't a game for seven weeks. Was it a disadvantage? I don't know. But Croke Park was a frightening experience. Jimmy Carroll had a fine game that day. My early recollection on the field was Galway's first goal. It was like listening to a noise boom, turning up the volume. That just went through you. That was nerve-racking.

I am not so sure if that seven-week break went against us, but for any of us who had never played in Croke Park, for us to experience Croke Park it would have been an advantage if we would have gotten a semi-final and obviously won the semi-final to get to the final.

But no, Croke Park was daunting. Galway had played a quarter-final against Kildare and a semi-final against Offaly during that time.

It was my first time playing in Croke Park. I would have loved to have got back there to play again.

"

JIMMY CARROLL

LIMERICK 2-14 CORK 2-10
Munster SHC Final
Semple Stadium, Thurles
JULY 20, 1980

Jimmy Carroll learned from the best, and offered his knowledge on... here managing Emmets in the 2010 Limerick senior hurling final against Kilmallock

★ **LIMERICK:** T Quaid; D Murray, L Enright, Dom Punch; P Fitzmaurice, M Carroll, Sean Foley (capt) (0-1); **J Carroll (0-1)**, David Punch (0-2); L O'Donoghue (0-1), J Flanagan, W Fitzmaurice (0-1); O O'Connor (1-1), J McKenna (0-1), É Cregan (1-6).

★ **CORK:** T Murphy; B Murphy, M O'Doherty, J Horgan; D Coughlan (0-1), J Crowley, D MacCurtain; J Fenton (0-6), T Cashman; T Crowley (0-1), P Horgan (0-1), J Barry Murphy; S O'Leary (1-0), R Cummins, E O'Donoghue (1-1). **Subs:** P Moylan for MacCurtain, C McCarthy for Cummins.

THE ACTION

THERE WERE EMOTIONAL scenes in Thurles, in a first win over the Leesiders in a Munster final since 1940 and Limerick's first championship victory over the Rebels since 1971.

After taking a 1-7 to 1-3 lead into half-time, thanks to a goal by Éamonn Cregan, Limerick held their four-point advantage until the final whistle, with Ollie O'Connor getting in on the goal scoring action after the interval.

Played in front of 43,090, Cork went in as hot favourites and were in search of a record-breaking sixth Munster successive title having won the five previous provincial showdowns – a feat only matched by Cork again from 1982 to '86 and Limerick from 2019 to '23.

Ahead of the game Cork had overcome Tipperary in their semi-final with eight points to spare, while Limerick defeated Clare in the other semi-final by 3-13 to 2-9 in the Gaelic Grounds.

In what was a major blow, Cork lost their captain, Dermot MacCurtain, midway through the second-half and were subsequently forced to make a number of other changes throughout the field. The Cork attack improved in the half with Tim Crowley and John Fenton launching attacks from midfield. Seánie O'Leary scored Cork's second goal in the 12th minute to reduce Limerick's lead to 1-10 to 2-5.

Five minutes later, Ballybrown stalwart Ollie O'Connor bagged Limerick's second goal after a pass from Donal Murray. The goal proved to be the match-winning, vital score and, although Cork were only three points behind, Limerick went on to win by four – their first of two Munster title wins in-a-row.

★★★★★

> 66

I JOINED THE panel in 1978… and we did alright! But then in '79 Noel Drumgoole came onboard and I found him a very, very interesting man straightaway because the first thing he did… there were 12 players from junior clubs brought on the panel. One of them was Johnny Flanagan… Séamus Flanagan's father.

Johnny and myself became good mates. We are both from junior clubs, we are both farmers… and we were both under pressure with cattle.

Noel was from Dublin originally, and he worked inside in Limerick with Bord na gCon. He had a great understanding of how under pressure we were. Was he the best coach in the world? I'd say probably not. Was he the best manager? I'd say yes.

We had 12 junior players and then you'd all of the senior hurlers. You'd the likes of Leonard Enright and all the Patrickswell group, then you'd that special hurler Éamonn Cregan and all the Claughaun boys, and you'd all the South Liberties' lads… and then you'd 12 junior hurlers from nowhere. Nobody knew any of us.

It was Noel Drumgoole's job to integrate us, and start a happy little family because that's what he created. And he started that in the 1978-79 season, and all of a sudden, we were one happy bunch after that.

We went on… we didn't do everything good, but we won a couple of leagues and we won a Munster final in 1980. That was a very special day.

The reason I remember the Munster final in '80 so well is because we were after playing the league final twice, down in Cork against Cork – a draw and a replay.

They beat us in the replay… and into the dressing-room afterwards, and I remember Noel just closed the doors pretty sharp and said, 'It was not a great performance… but we will be meeting these boys in the Munster final. I can guarantee you that… and I guarantee you we'll beat them'.

To say that after kind of being well beaten in the replay of the league final… it gave us all a lift straightaway. I know it personally gave me a lift anyway. I was actually ready for the day that we'd meet them in the Munster final.

I got involved from this little parish, Hospital-Herbertstown, and I was delighted to get my opportunity. I love my club and I've always played with them, and even sometimes I would have a discussion with Noel because if I was missing from a junior match, which might have been a week or two before a senior game with Limerick, we could be knocked out of the championship. He always facilitated that as well. I wouldn't abuse it, but if there was a match on, say maybe a week-and-a-half before a championship match, he'd let me play.

I was in awe going into my first training session with Limerick, particularly when it came to Éamonn Cregan. He was so much better than the rest of us, it was frightening. His skill level… he was a master. I was willing to learn. The first night I was inside in training we were pucking the ball across the field, and who was I picked with… but only Éamonn Cregan. We were pucking the ball back and forth and I was giving it as good as I got… high and low and left and right, and all that!

There was a noise off my hurley because the hook was loose. I was fine and fit at the time. I ram him into the ground afterwards. But then he came out to me after training and he says to me, 'Have you any interest in playing with Limerick?'

And I says, 'Éamonn, why do you think I'm here?'

'First of all, you've two socks and they don't match,' he says. 'And you've a hurley that only looks like a hurley'. Next thing, he goes over to the boot of his car and he pulls out two hurleys and he says, 'Take away one of them, they are good hurleys'. I was so close to telling him to do something else, but I said, 'Fair enough, I'll try it'. The following night we had training… that Thursday night, Cregan came in and he said, 'How'd you get on?' I was part of his team then because I was willing to learn.

I accepted his guidance then, and he made me a more confident person because I tried to become as good as he was. I could never, never become as good, but the harder you try the closer you will get.

Cregan had his skill, but what he used to say to me was that he appreciated that I had a good engine. I wasn't a very skilful hurler at all and my left side wasn't great, but I'd a great engine. Cregan would always tell me what way to strike the ball. If I was hitting say from the right-hand-side of the field on my right side that I should try and keep it to the left-hand-side of the goal and vice versa. It doesn't sound very special, but it worked!

If you needed a score, you had to get the ball to him… and my job was to get the ball to him. I didn't have to do anything more, but I had to get the ball to him. If I got the ball to him my job was done because he'd do the rest.

The drawn game earlier in the year in the league was down in Cork. We were about two or three points down at the end of the game and, all of a sudden, Ollie got a point to draw it. We drew it, and we deserved to draw it.

We felt we were a better team then, coming into the replay. The replay was on two weeks later. It was a beautiful hot day. It was a very hot day down in Cork. They brought on Jimmy Barry-Murphy with about 20 minutes to go, and the next thing he pulled on the ball in the air and stuck it into the back of the net. All of a sudden, we were four points down and they pulled away from us and won the league.

Johnny Flanagan was centre-forward that next day against Cork in the Munster final. The ball was thrown in. Dermot MacCurtain was wing back. Johnny was as strong as a bull. The two boys went at each other for a loose ball towards the wing, and they collided. Johnny got up. Dermot didn't. And that was it! Johnny had a flying good game. Dermot MacCurtain wasn't able to take the punishment that Johnny gave. He wouldn't have had the strength of Johnny.

We brought confidence with us into that match, and we won it. We were delighted, but we didn't over-celebrate it. We got straight to the All-Ireland final then and, unfortunately, we met a team that was ripe to win it, and that was Galway. I hated losing to them but they deserved to win that match.

After Ollie O'Connor got the goal which put us a point up, I was on Moylan in midfield; he was a hardy boy. The ball came out. I was after a good bit of hard work, constant pressure for four or five minutes… and next thing this ball came out. Didn't it go over me… and he ran out to it. I said, *This is it, oh my Jesus!* But wherever I got the legs… I thought my heart was going to come out through my chest. I kept going because he was going for goal with the way it opened up for him. But whatever way I kept going, didn't I put out the hurley and *just* hooked him by a quarter of an inch. I don't think I was able to breathe properly until the match was over! I thought my lungs had collapsed.

A minute or two later, another thing which stands out in my mind took place. Seánie O'Leary got the ball, broke out, and next thing he hit the ball. It was a rocket of a shot. It hit off the butt of the post, came straight back out about 20 yards, and one of the boys cleared it out the field.

I remember after the game, I went in and met Tommy Quaid. I said, 'Tommy, how did you get to that?'

'I didn't get to it at all,' he says. The size of the post was the width of a telegraph pole those days. It hit it in the butt in the middle and came straight back out. I'll never forget that. I knew that day after listening to the likes of Éamonn Cregan and that other special man, Joe McKenna, and other experienced guys like Leonard Enright that you had to have the heart. We were the young guys starting off and we had the legs, but you had to have the heart. We were told that, and we believed that, you had to use the very last little breath in your body… and that you had to get to the ball somehow.

I will never forget the agony and pain I had going through my body trying to get back to the ball that day with Moylan… because there was no point in fouling him. A point would have changed the whole match.

I had to get to him!

I don't know how it happened but I got to him. And after that, I could walk on air. Now, the match was nearly over, but after that, I was afraid of nothing.

Coming back to Hospital and Herbertstown then afterwards was a holy terror.

Everywhere we went… obviously we stopped at all the local places. There were people there that I hadn't seen out for years… old, *old* people. Everywhere you went there were people jumping, there were people shaking your hand, and they were hugging you.

It is a great thing and you feel very important, but you also felt that because of that you have to go again, and you have to do this again. If you want to achieve something you have to do better. It is a way of making you better.

There was a quick turnaround then and straight into an All-Ireland final. For me, it was fantastic, but I was so inexperienced that I didn't cop on. At that time, we had no semi-final. I thought to myself, *That was great*… that you'd a nice little rest and everything.

Not at all… it was a disaster. I discovered that in recent times when you saw where teams got beat when they'd a four-week rest, when they would have been way better off with a two-week rest. We had over a month of rest. I thought we were primed… we probably felt primed and everything.

But we weren't sharp enough at all. We didn't have that dirty hard match behind us. It is something very similar to what happened with the current crop of players in 2019. They've certainly learnt from that since.

In 1981, we played in the first round over in Thurles against Tipperary.

I'll never forget that day because it was the wettest, windiest, dirtiest day. It was early June. We had an established team, Tipperary had a young team. They only had about two or three of their older senior players. They had won the under-21 championship a couple of years prior. They went up and they just blew us off the field. They went 12 points up in the first-half.

We were inside in the dressing-room at half-time and there wasn't a word said. Things were bad. Noel Drumgoole said a few things then, but Joe McKenna, who used to never say too much... I was nearest the door and we stood up to get out, and he said, 'Where are you going?'

I said, 'We better go out and play'. He said, 'You were out there for the last half hour or more and you're doing nothing... like the rest of ye'.

He just LOST IT! He picked me out because I was the midfielder to get the ball in. I wasn't able to get the ball, or at least not enough anyway.

'Look,' he says. 'Get the ball in. We have to get three goals straightaway.' Pointing at me he says, 'You get in at least two to me... maybe three'. He really showed his experience there, like a captain would, by taking the pressure.

'You get the ball into me, and I'll do the rest'. It was like something Cregan would normally do. The first two balls I got went into McKenna... two goals! Third ball in... over the bar. Liam O'Donoghue got one into him and back of the net again. All of a sudden, we were nearly drawing. As it turned out, we actually drew that match that day. Joe McKenna had to score 3-1 to make a draw of the match. It was all Joe McKenna that day. I'll never forget it. I got injured near the end.

We took them on then in the replay inside in Limerick. It was a roasting hot day... an absolute scalder. Mikey Grimes came on and played for me, and had an absolute bomber of a game, and we bate them handy!

The change in the weather and the momentum made all the difference. I equate it to a lot of the great things I've seen with this lovely, good Limerick team that we have now, that when you are going well you will continue to go well and get better, and just get better and better which this team has done.

And then something will happen then and you'll have a bad day.

You'll get beat. A couple of your good players will let you down. That day in 1981, a lot of players let Limerick down, including myself, but once we got a chance to get back and redeem ourselves there wasn't a team in the country who could have lived with us the day of the replay.

Without a doubt, my mother Teresa was my biggest influence growing up.

All of her brothers played with the club here in Hospital, and all of her uncles played in and won All-Irelands with Tipperary. They are from Limerick Junction near Tipperary Town.

My mother always believed in me as a hurler, which was vital because I got an injury as a young fella below at my primary school. A slate fell off the roof of the school, which is a two-storey building, and hit me on the head. I was only five.

I ended up inside in St John's Hospital in Limerick city for roughly nine months, and had many, many operations. I wasn't allowed to play hurling of any kind until I was about 12. The only reason I was allowed to play hurling then was because my mother took me into Gleeson's sports shop in Limerick. It was there in the middle of William Street at the time. She got a helmet. There were no helmets around or worn at the time. I remember it was very expensive. It was £70 or something like that. Then, I was not allowed to play with the team, but I was hurling off the wall at home… I was breaking windows and everything. I was never allowed to play in the field with the boys. Can you imagine the frustration of that? I was as fit as a flea, but I wasn't allowed to play hurling with a team.

Eventually, my mother and my father gave me permission, but it was my mother who was the hurler. She would look after me then. She would take me to every match, and she would be watching me in case I got injured. Once I had the helmet on, I was fine. I couldn't go anywhere unless I had a helmet.

Then when I got going, I was like a little dog that was left loose.

There was no stopping me.

My mam would then always be at the matches. I know where she'd be. And of course, she'd have the rosary beads ready in the morning, and the whole lot. I'd have to meet her after the matches, and the joy that would just be on her face would just make the whole lot worthwhile.

"

PAULINE McCARTHY

LIMERICK 4-3 KILKENNY 2-6
All-Ireland Senior Camogie Championship Semi-Final
Ballyagran, Limerick
AUGUST 17, 1980

Pauline McCarthy and the Limerick camogie team in 1994

★ **LIMERICK:** H Moynihan; J O'Shea; V Mackey, M Neville, J O'Brien; B O'Brien, H Mulcair, B Darcy (2-0); A O'Sullivan, **P McCarthy (1-2)**, B Conway (1-0); B Stokes (0-1).

★ **KILKENNY:** T O'Neill; L Neary; Ann Downey, B Martin (0-1), B O'Sullivan; A Holden, P Muldowney, M Purcell; H O'Neill (0-1), Angela Downey, A Whelan, J Dunne (0-1).

★ GAME OF MY LIFE ★

THE ACTION

HISTORY WAS MADE in Ballyagran when Limerick qualified for their first All-Ireland Senior Camogie Championship final with a well-deserved victory over Kilkenny.

In an exciting game, during which both sides were level on five occasions, it was the home side, despite having the advantage of a strong wind, who started slowly and found themselves 1-2 to 0-2 down inside the opening 10 minutes.

After a nervy opening quarter, both teams exchanged goals before Limerick added a further point and a goal, to take the narrowest of leads into the half-time break – 2-3 to 2-2.

Coming into this All-Ireland semi-final, Limerick comfortably overcame Down in the opening round of the championship, before heavily defeating Derry, who were missing their inspirational midfielder, Sarah Ann Quinn, on a scoreline of 5-8 to 1-1 in their quarter-final clash in Nowlan Park.

Kilkenny were soon level in the second-half and the pre-match favourites looked set to take control. Limerick had other ideas, and hit back with a goal only to see their advantage wiped out with three well taken points by Angela Dowling and Helena O'Neill.

In a dramatic last attack by Limerick, Brigid D'Arcy cracked home the all-important goal that gave the hosts victory and a first final appearance. Outstanding for the winners were Joan O'Brien, Pauline McCarthy and Brigid D'Arcy, while Ann and Angela Downey, Helena O'Neill, and Bridie Martin were most prominent for Kilkenny

With Cork overcoming a disappointing Dublin outfit in the other semi-final in Blackrock, two Munster counties qualified for the All-Ireland Senior Camogie Championship final for the first time. After playing out an exciting draw – Cork 2-7, Limerick 3-4 – in Croke Park on September 15, 1980, it was the Leesiders who won the replay three weeks later, bringing a heart-breaking end to Limerick's first and only appearance in a senior camogie final.

★★★★★

❝

THAT YEAR WAS Limerick's first and only senior All-Ireland final in camogie. Hard to believe Limerick have never made it back to a senior final since. I suppose Limerick camogie has always had small numbers and not enough strength in depth. Every team I was part of, and I was part of lots of Limerick squads, had maybe 10 or 12 of the squad who always came to training; trained hard and prepared well for matches, but there was always a certain cohort who weren't in it 100 percent. That's what it takes though, one hundred percent focus, effort… commitment.

In camogie counties in general, a strong club scene usually meant a weak inter-county scene, or it used to back in the day anyway. It has always been difficult for girls to give the same commitment to club and county. Women are different. Full commitment for a woman is totally different because you could be talking about juggling work, minding children, whatever. A man can say, 'I'm going training'…. and off they go, especially back in the 80s when women had little expectation but be in the kitchen tied to the leg of the table, feeding and cleaning.

It was a struggle for many. Time off was another issue. It wasn't and still isn't as freely available to girls as it is to the fellas. Often, it is the girls who cover the lads when they are off. Publicity for female sports such as camogie and ladies' football was practically non-existent, as I am sure the author of this book will attest to when he went looking for reports and photographs of the 1980 All Ireland Senior Camogie semi-final between Limerick and Kilkenny.

When I was young, three or four years of age, if I wanted to play with somebody else it was always going to be with the boys… I have three brothers and no sisters. Two older and one younger. Children today have play dates, are always being entertained and it's always… what's next. Back in the 60s there was no such thing as play dates, and you certainly wouldn't be taken anywhere just to play. If it wasn't within walking distance, then you weren't going anywhere… so I played in the yard and fields at home with my three brothers.

I didn't have any role models when I was young, or rather, I didn't have any female role models. I wasn't aware any other girls were playing hurling like me. It wasn't until I was 11, when we started a local camogie team in Ballybricken for a couple of years, that I realised, Girls play too ….and in a team. Up to that, I was just playing away with the boys. It had no big significance to me that women were or weren't involved in sport. I was just playing for the fun of it. My mother was a South Liberties woman, so we went to all the South Liberty matches.

My hero that time was Eamon Grimes. I imagined I was Eamon Grimes when I was out hurling in the field by myself and the commentator on my games was always Michael O' Hehir. I'm not sure Eamon will appreciate this information, but he was a god in my eyes.

Camogie teams were few and far between when mam was a girl. It was difficult to arrange games and keep teams together. My mother didn't play, although she did tell stories of going to camogie matches and of a team in Fedamore and Pallasgreen. They had to wear so many clothes too while playing. Teams appeared and disappeared regularly. All those teams were gone when I came along.

Ballybricken was a small rural parish and wasn't endowed with many players, so if the boys were short at under-14, then I'd be asked to play. My brothers were playing anyway so I would always be at the matches. A girl can play up to 14 years with the boys but after that, the boys are too strong and can hurt you. One day I was corralled into playing in goals for the under-21's in Caherconlish against Doon. We got riddled! They beat the living daylights out of us that day.

I suppose to come from not having a local club to play with growing up or a camogie role model, and go on to play for Limerick at all levels, is very satisfying and, I suppose, I am proud of those achievements. There was no local club for me until four years ago when St Ailbe's started an adult Junior B camogie team. I jumped at the chance to play with them even though I was well past my sell by date, but it gave me a chance to carry on playing and the best part was the field was only a mile and a half away. I was off winning club championships and playing for Limerick, but none of the neighbours ever saw me play... only an odd one here and there. They might come to a match but mostly it was some other parish I was playing for. I'm extremely grateful to all the clubs I played for down the years.

The players I played with were some of the best camogie players in Limerick and the country at the time. Limerick clubs were very successful and won county, Munster and All-Ireland club titles in the 1970's, 80s, and 90s. Clubs such as Croagh Kilfinny, Ballyagran and Granagh Ballingarry all have All Ireland Senior

Club titles. Ahane won county and Munster titles too and were unfortunately beaten in two All-Ireland club finals. Without a doubt, I have been extremely lucky to have played with those players and teams, and to have been around at the time of the late 70s and early 80s at club level. That was obviously my time because I went over 30 years before I won the next senior title.

When we played Kilkenny in the All-Ireland semi-final in 1980, I was playing with Ballyagran - a club in south Limerick and 25 miles away from home. I often think my father was stone mad bringing me to Ballyagran twice a week for club training and then off to Adare twice a week for county training. If that wasn't enough, I started playing football with Newtown Shandrum and he used to bring me to that training too and their matches all over Cork. I never had to beg for a lift from anyone. He always brought me. He loved the camogie especially, but all the games, and we had great times travelling here and there. When I got my own car and had to pay for my own petrol, I was forced to re-assess all that travelling and eventually left Ballyagran and Newtown Shandrum for a club nearer home. That win against Kilkenny was an absolutely massive achievement for us because we weren't supposed to win that game. Kilkenny were serial All-Ireland winners.

Limerick weren't a hugely successful camogie county at that time. Our All-Ireland appearances were few and far between, and we had only become senior in 1977. We were missing our centre-back and captain, Geraldine O'Brien for the match, so were up against it. Geraldine was a brilliant centre-back and playing against Kilkenny we couldn't afford to be without anyone. I remember coming off the field in Croke Park in 1977, having just won the Junior All-Ireland and meeting that same Kilkenny team running out to play in their senior final that same day.

Here we were then, three years later, playing them in a senior semi-final. Unreal!

We started that senior championship without much hope, but we did have a very nice draw. We had an injection of younger players coming onto the panel which was a shot in the arm for the team who had lost two Senior National League finals in 1978 and '79 and been knocked out of the championship on both those years. We had 19 on the panel for the 1980 championship, who were never listed for games, but those girls were very important to our success that year. Players such as Liz Moloney and Helen Clifford (Bruff), Anne Sheehy, Helen Sheehy, Martina O'Donoghue (Croagh Kilfinny), Elizabeth Hayes (Ballyagran, but from Bruff) and Bridget Darcy (Croagh Kilfinny, but from Patrickswell)

We played Down in the first round, and we beat them handily enough. Then we travelled to Derry to play them in the quarter-final. Derry were missing a few of their good players and we hammered them up in Swatragh. That got us to the semi-final, and we were down to play Kilkenny and, of course, we were to have no hope. Not only playing against the vastly experienced Kilkenny, but also without our regular centre-back. Kilkenny had Angela and Anne Downey, Bridie Martin, Mary Fennelly, Helena O'Neill and many more. Their team was littered with stars, and nobody knew who Limerick were. Maybe we were using a siege mentality to motivate ourselves by building up Kilkenny, I can't remember, but whatever it was Carrie had us ready to go that day.

That was back when it was 12-a-side, so once the ball was thrown-in we were in the game, all the time.

We were playing with the wind in the first-half against Kilkenny, and we started poorly. They were 1-2 to 0-2 up early and our two points were from frees. We got a lucky goal to get back into the game. Anne Downey, of all people, favoured one side over the other back then and we knew that. She threw the ball up inside her own square right in front of the goal… Betty Conway blocked the ball into the net… GOAL! That levelled the game 1-2 each.

It gave us a bit of confidence, but we got brought back down to reality again when they scored a second goal. However, we managed to get a goal of our own just before half-time and went in a point up at the break. Geraldine O'Brien was missing, but Margie Neville moved from the corner-back position to centre-back and played a stormer, and Vera Mackey was brought back from the forwards to play corner-back marking Angela Downey. Anne O'Sullivan, a native of Ballylanders, was promoted from the subs to the forward line.

Vera was fast to run. She was always our girl for Angela Downey, because Angela, while she was a brilliant hurler too, her biggest attribute was that she was lightning fast. We needed someone to keep a hurley in her face all the time, so Vera was assigned to do that… and she did. Angela Downey only scored a goal and three points. That was an amazing result for us because she normally scored two or three goals, and seven or eight points in every game. Kilkenny were kingpins in camogie at the time so to beat them that day was surreal. It took a while to sink in.

In the second-half, I got a goal. It was just one of those sweet strikes you sometimes get. Ber O'Brien pulled on a ball out in midfield and, as it was just passing me, I let fly. I just met it on the full and it flew off the stick past the goalkeeper before she even saw it. That put us up again. Angela Downey scored three points then and I suppose other years we would have collapsed… but they couldn't shake us off that day. We managed to claw them back and Bridget D'Arcy scored a goal right on the stroke of full-time… and that goal won us the game.

Kilkenny didn't take the defeat well at all. They were supposed to win, like! Who the hell were we? They tried to make out there was a hole in the net and that is how the last goal went in. They took photographs of the net, and everything. They said the goalkeeper was on her knees and the ball couldn't have gone in. But that ball was behind her before she ever got to the ground. It was David vs Goliath stuff… fantastic. I remember coming off the field and thinking, Mother of God, we're going to Croke Park for the senior final.

There were no dressing-rooms in Ballyagran back then, so we had to come off the field and walk down the road with the supporters to the local hall to change. And we came down arm-in-arm, singing down the road.

We should have won the first day against Cork in the final.

There was a disputed point for Cork. One of the umpires waved it wide and the other umpire put up her hand for a point. The referee conferred with them, but Cork got the point. We eventually had to level the game at the end, but that point still sticks in the craw a bit. I had a good view of it and would still swear to this day, it was wide.

In the replay, they got off to a great start. Cork are always the same, and they still do it. If they can beat you in the first 10 minutes, they'll do that. They came out of the blocks absolutely flying, and they caught us early in the match and we just couldn't catch them. We did make a late comeback and nearly scored what would have been a winning goal when a Geraldine O'Brien free just flew centimetres wide. But we lost and with that, the chance of winning an All-Ireland senior title for Limerick. I suppose that is why I have played for so long, searching for the chance to get back there and try again. It was a sad ending. It is still a feeling of a missed opportunity. We had was a good team. Carrie Clancy was our manager, and she had a special way about her. Honestly, you'd go through a wall for her. Just for that particular group, that was the match... we should have won it. The chance never came again.

There is self-doubt going into a big game like that. While we talked the talk of being positive and winning, we knew in the back of our minds we had always been beaten at senior level by Cork. You believe, and you have to believe or otherwise you'll go nowhere, but if you are constantly being beaten at that level by the same teams, there is always going to be that doubt until you beat them... then the fear goes.

Since then, Limerick have had an odd victory over Cork, but the next time we played them, they would hammer us again. We don't have a history of long-term suppression of Cork or Tipp. Limerick camogie, since then, have won junior titles and intermediate titles but have never reached the top level of senior and co-exist with the Cork's, Kilkenny's and Galway's on a continued basis. Like the hurlers, it is extremely difficult to get over one of the traditional winners and you need to do that to get confidence and drive on from there.

It takes a long time for work done in the clubs to reach inter-county level. There isn't a history of total sacrifice and total focus, even in the current team. The best players in the county aren't playing with the current Limerick team. Why?

I have no understanding of that, that you don't want to play for your county team.

It is amazing how camogie has grown since the 1980s.

I went to secondary school in Hospital, Presentation De La Salle as it was known then and I'd say, I was probably the only one playing camogie... and I was playing for Limerick by the time I was in second year. I was playing county, and nobody knew. At the time, camogie didn't exist in any city schools, just a few out the county like Hospital, Kilfinnane and Rathkeale. It has been one of the reasons for the upsurge in numbers playing that eventually the city schools introduced camogie.

After playing in the 1980 All Ireland final, Limerick camogie disappeared for a while. Most of the 1980 team retired, and I and a few other younger girls were left. There was a good junior team, but those players were not allowed move on to the senior team because the executive at the time decided they could win a junior

All-Ireland with that group, so the senior team had no new blood coming into it. I suppose that is why I still play because I was robbed of what should have been my best years in my twenties.

It's easy to retire from camogie when you have five or six All-Irelands in your back-pocket. I played with Limerick for a long time and that was always the thing for me, to try to get back and win a senior All-Ireland. The junior team didn't win either and eventually in 1988 Limerick regraded back to junior level. We were still in disarray and started that 1988 Junior Championship without a coach or selectors. We managed to beat Cork in the first round of the Munster Championship and organised ourselves a little bit after that. We reached the All-Ireland final on pure hurling ability alone.

We weren't fit or prepared enough for it though, and we lost it to Galway. It took until the early 90s, when Phil Bennis came on board initially, followed by Éamonn Cregan for attitudes to change and some success to arrive again. The fact that Phil Bennis would want to train us! That's the way we used to look at things. Phil was a great motivator, and we won the National League that year but were beaten by Tipperary in the Munster final. Phil only stayed with us for one year but the change in mentality of the entire set-up was the basis for further success in later years. Éamonn Cregan came in then, and that was like, God, we got Éamonn Cregan. Wow!

Éamonn stayed with us for four or five years. It was fantastic for Limerick camogie that Éamonn, this huge star of Limerick hurling would give his time to us. That's the ridiculous way we looked at things, instead of looking at it and saying, Why wouldn't he give his time to us? We were very successful with Éamonn at the helm and won the junior All Ireland in 1995 and the intermediate in 1996 to regain our senior Status.

In 1980, when we were in the senior final, Carrie Clancy tormented everyone for sponsorship of new gear… but she wasn't able to convince anyone to come on board. I suppose our 1980 adventure was swallowed up by the Limerick hurlers who were also in the 1980 senior All-Ireland hurling final. Times were tough and any sponsorship available went to the hurlers. There was little or no publicity for a company in sponsoring a camogie team.

When I started playing with Limerick in 1974, we were playing in these heavy green pleated skirts with a red sash belt. I was told that the skirts were previously green pinafores that had the top cut off them to make a skirt. At least I managed to miss wearing the pinafore and the black tights with white socks rolled down. It was like wearing a tweed blanket during a match. You can imagine the weight of it when it got wet. We used to wear polo shirts for jerseys.

We had those polo shirts from 1974 to 1980. The sleeves were ripped, and the buttons had fallen out, but they did us, they had to. In 1977, we got new skirts. They were green wool. Hot too, but way lighter than the tweed, and had a red waist band. I still don't know what the significance of the red sash and red waist band was? Those were the skirts we had for the 1980 final.

The county board bought 20 plain white polo shirts before the 1980 final, and myself and my mother sewed the numbers onto the backs of the polo shirts the Thursday night before the All-Ireland. My mother was great to sew. Carrie Clancy managed the Genelle shops on William Street and O'Connell Street at the time. The William Street shop was near the Limerick Sports Store, and I'd say she tormented Christy Williams for gear or anything, for the final. He did give us a set of green soccer jerseys – the ones that had the long peak collar and a white V neck.

We wore those as a tracksuit top for the final over the white polo shirts going out onto Croke Park. We had asked the county board for some part of the hurlers' money and, to be fair, they gave us £100 the day of the All-Ireland and got a nice photo of the presentation with the backdrop of the old Cusack Stand in Croke Park. Different times back then.

Limerick camogie would have worn white tops and green skirts with white socks up to fairly recent times, when they moved to all green. I think the first time we got actual jerseys was for the 1988 junior semi-final. They were white with a green pin stripe. They were class! Since then, the skirts have changed too from wrap arounds to pleated skorts, and now the skort with the in-built shorts. All of which were and are very uncomfortable. I suppose we will never see the shorts which would be way more convenient. We are asking for shorts since I was 16. I don't know what the issue is. The LGFA wear shorts. Mostly, it's the same players. We train in shorts, we play challenge games in shorts, they are less expensive… but we must wear skorts for official matches. Beyond logic.

"

GER HEGARTY

LIMERICK 3-11   CORK 3-11
Munster SHC Semi-Final
Semple Stadium, Thurles
JUNE 14, 1987

Ger Hegarty powers out of defence in the 1994 All-Ireland final against Offaly

★ **LIMERICK:** T Quaid; P O'Connor, P Carey, D Barry; L O'Donoghue, N Leonard (capt), P Creamer; D Punch, J Carroll (0-1); **G Hegarty**, T Kenny, P Kelly (0-5); S Fitzgibbon (1-1), P McCarthy (1-3), G Kirby (1-0). **Subs:** L Enright for O'Connor, A Carmody (0-1) for Leonard, M Ryan for Kelly.

★ **CORK:** G Cunningham; D Mulcahy, R Browne, D Walsh; T Cashman, P Hartnett, J Cashman; T O'Sullivan (0-3), J Fenton (0-5); K Kingston (2-1), T Mulcahy, T McCarthy (0-1); J Fitzgibbon (1-0), G Fitzgerald (0-1), K Hennessy (capt).

★ GAME OF MY LIFE ★

THE ACTION

A YOUNG LIMERICK side came into this Munster SHC semi-final full of confidence after overcoming a strong Waterford side in the quarter-final, and showed great value to secure a replay after coming back from being seven points down in this highly exciting clash against their age-old rivals Cork in Thurles.

The last sensational, yet controversial, score fell to Cork but in truth this game was really a case of the favourites failing to win and Limerick showing great heart and determination to earn themselves a draw. Inspired by a brilliant display of goalkeeping masterclass by Tommy Quaid, Limerick rallied magnificently to wipe out that seven-point deficit and even took the lead when Shane Fitzgibbon rattled the back of the Cork net three minutes from time.

Cork supporters watched dejectedly on as it looked like Limerick were on course for a famous win against a hotly favoured Rebels side who were in search of six Munster titles in-a-row, until Kieran Kington's last-grasp equalising point, 45 seconds into injury time.

It was a dramatic climax to a game that went very much Limerick's way in the early stages, swung in Cork's direction after the vital decision to switch Teddy McCarthy to midfield, and victory stayed within the Leesiders' grasp after Kingston found the net 13 minutes into the second half. However, just as it looked Cork had one foot put into the Munster final, the Rebels were left to rue their missed scoring chances when Gary Kirby scored Limerick's second goal just after the hour mark.

Limerick supporters, so accustomed to heartbreak and near misses, could only watch on as Kieran Kingston got the latest of late equaliser to set up a replay. In the second game, Cork's John Fenton scored what is often regarded as one of the greatest hurling goals of all-time as the Rebels ran out comfortable 13-point winners – 3-14 to 0-10 – to set up a Munster final against Tipperary.

★★★★★

> 66

THE GAME THAT stands out in my memory was a match that had many twists and turns in it, and had we held on to win it would have propelled us down a road to a whole new chapter in Munster hurling history.

We were on the attack and we went a point up going into injury time. I remember the ball was pucked out by Ger Cunningham in the Cork goal. We won possession at midfield… and what I thought was an obvious free. I was on the ground and our team doctor, the late Dr Richard O'Flaherty, came over and I think we both were thinking, *This is great we are in the Munster final.*

The next thing, I was looking up from the ground at the referee John Moore, who was pointing the other way and giving a free to Cork. John Fenton stood over the long distance free but it went wide.

Someone threw a billiard ball from the terraces onto the field and it delayed the puck-out, which I think allowed the referee to add another minute or two. Cork went down the field a couple of seconds later and Kieran Kingston got the equaliser to set up a replay which Cork won.

That was an ageing Cork side against a new-look Limerick side. If we had won that, we would have been in the Munster final against Tipperary, rather than Cork playing Tipperary, a game which famously Tipperary went on to win in Killarney and end a famine for them.

Tipperary were emerging with a very young side under 'Babs' Keating and went on to dominate in Munster until the early 90s and picked up a few All-Irelands along the way.

I sometimes wonder, had that free gone to Limerick, as I felt it should, and had we made it to the Munster final to play Tipperary, how things might have worked out?

That Limerick team of 1987 was filled with many players from the under-21 side that had won the All-Ireland earlier that year, and when merged with players like the great Leonard Enright, Shane Fitzgibbon and Danny Fitzgerald, it had huge potential.

Cork on the other hand had well known stars like Kevin Hennessy, John Fenton, Teddy McCarthy, Kieran Kingston, and Tony O' Sullivan, but with the under-21 success we were going into the match with great confidence.

My memory of the match is clear and I really enjoyed it even though Cork went on to beat us fairly well in the replay a fortnight later. Even so, I think that game was a starting point for the Limerick side of the early 90s that had many great players in it.

The disappointing thing was that we got to two All-Ireland finals, but lost them both. I always believed that if we had got over the line in one, we could have gone on to win a couple.

But unfortunately, we didn't.

That first All-Ireland, as the current side found out, is just so tough! Limerick won by a point against Galway in 2018 when they could have won it by a lot more. But just to get over the line and to win it by one point was so important, because all the pressure and baggage of 1973… 45 years of history, is suddenly gone in an instant.

And Limerick have hurled away without baggage since that time.

The similarity with the current side is that a lot of the current Limerick team won an under-21 All-Ireland in 2015, and three years later won the All-Ireland.

The sooner you make the breakthrough, the sooner you get that baggage off your back. There are massive similarities between 2018 and 1992, 1994, and 1996 when we were so close but didn't do it.

A lot of it, I think, was the pressure of getting the 1973 thing closed out. Getting that monkey off the back was a difficult thing to do. We couldn't do it unfortunately.

The current side did it, and even though they fell over the line against Galway, they got it done. That was the most important thing. They got it won. Whether it was by one point or by 10 points, it was won… it was over. And in 2019, 2020, 2021, 2022 and now again this year with four in-a-row completed, they continue to write history.

I have no doubt about it, if we had won that game against Cork in 1987, it would have set us up for a golden seven or eight years.

At that time, you'd Mike Houlihan, Gary Kirby, Ciarán Carey, and you'd the Nash brothers… we'd quality players coming through all over the park. It was just all about getting that breakthrough game to get you on the road. Limerick had gone through a barren spell. We won the Munster Championship in 1981, but '82, '83, '84, '85, and '86 were barren years. It is very hard to make that breakthrough to win an All-Ireland, even after a four or five year difficult term, never mind 45.

The following year, 1988, we got beaten by Tipperary who had won the Munster Championship in '87. They had beaten Cork in the Munster final that we felt we should have been in and would have had a great chance of winning, and suddenly, Tipperary – a bit like the current Limerick side – were established and they beat us in 1988, '89, and in '90.

Suddenly, Tipperary had got their All-Ireland under their belt and they were hurling with the freedom that the current Limerick side are hurling with today. It was all because they got that Munster Championship win in 1987.

That was a critical year for me in '87. It was a critical year for what might have been, especially if we had got the win in that so-called drawn match.

But I have no regrets.

That was a very memorable game. It was a great game. I can remember there was a very big crowd there. It was my first time playing in front of a full house. I really enjoyed the game.

I got my love for the game from my mother and father. I have three brothers, John, Paul, and Joe, and we all played for our club, Old Christians. John was certainly at the level that was required to play inter-county, but work pulled him to Dublin and he played little after that.

My other two brothers, Paul and Joe, were also very, *very* good hurlers, but they had no aspirations to play at inter-county level, but were and still are great servants for the club.

I'm not so sure if Gearóid was massively influenced by what I did in a Limerick jersey when he was growing up. He was born in 1994 and I retired from inter-county hurling in '98 so he was only a little tot when I was still playing.

I actually saw Gearóid as having huge potential as a footballer. I didn't see that ability with hurling, if I am honest. When he emerged at around 21, I would say that University of Limerick and John Kiely played huge roles in bringing him to where he is today and giving him the confidence that he now has.

I really enjoy modern day hurling, and the levels of skill and fitness versus my day are off the chart. Thirty years ago, you got the ball and hit it long time after time, whereas today you need to think more and play is much more varied. I suppose you could say keeping possession is *everything* now.

Now, you get the ball and you've got to be thinking on your feet as to where the ball is going, where to play it, and who is in the best position to get the ball. That whole side of the game is evolving.

Certainly, the players of today are stronger, fitter, faster and they use the ball so well. The behaviours today are so different. This is professional hurling that is going on at the moment, bar payment. The current Limerick side are prepared as well as any side in any professional sport.

Did we enjoy our time? We had an absolute ball.

Along the way we met great personalities, like Noel Drumgoole who gave me a start in 1985, and Phil Bennis and Éamonn Cregan and Tom Ryan, all men who gave so much for the game in Limerick.

While we didn't have the resources that Limerick have today, we still trained hard, maybe three nights a week and played a match at the weekend if there was a game on. We thoroughly enjoyed the bit that we did, and we gave it our best. We came up a little bit short, but no regrets.

That game in 1987 is certainly a case of what might have been. A young Limerick side just came up that little bit short.

Inches.

I have no doubt that all the lads I played with over the years are enjoying this golden era that we find ourselves in and hoping, like me, that there is more still to come from this wonderful bunch of players now wearing the green and white of Limerick.

"

CIARÁN CAREY

LIMERICK 0-14 TIPPERARY 0-13
National Hurling League Final
Gaelic Grounds, Limerick
MAY 10, 1992

Ciarán Carey shakes hands with Wexford captain Martin Storey before the 1996 All-Ireland final

★ **LIMERICK:** T Quaid; B Finn, P Carey, D Nash; M Houlihan (0-1), **C Carey (0-2)**, A Garvey; M Reale (0-1), G Hegarty (0-2); M Galligan, A Carmody, G Kirby (0-4); L Garvey (0-1), J O'Connor (0-1), S Fitzgibbon (0-1). **Subs:** R Sampson (0-1) for Garvey, P Davoren for Galligan.

★ **TIPPERARY:** K Hogan; P Delaney, N Sheehy, G Frend; B Ryan, C Bonnar, R Ryan; D Carr (0-1), A Ryan; M Cleary (0-4), J Hayes, C Stakelum (0-3), P Fox (0-3), D Ryan, N English (0-2). **Sub:** J Leahy for Hayes.

THE ACTION

LIMERICK CAPTAIN JOE O'Connor was a happy man as he held aloft the National Hurling League trophy in front of 35,000 supporters packed into the Gaelic Grounds after the Treaty men secured their 10th league title – their first in seven years.

After topping Division 1A, following wins against Tipperary, Kilkenny, Down and Laois, Phil Bennis' charges overcame Cork in the league semi-final in the Gaelic Grounds before facing the Premier County again in the final.

A pre-match move by Phil Bennis, switching his fellow Patrickswell man, Ciarán Carey to centre-back proved dividends as the Shannonsiders secured the title thanks to a late point from substitute Ray Sampson.

Yet when Tipperary, who had made easing pickings of Limerick at the semi-final stage of the previous four Munster Championships in 1988, '89, '90, and '91, marched into a comfortable half-time lead of 0-11 to 0-3, even the most optimistic of Treaty supporters wouldn't have predicted the outcome. At one stage, Tipp were 10 points up.

However, once Gary Kirby pointed from a free 40 seconds after the restart, the Ennis Road venue became a sea of green, the sense of belief grew on both the pitch and in the stands, and the pendulum slowly began to swing in Limerick's favour. And in an almost reverse outcome of the opening half, Limerick outscored their neighbours by 0-11 to 0-2 in the final 35 minutes.

Just three minutes into the second-half, Limerick had narrowed the deficit to seven – 0-12 to 0-5. Tipp struggled to get going again and for the next 10 minutes Limerick scored five points without response, as efforts from Mike Houlihan, Ger Hegarty, Gary Kirby, Shane Fitzgibbon, and Mike Reale made it a two-point game going into the final quarter.

With six minutes left, the impressive Carey brought the sides level for the first time, and when the Gaelic Grounds erupted in response there was always only going to be one winner.

★★★★★

>

THE GAME THAT sticks out in my head is the National League final in 1992. The reason I remember that game well is because it would have been in the group stage that I would have played centre-back for the first time.

We played Kilkenny on a Sunday. On the Thursday night beforehand, we were in Punch's Bar in Patrickswell. There was a night there where Patrickswell were either launching a book or talking about a book, and they wanted present players and ex-Limerick players there.

I was down at that, and at the same time there was a Limerick management meeting upstairs with Phil Bennis and the selectors. I can remember going to the loo and Phil landed alongside me. He must have come downstairs to use the toilet, and he just turned to me.

Prior to this, I'd have played corner-forward, half-forward, and corner-forward again, for Limerick. He landed alongside me and he said, 'Hi Ciarán, we're playing you centre-back now Sunday'. That's when I first heard it. It was a shock, but would I have relished it at the time? I would, of course.

I remember the league final then, because it was my first league final playing and it was my first league final playing centre back. It was a terrible day… wind and rain. We were down 10 points by half-time. We clawed our way back and we won the game. Up until that point, Tipperary would have given us a nice little toasting in the championship. It was my first experience in overturning them in a big occasion and on a big day.

Phil Bennis was an outstanding manager, a manager before his time; he was brave enough to see it and he trusted me.

I'd a bit of experience at that time with the club, so I knew he trusted me to the hilt and I knew if he put me in there, it was to do a job. It was a huge thing at the time. Looking back on it, one would have liked to have been a bit like Brian Whelahan having No 5 on his back throughout his whole career, near enough, until at the tail-end of it they put him in full-forward.

I was a bit unfortunate… I started at 13, went to 10, back to 13… and then 6, 8… back to 6, 8, a little venture at 11… and then back to 6. It would have been nice to have been left in a position and to fulfil your potential then in that role, where you would have felt you were most comfortable playing.

It is hard to know if my career would have been different if Phil hadn't decided to put me back to No 6 that day against Kilkenny. At that stage of my career, I was well and truly into good habits and no matter what number I had on my back, I was going to empty the tank… and the spare tank.

Phil was clever, and cute enough, and if you ask players where they would like to play, they'll answer you. If you asked them where you think you might fulfil your potential, the answer might be different.

I think Phil was able to spot that in me, he reckoned having 6 on my back would be the greatest chance of me fulfilling my potential as a player… and I think he was right.

I would have always admired Kilkenny, and I still do, but especially in the Brian Cody era. Even back then, I can remember watching Kilkenny and there was a fella playing corner-back, Dick O'Hara – a very good player. I remember Cody playing. I remember watching Frank Cummins, 'Fan' Larkin, Noel Skehan, Matt Ruth, and Ger Henderson at centre-back… another great player. I was only a young fella. Then Christy Heffernan, a different era, came along… so beating Kilkenny was massive.

The league final in 1992 stands out for lots of reasons. In our journey to winning the final, we were after beating Kilkenny, Cork, and now Tipperary. Tipp were All-Ireland champions the year before. Without a doubt, what we did in '92, winning the league, gave us huge confidence to go on and do what we did in 1994, winning Munster and getting to an All-Ireland final. It stemmed from there.

I would look back on that period – 1992 to '96 – and what I did in a Limerick jersey, I did with huge pride. Looking back on it now, we had to navigate a lot of stuff ourselves. We had to think on our feet. There were no sports psychologists back then. We had to gear ourselves up and get ourselves ready for every match.

It was lashing raining.

It was a huge win at the time. There are a few brilliant interviews on YouTube. Phil Bennis gives a great interview. Marty Morrissey asked him, 'What did you say at half time, Phil?'

'I said nothing to them, Marty… only to go out and hurl'.

Without a doubt, I look back on it with huge pride having won the league that year. That was an outstanding win because that Tipperary had Nicky English, Pat Fox… they'd Declan Carr, Joe Hayes, Bobby Ryan… they'd Aidan Ryan. They'd a packed team. I got major confidence and major self-belief from that game because you are beating the biggest gun in the country at the time in Tipperary.

It was a great period. Munster was so strong. It was brilliant. If we had jumped the fence in 1994, I believe we were on a run then, but that's all ifs. But that's the way it goes. You can't change the past. The only way you can deal with the past is to live well today.

We were after being beaten in 1989, '90, and '91 – three years in-a-row by Tipp. Myself personally, I was after playing and being beaten in – in the middle of it and before it – four under-21 Munster finals, so for me it was my first jump at a medal and there was a bit of relief because it was all beatings… beatings, beatings before that.

Back then when you were beaten… GONE!

Balloon burst for 12 months. That's the way it was unfortunately, so it was a huge moment in my career, a huge moment that we finally won a small bit of silverware. And not only did we win silverware, it made it that bit sweeter beating Tipperary.

In the championship that year we lost to Cork in the Munster final; Clare beat us in 1993, and we'd new management in '94. With new management you want to impress and you want to leave your mark as well.

Tom Ryan brought in his crew. Tom would have picked up his own reputation at club level but, to be fair, by the time he finished his career, everybody in the country knew him. He was an exceptional manager, and you would want to play for him.

There were certain players he might have spoken to, other players he mightn't have to say a whole pile to, because he trusted them and he knew their pedigree. My relationship with him was always good, always top class, and he always had the utmost faith and trust in me. He didn't have to say a whole pile to me.

Him looking at me said enough. I knew what he would have meant.

The journey in 1994 was absolutely brilliant. The '94 All-Ireland would also stick out for a big reason for me. It was my first All-Ireland final ever attending, and it was my first one playing in. I killed two birds with the one stone that day.

Even if you think of the enormity of that, I'd never been at an All-Ireland final and I'd never soaked up all the atmosphere and all that goes with it.

My philosophy was, whether it was Croke Park, Thurles, or Patrickswell, I still saw it only as a field. Still only a game, but it was a different arena, a different title… and a different type of circus. None of that really would have impacted me. I would have moulded myself into that kind of ruthless thinking.

If I have to be ruthlessly honest, looking back on that era, and not to be kidding ourselves, there were super teams in that era. Kilkenny were exceptional… Cork were good, Tipp were good, Clare were good, Limerick were good… Offaly were good, as were Wexford. You had a pick of seven teams that had the potential to win an All-Ireland.

I don't have any regrets. None at all, because my frame of mind really is when you go to Croke Park – and back then the quarter-finals, semi-finals, and final were always in Croke Park – the bottom line is, it's a given that you have to produce the goods if you are going to get the results and if you're going to get across the line.

Automatically, that would have been my frame of mind, so there is nothing I would change really to be fair; if we didn't travel the road we travelled and got the experience that we got, that in itself has moulded us into who we are today and now.

For those reasons, I certainly wouldn't change anything.

I remember this particular game, and when I am telling this story we are being mindful of concussion.

We played Galway in a National League game above in Ballinasloe. Stephen McDonagh was corner-back and Declan Nash was in the other corner-back. In fairness to the two of them, and definitely to Stephen… Stephen would have got belts, but he never would have got belts from the shoulders up, they'd be used to getting clatters on the hands and legs. Like us all, you get immune to that.

But the same day, Stephen got a belt in the head and it knocked the stuffing out of him. Declan got a bad belt in the nose. There was a lot of blood. Declan was allergic to blood. He was kind of fainting.

The ironic thing about it was, 10 minutes into the second-half I got a bad belt and we'd no doctor. The doctor from Galway came in. I was down on one knee. In the middle of the field, he banged in four staples.

The game was over and he saw me again, and banged in another four staples. I walked into the dressing-room and Declan was in the corner with an entourage around him with a bit of blood still coming from the nose. Stephen was over with another entourage around and he was nearly getting sick. I walked in on my own and I'd eight stitches on the back of the crown, and I'd say no one even knew about it.

There were no helmets in those days! That will tell you the changes in hurling… any bit of blood now and you're off. That would have happened a few times. I remember playing Cork in a league game in Kilmallock.

Dr Richard O'Flaherty was our doctor, Lord have mercy on his soul. The same thing happened, I got a belt in the eye in the second-half. Straight into the dugout… two or three stitches. Back out onto the field.

There are huge changes. The modern game with the science behind it, the strength and conditioning behind it, the planning behind it, and the coaching behind it, it's absolutely outstanding the way it's moved.

You'd be often asked the question, 'How would ye fare out in the modern game?' It is a simple enough answer. If we had the same preparation, and the same training, to me it would be like a glove in the hand. Even at centre-back in my time you are covering 5, you are covering 7, you are covering across the way. We were sweeping when it wasn't fashionable to be sweeping.

I think when you look at a lot of the players back in my time, you could pick the players that could slot in in the modern era. You know the ones that, if they got the same type of training, they'd slot in there. You see people now comparing the current Limerick team to the Kilkenny team in the 00s. I think it is probably a bit wrong because it is different eras and different styles and types of hurling. You are not comparing like with like.

With the club, we played O'Donovan Rossa above in Kilmallock in the All-Ireland club semi-final in 1988. That game stands out for me for different reasons than the Limerick game, unfortunately.

The reason that particular game stands out the most for me, at club level, is poor Tony O'Brien – he was our selector, Lord have mercy on his soul – got a massive heart attack inside in the main hall in Kilmallock. I can remember his poor wife, Joan crying, and the ambulance coming in and everybody doing their best, but unfortunately, he passed away.

That sticks out for that reason.

Tony had hurled with Limerick. Himself and his wife had seven kids at the time. I was young at the time. It was my first time experiencing something like that. It is something we don't see, it is something we don't expect in the game, and it is something you don't expect to see at your own doorstep. It definitely left a huge impact on me at the time.

We were after winning the Munster Club and we were playing O'Donovan Rossa from Antrim. It happened after the match. They were after beating us. It was a horrible journey back to the 'Well. You are not prepared for a sudden death and when it hits as hard as that did at the time, it just felt that you were in the twilight zone… this wasn't real. Sudden death and suicide are probably the worst deaths, and this was as sudden as you get.

He was talking to us in the dressing-room, and a half an hour later he is in the middle of the clubhouse and the ambulance crew were around him trying to revive him.

I hurled with all of Tony's sons. All brilliant guys. They were all young at the time, so Joan deserves serious credit for how she had to mother and father her seven kids for the rest of her life.

Patrickswell as a community was brilliant.

The local community was also brilliant at the time when it came to my own brother, Paul but when the dust settles, it is difficult. His poor wife, Anna to this day is left with her two sons, Fíonn and Paul Óg, and she is still finding it difficult. I am still finding it difficult myself, but you do find strength somewhere deep in your soul to keep going and drive on.

Inevitably, everybody will go through that type of grief because nobody can sidestep it. It is different when it is someone young however.

The GAA community was a huge comfort at the time. The GAA don't get everything right but they get a lot of things right. Anytime there is a bit of a tragedy in any community in the country, the local GAA club will be the first one to be there, and to back and support any family or family member going through that type of grief.

I know hurling has gone totally professional in all but name, but when we were playing it was as professional as it was at the time – you were still giving it the full seriousness.

There were serious characters there. Mike Houlihan, a great character. Ger Hegarty, Stephen McDonagh, Joe Quaid, Gary Kirby… there were brilliant hurlers. The Nashes, Davy Clarke, and Mark Foley… great characters.

You are gone from it so long, what would you miss from it? I was often at various 'questions and answers' events and everybody would give different types of answers, but commonly the answers would be the roar, the crowd, the camaraderie, walking behind the band, and running onto the pitch in Thurles, Gaelic Grounds, or Croke Park. They're the things you miss most.

But if I had to pick one thing or credential that I miss from the inter-county scene, and I suppose it was my own doing, though it worked because that's where I needed to go… it would be the pressure that I put on myself to perform.

I am at my best when the pressure is on. I am bringing that into my everyday life now in every area, because when you are working in the field of addiction and mental health, the pressure is on. Yet I can be cool, calm, and collective, and composed in the middle of that pressure.

That's where my skill is. I would have thrived under pressure as a player.

When I stopped playing hurling, it took me a while to navigate life because I believe whether it is football or hurling you are playing, club or county, your personality has to shine, your personality has to come out on the field.

You have those same credentials off the field. It took me a while to see it, become aware of it, and tap into it, but now the same credentials are there and I am utilising them in different ways in my profession today.

99

MIKE HOULIHAN

KILMALLOCK 1-12 PATRICKSWELL 0-12
Limerick SHC Final
Gaelic Grounds, Limerick
SEPTEMBER 27, 1992

Mike Houlihan breaks up the field against Waterford in the 1997 Munster Championship

★ **KILMALLOCK:** G Hanley; S Burchell, JJ O'Riordan, S O'Grady; G O'Riordan, D Clarke, D Barry; M Nelligan (0-1), S Barrett (0-1); T Nelligan (1-1), **M Houlihan**, P Barrett (0-1); P Tobin (0-2), B Hanley, P Kelly (0-6). **Sub:** D Hanley for B Hanley.

★ **PATRICKSWELL:** J Murphy; Philip Foley, Paul Foley, E Kelleher; D Punch (0-1), C Carey, Pa Foley; A Carmody, S Carey; D O'Grady (0-3), G Kirby (0-6), P Carey; N Carey (0-1), R Fitzgerald (0-1), S Kirby.

THE ACTION

A TOM NELLIGAN goal proved to be the difference as Kilmallock were crowned Limerick SHC champions for the seventh time, and their first since 1985, in front of a crowd of 7,500 in the Gaelic Grounds.

A team that was built around an excellent minor team from 1987, it was the veteran of the pack, Kilmallock captain Paddy Kelly who rallied the troops at half-time. Kelly, the motivator over the half-time cuppa, proved to be more than a talker. He led Kilmallock's charge with a point six minutes after the restart, before bringing his side level at 0-10 to 1-7 midway through the second-half.

While the former Limerick star, now having played senior hurling for his club in three different decades, was furious that Kilmallock had not played anywhere near their potential against pre-match favourites Patrickswell, he was believed to have been left more frustrated by the fact his side were behind 0-9 to 1-3 after a lacklustre opening half.

However, as the dust settled, Kilmallock, boosted by the shrewd move to deploy Kelly as an extra midfielder alongside the youthful Mike Houlihan, put a disjointed 'Well to the sword.

Kelly had earlier told his team that they could not return south on the R512 road as defeated finalists for a second successive year. That they didn't, but truth be told, were it not for an opportunist first-half goal by Tom Nelligan, after a long clearance by Houlihan, the 36km trip to south Limerick may have felt a lot longer for those cheering on the men in green and white.

After seeing off Cappamore, Adare, and Ballybrown to reach this county final, the journey did not stop there. This youthful Kilmallock side defeated Sixmilebridge to claim the club's first Munster title, before losing out to Sarsfields of Galway in the All-Ireland final.

★★★★★

>

WE WERE BEATEN in the county final the year before against Ballybrown, and it was redemption to win my first county medal. We were underdogs going into that final. We were going up against a Patrickswell team that had the likes of Ciarán Carey, Gary Kirby, Pa Carey, and Anthony Carmody… a lot of household names. I'll always remember the build up to that final. We were togged out in suits for the final… a club team togged out in suits! Phenomenal stuff really, because when we were going into the match some people were saying, 'Jaysus, where are ye going with the suits?'

And they were saying, 'Ye will only want them for the one day'.

But, as it turned out, we wound up in Croke Park. What is sticking out for me in that game is that I was marking Ciarán Carey. I would have traditionally started out as a midfielder or a wing-back for Limerick, and both of us were in the half-back line for Limerick that year. We played there together in a league final and a Munster final.

Ciarán had to be curtailed. We would have respected each other as players, but when it came to playing against each other, all bets were off.

It wasn't as if it was a classic game – it was only 1-12 to 0-12 points – but the second-half went into a big tempo game. It was played in front of 7,500 people which is a big crowd for a county final in Limerick. It was just the fact the build-up and the aftermath of the game was massive.

Every club should experience what we experienced that year. I know that's not possible, but at least in this day and age there is intermediate, and there is junior. More clubs can get the experience to follow a Munster path or an All-Ireland path.

It is the same at senior level. It does bring everyone together. The whole county comes with you, supporting you; maybe more so in them days because that's the way the affiliation went. It might not be as much today, but, still, they will go and see matches, even though they might not follow you with the same passion.

We had some great teams in Kilmallock but they never passed the stage of winning a Munster club, and we were just fortunate to win it that year. It was a surreal experience – I was only 23 at the time.

It would have been my third or fourth season with Limerick, and at that time you would have been regarded as a county player so people would be expecting county players to perform. The winning factor and coming back to your club is why that Munster campaign stands out for me.

But unfortunately, after the Sixmilebridge game in the Munster final, they lost a player a week after. We all went down to the funeral. Padraig McNamara was his name. That throws it to the other side then too, that even though winning is brilliant there are other sides to life in that they had a tragic loss after that game… they did appreciate us going down.

After winning Munster, we played Desmonds of London in February in the All-Ireland club semi-final… but my mother passed away that week. In fairness to the club, they did ask if we wanted the game called off, but we said that there were people coming from England, so you can't rearrange plans. We played the game. I was delighted to play because life still has to roll on.

All that year had a lot of little different things in it.

Maybe it wasn't a game that I starred in totally, but with Ciarán Carey and other players, you had a duty to mark your man or take control of the situation. They'd be doing the same, it was just that you had to step up to the plate.

There were lots of things in the game. Davy Clarke was centre-back on Gary Kirby, and I was centre-forward on Ciarán Carey. He had as much of a job on Gary, as I did on Ciarán. Gary had his first All Star won at that stage, and then he came again in 1992 with a big performance, so that would have been a big game for Davy, and it would have been a big game for me on Ciarán Carey.

They had won the All-Ireland Under-21 Championship with Limerick in 1987, and won Munster at minor level, so they were big reputation players. Patrickswell always had a big reputation, but we always had a *reputation* against them too that we would be able to perform. In the game itself, it was exactly those battles that took place. Possession hurling isn't the same as it is now, but at that time you had to hurl the ball or you had to keep the ball moving. There was a sense that if you don't keep it moving away from Ciarán Carey and he gets it, and you try to follow him, you'll know all about it. He definitely showed that later on in his career with his scoring, the pace that he had, and the athleticism… sure Ciarán Carey is 54 and he is still playing football with the Limerick Masters team. It shows the athleticism he had, and still has.

We were underdogs going into that final, even though we were in the county final the year before. You should think, *Why would you be underdogs if you made the county final the year before?* But it was just that Patrickswell had a lot of key players.

They had won a Munster Club Championship a couple of years before that. They were only after coming off the back of being in an All-Ireland Club final against Glenmore of Kilkenny in early 1991, so they would have been seen as bouncing back in 1992. That Patrickswell team went on to win three Limerick senior titles in-a-row in the mid-90s so that sums up why that game stands out for me. It brought respect to your team, and your players, from people in your county when they see you winning a county championship.

Success like that helps create tradition and strengthens the club going forward.

For the next generation after us – the likes of Graeme Mulcahy – they came along and were part of a five in-a-row under-21 winning team for Kilmallock. Now, they didn't all win five in-a-row but they were in different age groups participating in it.

It is what goes before you and what you see… and you go up to the field and you are imitating it and, next thing, when your time comes you want to achieve something. Hurling is hurling, and it is one part of it… getting on with life is another part of it. Meeting your friends and playing with the people you grew up with and going to the field is good for fellas, and it sets them in the right vein.

I am very proud of my time playing with Limerick. I was with Limerick for 11 years. In our time it was knockout championship hurling, so if you were beaten in the first round, whether it was the start of May or more than likely the end of May, you were gone.

If you got a run, you'd have a longer summer. We met some great teams! We might say we should have won more games too, but you were meeting good teams… Cork in the 90s, and Tipperary in the 90s. We came along then and had our run in 1994, '95, and '96. Then you'd Clare to contend with.

These days, you've four games in Munster so it is a different platform. People say to me today, 'Sure, would you do today's thing?'

Of course, you'd do it. If you were at the top as you were back then, you would be doing what they do today. We had a dietician in our day, but how you implemented it was the biggest thing. Today they implement it because they give you meals at training and you get your meals going home.

In our day, you had to implement the diet yourself, but who monitored it? My mother unfortunately passed away in 1993 so we didn't have anybody at home to cook a meal. One of my sisters was working and another sister went to England. I was working in a meat factory, so you got your food whenever you got it You went into training to a man called 'Mick the Griller', Lord have mercy on him… he was a famous man for cooking at that time; he'd have the food ready for us, either steak or chicken. If you didn't have a dinner, and you said to yourself, *Steak or chicken*? You are not going to refuse a steak. And if Mick said to you, 'There's an extra few spuds', you're going to take them too because you are saying to yourself, *That's my dinner for the day.*

The point is, it wasn't easy to monitor the diet and it wasn't easy to monitor the body fat content. It was difficult to implement it. The ideas were good but you need a base and you need funds to deliver the whole project. Limerick, and every county, are delivering these projects now; some maybe a little bit better than others.

It is different now. Players back then had more physical jobs. My job was loading hind quarters, front quarters, and dropping pigs to Loughnane's butchers at eight o'clock on Monday morning. It would have been a lot of physical work you would have been doing at the time. But it was just like a farmer or any other type of similar work.

I'll always have huge pride having got to play in two All-Ireland finals with Limerick. We had some fantastic occasions, but, unfortunately, there has to be a winner or a loser. They are some of the things I don't dwell on particularly because you had your chance… we got two chances.

My mother-in-law, Mary Kelly of Bulgaden Castle passed away recently and JP McManus came to the house. I was doing a bit of painting and tidying up before the removal. JP would have been great friends with them – they came to the parish nearly at the same time. Noreen, JP's wife, was a very good friend of Mary. JP was asking me about 1994 and 1996.

I said, 'JP, I don't remember too much about it, to be honest with you'.

PADDY KELLY

KILMALLOCK 3-11 SIXMILEBRIDGE 2-11
Munster Club SHC Final
Gaelic Grounds, Limerick
NOVEMBER 29, 1992

Paddy Kelly in full flow for Limerick in 1984

★ **KILMALLOCK:** G Hanley; S Burchell, JJ O'Riordan, S O'Grady; G O'Riordan, D Clarke (0-2), D Barry; M Houlihan, S Barrett; T Nelligan, B Hanley (1-1), P Barrett; P Tobin (0-2), D Hanley (0-1), **P Kelly (2-5)**. **Sub:** P Dowling for Nelligan.

★ **SIXMILEBRIDGE:** D Fitzgerald; M Halloran, J O'Connell (0-2), K O'Shea; K McInerney, S Stack, J Chaplin; N Earley (0-1), C Chaplin (0-1); D Chaplin, P Morey (0-1), P McNamara (0-1); O Quane (1-2), E Healy, G McInerney (1-3). **Sub:** A White for Morey.

THE ACTION

DESPITE HIS MATURING years of 37 years, stalwart Paddy Kelly proved his worth, and experience, to score an impressive 2-5 as Kilmallock claimed their first Munster Club SHC title.

Kilmallock, a team that doesn't know the word defeat, once again defied the odds to overturn an early second-half seven-point deficit, into a one goal winning margin in what was a tremendously exciting Munster club final. Kelly was enjoying his 19th season in the famous green and white.

Four minutes into the second-half, and despite having gone a further point behind to a Christy Chaplin effort, Kilmallock reduced the gap to just one score thanks to two points from Kelly and a Brendan Hanley effort. But any raised hopes that came about following this flurry of scoring quickly came crashing right back down to earth when two defensive errors dearly cost the Balbec.

Sensing danger, Sixmilebridge moved up the field straightaway, and were duly rewarded. In a lovely four-man move, involving Seán Stack, Noel Earley, Christy Chaplin, and Gerry McInerney, the latter stroked the ball to the Kilmallock net. Worse was to follow for the south Limerick men. By the time Owen Quane raised the green flag for the second time in the game, it was 2-8 to 0-7 in the Bridge's favour.

The game was, however, changed dramatically in the 40th minute. When Brendan Hanley was floored by John O'Connell, Kelly knew only a goal from the resulting penalty would suffice. He obliged, giving Davy Fitzgerald no chance in between the Bridge posts.

Kelly was the hero once again, darting through a stretched Bridge defence to make it a one goal game. Fitzgerald was, once again, helpless. With the momentum behind them, Kilmallock were in front for the first time when Dave Clarke pointed minutes later. There was no looking back,

The All-Ireland stage saw Kilmallock reach the final after defeat of London club, Desmonds, before Galway and Connacht champions, Sarsfields, proved too much for the south Limerick men in the St Patrick's Day Croke Park showdown.

★★★★★

> 66

IT HAS TO be the 1992 Munster club final against Sixmilebridge played inside in the Gaelic Grounds. It was coming to the end of my career. It is a match I keep going back to, because in 1991 I missed three frees against Ballybrown in the county final in the last few minutes of the game... and they won by a point.

I was retiring in '91, but I didn't. I kind of went back... reluctantly, in 1992. I had been captain of Kilmallock a few times, but the boys made me captain again in '92... and it just took off from there. We had a local man training us in Tony Moloney, and we had Mick Barrett and Mick Maloney as selectors, who were also local men. Jimmy Mulcahy was our physio, kind of... a psychologist as we used to call him.

It was a real local, good feel, trying to get back to the era when Kilmallock had good senior hurling teams, because we had good minors coming through... Mike Houlihan, Dave Clarke, Tom Hennessy, Patrick Tobin and Pat Barrett... a whole good crop of minors who won the 'county' in 1987.

By '92 that group were beginning to get into their early twenties. At that stage, Mike and Dave were playing fantastic hurling with Limerick, and then we had an older cohort of players in their thirties, such as Donie Barry, Shane O'Grady, Sean Burchill and JJ O'Riordan. Then we had Maurice Nelligan and his brother 'Tricksie' Nelligan.

Even talking about it now, there is a smile on my face thinking back. You are playing with the people you grew up with... and then I was the elder statesman, coming to the tail end of my career... but I got a couple more years out of it.

I kept going until I was one month shy of 40 in 1995.

Things just happened in 1992, that just kept happening... and it resulted in us winning a Munster Club final inside in Limerick against Sixmilebridge.

I remember particularly in 1992 we were playing Cappamore... in Cappamore. And if we didn't win the game, we were gone... and we won by two points. The last shot was going in. The Cappamore guy took a shot and it was going in at the butt of the post. Ger Hanley was in goal at the time and pulled off a miraculous save. Suddenly, we were in a county quarter-final against Adare. We won quite easily, and then we overcame Ballybrown in the semi-final, quite easily as well.

And then we had a titanic struggle against Patrickswell in the final. Mike Houlihan had a massive second-half. There were choice words spoken at half-time, and we came out all guns blazing.

We went down then to play Erin's Own in their pitch, and we were five points down with five minutes to go… and, somehow, we drew with them! Brian Corcoran, who was playing with Erin's at the time, broke his collar-bone in the last minute of the game. We weren't talking about Munster Club or anything… we were talking about winning this match. We got over that one and then we had Toomevara the following Sunday in our own pitch as well.

We were losing that one as well, and then we got a goal in the final seconds of the game to win it by two points. We were facing Sixmilebridge in the final. Maurice Nelligan, along with a guy from Toomevara, had been sent off in the semi-final so he was a huge loss for us.

A *huge* loss, because he was a county player with Limerick. Our expectations would have been… we approached the game as if we had a chance, but we certainly weren't favourites in any shape or form.

The 'Bridge would have been seen as a good, solid Munster club team in that era. Surely enough, we were down at half-time. We were seven points down at one stage in the second-half. I happened to get a 21-yard free with about 15 minutes to go. Davy Fitzgerald was in goal. I used to always go for the left shoulder of the goalkeeper, no matter who was in the goal, because it wasn't going to go wide anyway.

It had to be saved.

We got that goal, and then a couple of minutes later I got another cracker of a goal. It was probably the best goal I've ever scored. I often tried it in training afterwards and I could never even hit the target.

Coming towards the end, it was a draw, and this long ball comes in and Brendan Hanley flicks it into the back of the net… suddenly the whole place just erupted. It is all the people who have supported you down through your career, people who even helped me when I was a young lad. I remember Jimmy Millea, Joe Naughton, and Dan Connolly cheered me off the field for the presentation of the cup.

It was just magical.

We were under no illusions, because Sixmilebridge had the Morleys and the Chaplin brothers. They had Seán Stack centre-back, Gerry McInerney corner-forward, and then Davy Fitzgerald in goal. But we had our own All Stars.

Coming home to Kilmallock with cups, and then getting ready over Christmas for the All-Ireland series was just unbelievable really. The expectation now is different because we have three Munster Clubs won. At that time, Patrickswell and Ballybrown had already made the breakthrough at Munster level, but nobody from Limerick had won an All-Ireland club at that stage, until Na Piarsaigh did it a few years later in 2016.

We had a fantastic chairman in Tom Nelligan. He was really an unbelievable man. I remember inside at the county semi-final he stood up on the seats inside in the dressing-rooms in the Gaelic Grounds, and he announced to all of us that he'd rig us out for the county final. We got shirts, ties, blazers, and pants, as well as the bag and the playing gear, which was unheard of for club players at the time.

We went into the county final dressed up like this. I think the 'Well boys were looking at us with the corner of their eyes, 'What's happening here?' We wore those blazers, shirts, and ties 20 or 30 times over the next few years with the success we had, especially with all the functions.

A couple of years ago, we had a reunion of the 1992 team.

There was a video playing in the background. We were nearly ahead of our time. We had all our big matches videotaped by a local man in West Limerick, and Billy Mulcahy was the commentator. I was looking at the video and you are looking at all the people who had passed away in the 25 years between the match and reunion… and the joy on their faces. We had a past players' organisation which had developed in the late 80s and early 90s. They were supportive of us as well, and gave us a lot of help. There was a real bond between the club, the players, the past players, and the supporters.

I can't separate 1991 from '92. I really can't because nobody knows what is around the corner. I had retired in '91, but it went so badly for me. I remember the boys came up to me in the house. I didn't want to go anywhere, but they dragged me down town. At that stage, we used to go to The 41. Jimmy and Kathleen Foley had the pub downtown, and that was the place where the players gravitated towards after matches, particularly after our home matches. Mike Houlihan owns

The 41 now, so there is still a connection with it.

In that era, you still had the bonfires, which you can't have any more with health and safety. Karl O'Donnell was our main bonfire operator. He was another past player from back in the 50s and 60s. He went to London for a while and he came back, and he was chairman.

The first thing you feel when the whistle goes is relief.

Every player has bad memories of a ball going two inches wide or going inside the posts. What happened in 1992 was Patrickswell had us in trouble in the county final. It was a second-half display that got through that. Erin's Own had us in trouble with a few minutes to go and we got out of it with a draw. Toomevara hit 20 wides that day in Kilmallock and we got a goal in the last seconds of the game. Sixmilebridge were seven points up with 20 minutes to go.

When you win games like that it just adds to the whole general excitement for everybody in the stands.

In terms of our expectations, we didn't really know what we were getting ourselves into, or the level of interest that was out there. When you get to the Munster stage, it is not only the local crowd that follow you; now you get the county supporters, who go to all the Limerick games. They row in and swell the numbers, and these are all big occasions.

I'd say for Tony Moloney, we were very easily coached because there was a lot of communication, on the field. I had Podge Tobin and Brendan Hanley in the full-forward line with me. They were two guys I coached from under-12s up. Pat Barrett was wing forward. He is another great player from that team. 'Tricksie' Nelligan was the other wing forward. James Connery was wing back.

Seven or eight of that '92 team came from the successful minor team of 1987. We beat Na Piarsaigh in the semi-final and we actually ended up winning the '87 minor final in Kilmallock because the Gaelic Grounds was being redeveloped at the time with the building of the new Mackey Stand.

That connection was there, but it took us a while to win a county championship. We were beaten in county semi-finals by Adare and Ballybrown, and never could get to the final. Then we got to the county final in 1991 and things went pear-shaped, but everything came together in '92 and again in '94.

Expectations were small but then we just started on a rollercoaster in '94, and we repeated the whole thing over again. That probably made it that bit sweeter in

'94 because when you are doing it the next time it happens, you kind of appreciate it more.

You say, 'We've got to enjoy all of this because it comes and goes very quickly'. The three in-a-row team in 1973, '74, and '75 that I was playing on were twice beaten in the Munster Club Championship by the teams that went on and won the All-Ireland. St Finbarr's, and Blackrock beat us in the early rounds of Munster, and they all went on to win the All-Ireland.

But we had no motivation in those years. I don't think we even trained for the Munster matches after we won the county titles.

I first came on the senior inter-county scene with Limerick in 1974.

I was a minor in 1973, and I remember I played in the minor final that year when Richie Bennis put the ball over the ball for the seniors to beat Tipp in the Munster final.

In those eras, it was different. It was a 21-man panel. And trying to break into an All-Ireland winning team was very difficult. Kilmallock had won the county in 1973 so therefore my name was known. I was playing very well in that era and I broke through into the Limerick 21-man panel for 1974. I came on in the All-Ireland final in '74.

It was different back then because you could be gone, knocked out, after one match... and we'd good teams. We'd great teams in the 1980s, especially in '80, and '81.

We contested three league finals in 1983, '84, and '85. We had players such as Joe McKenna, Éamonn Cregan, Jimmy Carroll, Liam O'Donoghue, Paudie Fitzmaurice, Leonard Enright, Tommy Quaid in goal, Ollie O'Connor, Mossie Carroll, Brian 'Bomber' Carroll, and Danny Fitzgerald... all household names in Limerick hurling.

They were teams that if they played in the present era with the round-robin, they would win a lot more. I remember in 1983, '84, and '85 Cork beat us in our first game on each occasion. That was the Cork three in-a-row Munster winning team that won All-Irelands.

We are very lucky in Kilmallock. Where is the pitch? Smack bang in the middle of the town. So where is the meeting place? The meeting place for all of us is the pitch. It is the same in Patrickswell. It is smack bang in the middle of their community.

We only got the one pitch down there, but that is where everybody goes. And when you go there, what do you do? You bring a hurley and a sliotar with you.

A lot of the coaching that goes on goes on from just puck-abouts and talking to players; older players passing on little nuggets of information. You wouldn't know it at the time, but players like Bernie Savage, Jackie McCarthy, and the Hayes brothers were actually coaching you at the time.

When you are in a club like Kilmallock, every time you go training you are talking about games to win a county title. For a lot of clubs, it is just all about how to survive, but when it comes to clubs like Kilmallock, Patrickswell, or Na Piarsaigh, the county final is on their radar. We have won three county titles in the past 11 years, which is good going. We were in a county final again in 2022, and we were in a Munster final the year before and Ballygunner beat us. It was the first Munster final that Kilmallock lost. We won all the other three. The present team won one back in 2014.

That is the new era of hurling coming through, and they are generating another era of young players in Kilmallock. When you have tradition like that on your side, it does make it that little bit easier.

It is nice to keep having a bit of success.

It was a long career. I got to play senior club hurling in three different decades. Injuries didn't affect me that much… a few broken fingers, a few broken teeth, and a few stitches, but I don't think hamstring and ACL injuries were around in that era at all, for some reason.

The level of training was different. That was a time where you'd be training with Limerick, but on a Tuesday evening you'd still come out to your club and play a league match.

I'd be playing against Patrickswell and I'd be marking David Punch, which would be a far better game for the two of us. Inside in the Gaelic Grounds, if we were marking each other in training, you'd be trying to be loose on one another to try and get plenty of ball to impress, whereas when it was Patrickswell against Kilmallock in a league game there is responsibility on you to pick up your man and mark him.

During that era, we had a lot of club hurling, as well as inter-county hurling, and we'd a lot of tournaments. The big tournament here was the Kilmallock Tournament, the summer festival.

There would be massive crowds on a Sunday evening down the field. We used to always bring a Cork team down for the final day of the festival to play Kilmallock. St Finbarr's used to come up often. When I was growing up, you would have Charlie McCarthy down the field, and all these Cork hurlers, taking on the Kilmallock fellas.

And just by looking, you learn. You don't realise then that you have the same effect on the people coming behind you.

It was nice to be able to finish your career successfully because not too many people get to retire in a good era. Most people retire after maybe staying a year or two too long, or they picked the wrong year to retire and things happen the following year.

"

JOE QUAID

LIMERICK 4-14 CORK 4-11
Munster SHC Quarter-Final
Gaelic Grounds, Limerick
JUNE 5, 1994

The stylish and brave Joe Quaid in action against Tipperary in 1997

★ **LIMERICK: J Quaid**; J O'Neill, M Nash, S McDonagh; D Clarke, G Hegarty, D Nash; C Carey, M Houlihan (0-2); F Carroll (0-2), G Kirby (capt) (2-5), M Galligan (0-3); TJ Ryan (0-1), P Heffernan (2-0), D Quigley (0-1). **Subs:** L O'Connor for Quigley, D Flynn for Hegarty.

★ **CORK:** G Cunningham (capt); B Corcoran, S O'Gorman, D Quirke (0-1); C Casey, J Cashman, I Forde; P Buckley, T Kelleher (0-1); M Mullins (1-2), T Mulcahy, T McCarthy; B Egan (0-5), G Manley (1-0), T Sullivan. (0-1) **Subs:** K Murray (2-0) for McCarthy, S McCarthy (0-1) for O'Sullivan, D O'Donoghue for Mullins.

★ GAME OF MY LIFE ★

THE ACTION

A DAY FOR ducks, as the goals rained down in wintry conditions on the Ennis Road.

Kevin Murray bagged a brace for Cork, but at the other end Gary Kirby and Pat Heffernan scored two each as Limerick triumphed on their way to Munster glory.

Youthful Limerick salvaged the superb victory by wiping out an early eight points deficit, then drew inspiration from a goalkeeping masterclass from 22-year-old debutant Joe Quaid, the midfield mastery of Ciarán Carey and the quick-thinking of full-forward Pat Heffernan.

It was a historic occasion, only the fourth time in 23 clashes since 1940 that Limerick had beaten Cork – the last time the 1980 Munster decider.

Such was the shock of the result, Cork had contested in 10 of the 12 previous Munster finals, winning seven of them. Saying that, there is no taking away from Limerick's wonderful victory after trailing by eight – 2-4 to 0-2 – as early as the 16th minute when Ger Manley found the net, adding to Mark Mullins goal with 12 minutes on the clock.

Credit to Limerick, Tom Ryan's charges responded well and by the 27th minute both Kirby and Heffernan and their first of two goals each. And just five minutes later, the Shannonsiders were miraculously level with Kirby pointed, before the classy Patrickswell centre-forward was put through by Heffernan for his second goal – Limerick's third – immediately afterwards.

Cork, in total disarray at this stage, grabbed a late free to stop the rot of 16 minutes without a score, as Limerick took a 3-6 to 2-5 lead into the break. After Quaid denied Cork a certain goal three minutes after the restart, the home crowd really started to get a sense of belief. When Heffernan got his second goal in the final 10 minutes, Limerick went four up.

Half-time substitute Kevin Murray got in for his second goal, two minutes from time, but it was too little too late for the Rebels as the Treaty men set up a Munster semi-final against Waterford.

★★★★★

> 66

IT WAS MY debut, we hadn't beaten Cork in 14 years… and after 15 minutes were down 2-4 to two points, and I probably went on and had the best game of my life after that.

I don't think that if we had won an All-Ireland that the dressing-room would have been any better than the dressing-room was in the Gaelic Grounds that day. It was just PHENOMENAL! The place was full, there were supporters inside everywhere… there wasn't room… it wouldn't happen today.

It was a rollercoaster of a day, but WHAT A DAY!

I woke up that morning and I looked out, and it was raining.

The last thing you need when you are making your debut in goals, and when you are trying to follow in the footsteps of your cousin, who was in goals for Limerick for 18 years… and you are just looking and you are going, *Ah Jesus Christ, I wish the rain would stop now for the day.*

Coming out then… there was a massive crowd, but it was an awful day with the weather. I think, after we went down 2-4 to two points, an awful lot of people even left and went to the Davin Arms. They kind of thought the game was over at that stage. A lot of them missed the game.

The comeback then was just phenomenal. Pat Heffernan got a goal, Gary Kirby got a goal, and we even went in up at half-time. We were ahead, and then they came back… it was a battle to the very end. Then you had all the supporters afterwards coming onto the pitch and into the dressing-room.

You are walking down the street then in Newcastle West or Abbeyfeale and, all of a sudden, everyone knew you. Whereas before, nobody knew me. It certainly takes getting used to. I found it very strange that someone would walk up to me and say, 'Howya Joe'… and you'd be thinking, *Do I know them?* But it was brilliant. It was the start of something really good there from the mid-90s from ourselves as a team.

When you are starting off, you are under pressure all of the time. There is no God-given right to be there. You are under pressure at all stages and I suppose what made it harder was the likes of Tommy being there before me. That added its own pressure. Not only was I coming into the Limerick team after Tommy, I was taking over the same position as him.

Certainly, the first year I took over I was under pressure every day you went out because you had Tommy's shadow casting over you all of the time. Even after the Cork game, I needed to back it up. One game certainly wasn't going to please the Limerick public.

Every day that you went out was a day that you felt pressure, but that's a good thing.

I look back at my time playing with Limerick with huge pride. It was massive. Before, there might have been that worry that if Limerick won an All-Ireland after I was finished would you kind of feel hard done by, that it wasn't you, but that wasn't the case at all.

It was just huge pride and it was just great to have your own flesh and blood there as part of it in Nickie.

The mid 90s really was a golden era for hurling with the changing of the guard. In 1996, we beat Cork and Clare – the All-Ireland champions at the time – and Tipp in the Munster Championship so that was massive for us. It was a golden era and a lot more teams were involved in the championship. Any year there were 10 teams that could possibly win it.

The whole game against Cork that day in 1994 stands out for me.

In particular, it went from the fact that there were two goals gone in after 15 minutes, to us then taking over for the next 20 minutes.

We came out in the second-half and there was just an onslaught from Cork. It was just save after save, after *save*… and then we ended up saving a ball and they ended up scoring from a rebound.

It was just non-stop. You didn't get a minute or a second to turn around and relax. As a debut goes, it was probably the best you could have got because you had everything in it.

Not much can prepare you for a day like that. I had played in the National League, but the league is completely different to the championship. Playing in the first round of the championship and it being your championship debut, is massive, but I remember even the difference between that and All-Ireland semi-finals and finals which were completely different again.

Every game and every final, takes on a different meaning, which makes it hard to prepare.

I remember ahead of the 1994 All-Ireland coming out of the dressing-room at the Canal End and the noise from the Limerick supporters… I actually thought my eardrums were going to burst.

You can't prepare for the pressure and attention playing for Limerick brings either. You can either deal with it, or it engulfs you and swallows you up.

We went to Florida in 1997 on a team holiday, and that created a great bond between the players. I suppose like in any county set-up, the club rivalries can infiltrate in, but when you are in that set-up and in that group environment, you get on well with people. You needn't be best buds with everybody, but at the same time you'd have huge respect for everybody and for the work they are putting in.

Looking back, I suppose not many can say they made their championship debut, won a Munster Championship, and played in an All-Ireland final in the same year.

If we'd won the All-Ireland that year, I'd have won a National League medal, a Munster medal, a Railway Cup medal, an All-Ireland medal, and an All Star… not a bad debut season.

Coming from a county that hadn't won an All-Ireland since 1973, that would have been the stuff dreams were made of. I nearly got the full package of full silverware in my first year.

To win an All Star that year was something very special for me. It was the golden era of goalkeepers. You had Ger Cunningham, Mikey Walsh, Tommy Quaid, Brendan Cummins, Davy Fitzgerald, and Damien Fitzhenry. They were all big names. It's esteemed company to be held in… to be even named in the same breath and to be able to play with them lads.

I think we all drove each other on. When you wouldn't be playing, you'd be watching Tipp or Cork or someone, and you'd see somebody doing something and you would be saying, *Jesus, that's the standard now to set*… and you'd be trying to better it the next day.

My dad won the All-Ireland Junior Championship with Limerick in 1954 and he would have gone on to win the Munster title with the senior team in 1955.

He was a massive influence growing up, but he was well finished by the time

I was born. I never saw him hurling. The main influence for me would have been Tommy. He was probably the reason as well I got shafted into playing in goals. Seeing Tommy so close by, playing with the same club, and playing for Limerick, gave you something to aspire to.

My earliest and first memory of an All-Ireland final – the only one I was at before the 1994 final – was the 1980 final. I was only eight at the time. Tommy was playing in that final.

I remember being above watching them and they were in the old tunnel that was there at that time. They had to come out under the crowd in the middle of the field. We had seats alongside and I remember looking into the tunnel while they were waiting to come out. You could visibly see the nerves in them. That was an absolutely huge moment.

Looking back, I should really have called time on playing in 1997 when I got injured during a National League game against Laois in Kilmallock.

The defining memory I have of Kilmallock… tragically, it probably ended my hurling career at inter-county level. It was the day that my sub-conscious gave up on me, and just kept bringing back bad memories of what happened there on the 27th of April, 1997.

Just before half-time, Laois got a penalty. David Cuddy took the penalty, lifted it, hit it, it hit the ground… I went down on my knees. I was after getting a belt into the testicle. It was only after the match that I found out it had exploded on impact.

The doctor came in. He was holding my head. I couldn't talk. I asked to be taken off, and they didn't take me off. I went into the dressing-room after, and I was still in fair pain. I went for a shower. Doctor Dave Boylan, I called him over.

I said, 'Dave, is this okay?'

He just looked and went, 'Jesus. Go Straight to the hospital'.

The doctor came in, and I'll never forget it… he went, 'Ouch!' He walked out, and brought in another doctor. The other doctor says to me, 'Is it sore?' The first doctor says, 'What do you think?'

He said, 'We're going to have to operate? When did you eat last?'

I said, 'About an hour ago, I had a McDonald's'. He said, 'We can't operate for a couple of hours'.

Friends of mine called in to visit me that night. To tell you the type of friends

I have, they brought grapes, plums, and Maltesers. To sort them out, I pulled the blankets back. I was black and blue. One of them actually slid down the wall with weakness.

I retired from the inter-county game in 2000, aged just 28, but I did return in 2002 to play one last season. My edge was gone. That just affected me. I kept playing club, and I kept playing for another couple of years with Limerick but, looking back, I probably should have called it a day.

I ended up with four fantastic kids. It wasn't all as bad as it could have been. As far as my hurling career, I'd put that down as ending my reign at the top, let's say.

I transferred over to Murroe-Boher from Feohanagh in 1999 and we ended up winning the Intermediate Championship that year. I had good times at both clubs. Your home club will always be your *home* club. To be fair, when I moved over to Murroe, when I was living here, they were intermediate at the time and a lot of GAA clubs came looking to know if I would go playing with them and I said, 'No'… because I knew if I ever had kids down the road that this would be their club.

It is nice to have them playing for the club you play for. I had moved out to Murroe after getting married in 1998. I was living out here. It wasn't a case of moving clubs for the sake of moving.

Hurling is my life.

It always probably will be, and as long as I can be involved in teams, whether it be club or inter-county level, I will be.

The alternative of sitting at home watching the soaps is not something that would ever appeal to me. That's my hobby now. Some people play golf, some people go drinking, some people like horse racing, or whatever… it is just what I do, and what I enjoy. The day I stop enjoying it is the day I'll stop doing it. I haven't stopped yet anyway. If it ever becomes a chore, there is no point.

People would be on about, 'Oh Jesus, they are doing it for the money'. There are very few people making money from it. You might get a few expenses but if you boil it down to the hours put in, wear and tear on cars and stuff like that, it would probably actually end up costing you money.

If you didn't love it, you wouldn't do it.

We'd good times, but from my side of it, some of my memories off the pitch would be more to do with the time I was over Cian Lynch's group in the underage set-up with Limerick and what we had to deal with.

One of the young lads, Darra O'Donovan from Monagea, passed away with sudden adult death syndrome. Another one of the lads, Dylan Dawson, his mom died from cancer while he was in with us. They are the real-life stories that test you. You can have all the fun and games, but they are the real-life events, and they are the battles that are harder won than anything else.

For families, hurling offers a massive support. I remember the time Tommy died, Diarmuid O'Sullivan said it was like a death in the family, and he said it actually was… that it was a death in the GAA family. I thought that was a really nice quote. I felt that that's what it is, it is a GAA family.

"

GARY KIRBY

LIMERICK 0-25 Clare 2-10
Munster SHC Final
Semple Stadium, Thurles
JULY 10, 1994

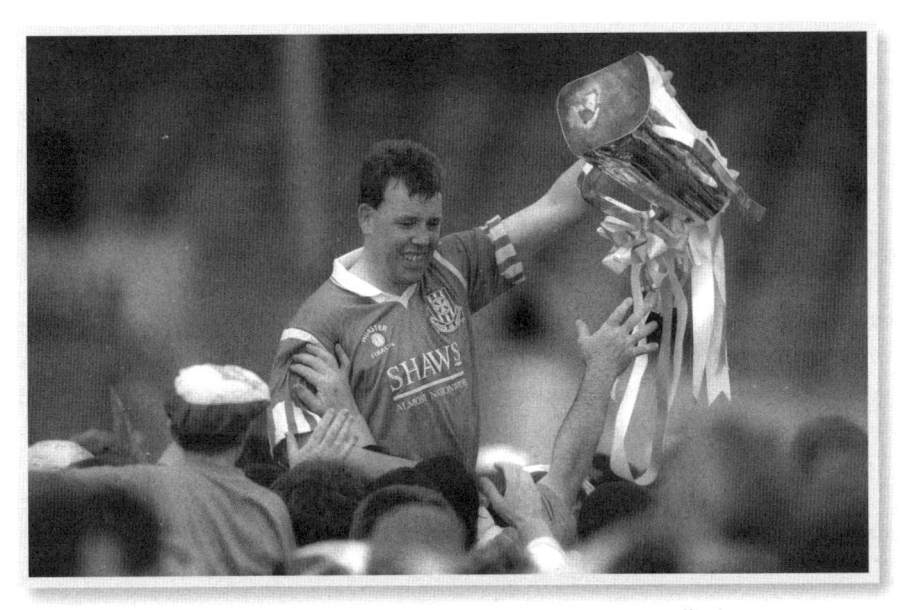

Gary Kirby rejoices with the Limerick supporters after the 1994 Munster final

★ **LIMERICK:** J Quaid; S McDonagh, M Nash, J O'Connor; D Clarke, G Hegarty, D Nash; C Carey (0-2), M Houlihan; F Carroll (0-2); **G Kirby (0-9)**, M Galligan (0-7), TJ Ryan (0-1), P Heffernan (0-2), D Quigley (0-2). **Subs:** J Roche for Heffernan, M Wallace for Ryan.

★ **CLARE:** D Fitzgerald; A Daly, B Lohan, L Doyle; J O'Connell, S McMahon, J Chaplin; S Sheedy (0-1), C Chaplin (0-1); A Whelan (0-1), PJ O'Connell, J O'Connor (0-3); G McInerney (0-1), T Guilfoyle (1-0), G O'Loughlin (0-3). **Subs:** F Corey for J O'Connell, C Lyons (1-0) for J Chaplin.

THE ACTION

'WE WERE BLOWN away... just blown away,' admitted a deflated Clare selector, Ger Loughnane, as Limerick captain Gary Kirby raised the Munster cup aloft. Limerick had waited 13 years for this day to arrive. Tom Ryan's men went in as favourites against the 1993 Munster finalists, and the Treaty County lived up to the hype to claim their first Munster final since 1981. Clare's two goals put a surprising gloss on the scoreline.

In fact, the Banner were blown away for their second Munster final defeat in two years, a tough blow considering Ulster champions, Antrim lay ahead in the All-Ireland semi-final.

Limerick were on top all the way through, and led by 0-11 to 0-7 at half time. The Clare half-back line were in trouble from the get-go with Limerick left half-forward, Mike Galligan ending up with seven points from play, as the Limerick half-forwards clocked up an impressive 13 points from play.

Clare spirits were lifted when Jamesie O'Connor pointed quickly after the restart, a mood that just as quickly changed when Limerick all but put one hand on the cup when they smacked over three swift points in response. Carey took over in midfield and as Galligan continued to give an exhibition of hurling, it felt like it was only a matter of time before a decade of frustration on Shannonside would come to an end, and Kirby would get to lead his beloved county to its 17th provincial title.

Fifteen minutes into the second-half, the men in green and white led by 0-20 to 0-9 and the Munster title was on its way to Limerick. Clare simply could not get a grip. Gerry McInerney and substitute Cyril Lyons got two late goals for Clare to make the scoreboard better reading.

But both goals were scored in the last eight minutes when the famous provincial trophy was already well out of reach for the Len Gaynor's charges – and room was being made for it on the mantelpiece in the Kirby household in Patrickswell.

★★★★★

>

A REASON WHY 1994 was a big thing for me was being captain as well.

That made a huge difference. And the build-up and the whole lot… into the final, and it a local derby against Clare.

It was a scorcher of a day… and the crowd was huge! We were getting into that time where Limerick and Clare were kind of taking over… getting involved. Two good strong sides. The whole occasion started at home. I was living at home with my parents at that stage. My mother always had a good breakfast for us. I wouldn't say it was the breakfast they'd go for these days, but it was a good breakfast for me… a good Irish breakfast. Things have changed now, which is fair enough. They look after their bodies a lot better now than we did.

The whole occasion, going down… normally I used to travel with Ciarán Carey; I would normally drive. We had a good laugh going down. It was on in Thurles. The home of hurling. A lot of my good memories come from Thurles, in fairness.

Going down that day… at the start of the year you are optimistic, whether we would or not achieve anything. We had a super win against Cork in the first round after being eight points down after about 10 or 15 minutes; we'd a good comeback.

Then we'd a good win over Waterford in the semi-final, so we were geared up well for the final. We were well prepped. Dave Mahedy had us well fit. He had us in great shape.

I remember I was down at the point-to-point in Kinsale with my wife – my girlfriend at the time – and it came through that Clare had beaten Tipp. We were playing Cork the following week, and I said to her, 'You know what… this could be our year!'

That gave us a lift.

Confidence was good. We didn't hurl exceptionally well against Waterford in the semi-final, but we got the job done. Sometimes to win games when you don't play well is good as well.

I think we hit it from the word go. It wasn't one of those games where we were under pressure in the last 20 minutes; we were kind of cruising at the end of it, which made it sweeter. It was, without doubt, a career defining moment.

We went through a good spell; we won the League in 1992. In 1993… I wouldn't say we were poor, but we were beaten above in Ennis against Clare in the first round of the championship. And then in '94, I remember being made captain. My mother said to me, 'What a year to get it!'

And I said, 'Sure, who knows? It is an honour anyway, one way or another'.

It just went from there. We'd a great year in 1994, we were unlucky in '95, in '96 we came back, and in '97 we won the league. The win in 1994 was the start of a lovely period. It is a shame we didn't win an All-Ireland.

There was a huge buzz that day in Thurles. We used to meet early in the day; and get there, chill out, have a puck-around, have a cup of coffee, and get to the ground. We'd stroll out to the ground and soak in the atmosphere. The minute you run out, you hear the buzz; that will always stick with you.

It was lovely to see… Galligan scored about six points from play that day. I'd a good few myself. We just seemed to be getting scores easier because our movement was good.

My biggest memory after the match was being lifted up to get the cup by all the crowd coming in, and then standing up in the stand and looking down at all the Limerick supporters on the pitch. There is no better feeling than standing up there, and you are just looking down… and it is full of green.

That feeling, without a doubt, makes all the tough days training worthwhile.

The biggest influence for me growing up was Phil Bennis. Phil was the manager when we won the minor All-Ireland, he was the manager when we won the under-21 All-Ireland, and he manager when I got involved with Patrickswell seniors.

His brother, Richie would have also given me a lot of advice. I would have gone to a lot of games with Richie. We still catch up with each other always; we still meet up most days.

It is moments like lifting the trophy that day in Thurles that makes you think of what fellas like that did for you. We are lucky enough; we are a strong family and we get on great. They take more pride with the win than even myself.

Without a doubt, you think of those moments. I remember I was below in the field about two weeks before the match, practising frees, and Richie came over to me and said, 'Why are you changing your style?' And I didn't even know I was.

It was only a small thing. My feet were in one position and I had the ball in one place instead of another, so he just gave me a small pointer. It is those little things that stand out to you. It might not mean much to anyone else on the outside, but it makes a huge difference to you, confidence-wise.

I don't have any regrets.

Disappointed we didn't win an All-Ireland? Yes! Without a doubt.

To be named one of the best hurlers never to have won an All-Ireland... it would be worse if they weren't talking about you. It is nice to be thought of in that sense. I have met a lot of good people from playing hurling. Even when I am working in Adare Manor – I do the night porter there – the amount of people that come over to you talking about hurling... I say to myself, *How do they even know me?*

They recognise you through the hurling. It is those memories that you can't take away. They will always be there. Yes, we had disappointments; we lost three All-Irelands, I always count the All-Ireland Club final we lost as well. But many players never played in an All-Ireland.

Deep down it was a disappointment that we didn't win one.

But regrets? Not really!

We definitely went for a few drinks after that game in Thurles in '94.

I wasn't one for drinking. Ciarán Carey came to my house for a while and we went out then. We just went to the local pub in Patrickswell. There weren't much celebrations after winning Munster. It was more after the All-Ireland final that they went out more so than after winning the Munster final because you have to remember, you are preparing for an All-Ireland semi-final as well.

The first place we called to was Tommy Casey, Lord have mercy on him. Tommy drove us for years. He drove Mick Mackey. He drove us when we were minor. We stopped outside his house and we brought the cup over to him. I remember that well. He lived across from the Parkway Shopping Centre.

Getting into Patrickswell, and getting into the pub... let's be straight; we were heroes with all the locals at that stage, especially with Ciarán and myself on the team.

I just see what the current Limerick team has done now, and I couldn't be prouder of the three Patrickswell boys involved. I'd be good friends with Aaron Gillane's parents, and what Diarmaid Byrnes has achieved is just immaculate… and what Cian Lynch has done is just unheard of.

I couldn't be prouder of what they have done for Limerick, and what they have done for Patrickswell and the community. I remember when we won the county in 2016 and I was over the team… and when the boys came in training, it wasn't with themselves they were training. Any young fella that was coming through the squad, they went with them and they helped them along. I remember seeing Diarmaid talking to them, and explaining things. You can't buy that; that experience and that willingness to give their expertise.

And, at the end of the day, the three boys are still young.

The future for the club is great because young lads locally have the boys to look up to. I look no further than my own two. I've two boys myself, John and Patrick. Two years ago, was John's first year playing senior hurling with Patrickswell – he had just turned 17. The first game he went into, the first fella to tap him on the back when he came on was Cian Lynch.

People were saying to me, 'Were you worried about him?'

And I says, 'He has Aaron Gillane here, he has Cian Lynch there, there is no need to worry… he'll be grand!'

I remember my first senior championship match; I was only 17 as well and I went through on a solo run and I was clocked going in. Richie was playing full-forward and he said to me, 'Keep doing what you're doing, I'll sort him out!'

You are looked after!

I see Diarmaid and Aaron going up to the boys; they look after them and they put the arms around them.

We'd a golden era for Patrickswell when I was playing.

I won 10 county senior titles.

But not to win an All-Ireland Club was very disappointing. It was actually nearly more disappointing not winning it with the club than with the county. Glenmore from Kilkenny beat us in the final. It was a day we didn't really perform. But then again, you've to put your hands up to the opposition too; they had Christy Heffernan, they'd Liam Walsh, they'd a few more inter-county players in their set-up.

We lost to them by four points. It would have been nice to win it. To win the two Munster titles was second to none. Anyone who plays hurling will tell you that nothing beats winning something with your club.

The friendships you make are one of the great things I got from hurling, but it is also the enjoyment you get from playing the game itself alone.

People say to me did I miss it when I gave it up? The part I miss most is the craic in the dressing-room beforehand, and inside in the training sessions having a laugh.

John Kiely was part of that 1996 squad with us and you had Mike Nash, whose young fella Barry is doing super at corner-back. And you also had Ger Hegarty in that team whose son Gearóid is in the current team, so there are connections all over the place.

When we are going to matches, if I see Joe O'Connor's son – his son, Aidan plays with my son with the Limerick under-20s – and Pat Heffernan's son has played with the boys – you take as much interest in their boys as much as your own, because of that connection we have.

Dave Clarke's son, Conor, is in goals for the under-20s so there is a connection everywhere and it is good to see it. We get to catch up at matches.

I remember for the All-Ireland semi-final against Antrim we went up to Dublin the night before, because the match was on at two o'clock.

I came down for the breakfast that morning… and who was sitting down, only Dave Mahedy, the trainer. I joined Dave, and we ordered breakfast. Dave ordered porridge and honey, and your one says to me, 'What do you want?'

'I'll have the full Irish'.

'Whatever you're used to,' he says.

But that was the times. I couldn't imagine a player having a full Irish before a match now. The game has changed so much when it comes to preparation.

I see that now with my two boys, John and Patrick. They were both involved in the last two Munster Minor Championships that Limerick won in 2019 and in '20, and both were then involved with the under-20s.

I got the schedule as a parent because they were under 18. We get their nutrition plan – what they have to eat – and my wife would be looking at it saying, 'What do I have to buy for them this time?' In fairness, she is good with them. She'd be better than me with it.

I was very pleased at how we played against Cork in the quarter-final – the first day out – in 1994 because it was lashing rain, and we were a new team coming out.

Lord have mercy on him, Tommy Quaid, had retired, and Joe Quaid started in goals. Cork got two goals at the start of the game, and… I had a '21' and I miss hit it… and it went for a '65'. From the resulting '65' I got a flick on for a goal, where I probably should have tapped the ball over for a point.

A mis-hit led to a goal… and it actually got us going! It was all down to one mis-hit, I firmly believe. Luckily enough we got that goal, then Pat Heffernan got a goal, and then I got another goal. Joe made some great saves then, and the crowd really got going. When we were going in at half-time, the crowd rose for us, and lifted us. They had seen what we had done to come back into it.

If you take the Joe Dooley goal in the All-Ireland final that year; we more than likely should have saved that shot. And if you look at the difference it made it history. No one ever thinks about the fact we missed a few chances ourselves that day.

I remember it well. We kept them in the game. We were six points up but we probably should have been up more. We weren't, we left them in it, and one moment from the free… has changed history. That comeback will always be spoken of.

Not too many people remember that moment against Cork, but I do. It was a wet day, the ball slipped. I didn't know where it was, I just didn't connect with it. We were lucky enough to get a '65'. It was just all momentum at that stage. If you were to pick one moment, that could be it! It is often just one little split-second moment and so many things follow!

You could say that in any game when a fella makes a block.

'If he didn't make that block…'

Joe Quaid made some good saves that day. I always remember, it was very funny… Tom Ryan used to say to Joe, 'Why don't you catch the balls? Why are you batting them out?'

'I make things look spectacular," he said.

'Would it not be easier if you caught it in the first place?' Tom Ryan was a great character to play under. His mother was a great player. The best player on the field was his mother.

'My mother can do better than ye, lads'. He was good alright, in fairness to him. I think people wronged him too in the sense that people said he sat in his dugout for the final, that if he got up off his bum we would have done better.

But he didn't get up in any other matches, and we won! It was okay for them games, but it wasn't for the final because we lost? The biggest mistake that day against Offaly was that Éamonn Cregan was in one spot, but if he was in a different spot he would have told Dooley to put that free over the bar. He said it himself, that he just happened to be on the wrong side of the pitch… or the right side as it turned out.

It is small things like that that make all the difference.

I remember in 2007 when Limerick were in the All-Ireland final. Richie Bennis was over the team and I was involved with him. Andrew O'Shaughnessy got a free with about five minutes to go, and Richie said we'd tap it over. I said, 'Richie, we didn't come here to do that, let's go for it'.

O'Shaughnessy told me afterwards that he was always going to go for it. With five minutes to go we said we'd just go for it. JJ Delaney saved it off the line.

There are defining moments in everything you do, that can change your life.

99

BRIAN FINN

OFFALY 3-16 LIMERICK 2-13
All-Ireland SHC Final
Croke Park
SEPTEMBER 4, 1994

Despite being an ever-present on the Limerick team for the previous seven years, Brian Finn (front row, third from right) had to watch the agony of the 1994 All-Ireland final loss to Offaly from the bench

★ **LIMERICK:** J Quaid; S McDonagh, M Nash, J O'Connor; D Clarke, G Hegarty, D Nash, C Carey (0-2), M Houlihan (0-2); F Carroll, G Kirby (capt) (0-6), M Galligan; TJ Ryan, P Heffernan, D Quigley (2-3). **Sub:** L O'Connor for Galligan.

★ **OFFALY:** Jim Troy; S McGuckin, K Kinahan, M Hanamy (capt); B Whelahan, H Rigney, K Martin; J Pilkington (0-2), D Regan; Johnny Dooley (1-4), John Troy (0-1), Joe Dooley (1-2); B Dooley (0-5), B Kelly, D Pilkington (0-1). **Subs:** J Errity for McGuckin, M Duignan (0-1) for Regan, P O'Connor (1-0) for Joe Dooley.

THE ACTION

THIS HEARTBREAKING FINAL continues to be talked about in Limerick to this day, but not for the right reasons.

The match is known as the 'five-minute final' due to the sensational comeback by Offaly, who scored 2-5 to win the game in the last five minutes. Such was the dramatic nature of and ending to this All-Ireland final, *The Guardian*'s Barry Glendenning, a native of Offaly, listed the game as one of six 'late sporting dramas' – alongside world renowned events from The Ashes and the Winter Olympic Games.

Damien Quigley had got Limerick's goals, and the Liam MacCarthy Cup looked destined for Shannonside for the first time since 1973.

With five minutes of normal time remaining, Limerick were leading by 2-13 to 1-11 and looked to be heading to their first title in 21 years, when Offaly were awarded a free 20 metres from the goal. Up stepped Johnny Dooley who beat Limerick goalkeeper Joe Quaid to score the resultant goal with a low-struck effort.

Momentum is everything in hurling and that proved to be the case when a quick and errant puck-out led to Pat O'Connor putting Offaly a point ahead moments later with a low shot to the net. Such was the quick-fire nature of both goals, those watching the final at home missed the build-up to Offaly's second goal as RTÉ were still showing a replay of the first goal. When live television transmission resumed, the sliotar was still dropping towards O'Connor.

★★★★★

>

I WAS A sub in the 1994 All-Ireland final against Offaly.

I had been an ever-present on the team from 1986 up until '93, but a change in management then led to the fact that I lost my place on the starting team. Coming up to the '94 All-Ireland final I was somewhat injured as well.

There was fierce anticipation in Limerick because we had been in the Munster final in 1992, and we were to some degree ambushed in Ennis in '93 against Clare – and you must remember at that stage there was no backdoor. I would have felt that had there been backdoors back in the 80s and the 90s some really good Limerick teams would have been a lot more successful.

If you look at the period from 1987 to '91, Tipperary and Galway dominated at All-Ireland level and at Munster level; and we were beaten three years in-a-row by Tipp. We still had a good team, and if we had got over Tipperary or if we had a second chance or even a third chance – in relation to a round-robin – I feel that Limerick would have been in a lot better place, but that facility wasn't there.

In 1993 we were ambushed, having been in the Munster final in '92, but we were still a very, very good team. A change of management brought a change of direction. Dave Mahedy was the coach, Tom Ryan was the manager, and the proof of the strength of the team was that we won Munster fairly handy that year. We beat Antrim in the semi-final and there was fierce expectation on that Limerick team.

But everyone knows really in Limerick what happened next – it is seared into their minds the events of the last three or four minutes against Offaly. It took from what was a very, very good team. They regrouped and were back in 1995 and were back in the All-Ireland final in 1996, but that experience stayed with Limerick people for a very, very long time.

In relation to Seán's career, and the 2021 All-Ireland final against Cork, I remember saying to my younger lad Patrick, even with three minutes to go… when we must have been 12 or 13 points up, and I was asking him continuously, 'How much is left? How much is left?' We're always going back to the memory of 1994.

I am so proud of what Seán has achieved. That team, Seán's team, were very young in 2018 and they didn't realise at all what they were after achieving. They hadn't suffered the hurt of 45 years that I had as a supporter and as a player.

Even though Seán was playing, the overriding thrill was the fact Limerick had won an All-Ireland for the first time in 45 years. Leaving Croke Park that day, we said if we never won again, we were happy.

People couldn't believe Offaly came back that day in 1994.

It was disbelief really. Croke Park at the time was under reconstruction. They were rebuilding the Cusack Stand. It was a strange occasion in one sense, and sometimes games can pass you by. I haven't ever looked back at the match so I can't really recall certain elements of it but you would be expected to close games out at that stage, with everything that was on the line for Limerick at the time.

People have been critical of Tom Ryan and the management, but I don't know if there was anything anyone could have done at that late stage to stem what actually was after happening. Having gone through that, it makes living through what Seán is doing now really great. I went onto the field to Seán after Limerick beat Tipp in the first round of the round-robin 2018.

Barry Murphy got the goal that day. He batted it in. I told Seán to stick with this team as I felt there was an All-Ireland in them. That was a turning point. When I saw the Tipperary team that day, I sensed that Limerick had a chance of winning it. For some reason, I felt there was complacency in Tipp and they put out a team that they thought was going to be good enough to beat Limerick. And it wasn't.

That was the spark that ignited the whole thing.

It was the fact Limerick, a young team that was coming from nowhere, had beaten a team like Tipp. I thought Tipp actually made a mistake in the team they picked. I got a sense of belief even at that early stage that this young team maybe were going to do something.

Subsequently, they got a win over Kilkenny in Thurles in the All-Ireland quarter-final. That was a major, *major* turning point. We beat Kilkenny by two points but we should have beaten them by 10 points that day. It showed that measure of that team.

I believe they were fearless coming through.

The 90s team was a seasoned team. The 1992 championship team that lost to Cork in the Munster final, that was a very seasoned team. Subsequently, a lot of them came through in 1994, albeit with new management along with some new players that had come through as well. You were looking at some of the players coming towards the latter stages of their career. They were certainly more experienced than the Limerick team of 2018 that won the All-Ireland.

There always is pressure.

Limerick had been in quite a number of All-Irelands. I remember travelling up to Dublin on the train in 1980, when we were beaten in the All-Ireland final, and then again in '81 when Galway beat them in the semi-final when Seán Foley was sent off in the first 10 minutes.

They were teams well good enough to have won All-Irelands, and that period of 45 years wouldn't have existed and wouldn't have been an issue at all.

That pressure to win an All-Ireland was absolutely there going into the final against Offaly in '94, especially when we felt we were probably better than Offaly. If you are a better team, there is that pressure to perform. We did perform and played very, very well. Being seven points up with four or five minutes to go in an All-Ireland would suggest that you are in a good place, but we all know what happened next.

This current Limerick team is better than anything that is around, since 2018. Whatever happened on the day in '19, we were poor against Kilkenny. We had an injury to Declan Hannon. If I was ever critical of the management, I just felt that they didn't deal with that particular injury because we seemed to change the whole team to try and compensate for Declan's absence, and that gave the initiative to Kilkenny.

That fact that we came back and probably should have got a draw was still a measure of that Limerick team. We had been better than teams and that brings its own pressure. If you are better and you don't perform, you can still get caught, but if you do perform you will win the game.

Anyone who was a member of that panel or that team in 1994 would always be identified with that final loss to Offaly.

Limerick were in the All-Ireland final in 2007 when to some degree we were beaten after the first 10 minutes. Having said that, we performed very well for the rest of that game. But 1994 is still the one people go back to. Either ourselves or the media always refer back to that, but thankfully not as much now.

I remember in 1992 I was playing corner-back in the Munster final. It was a fantastic occasion down in Cork in Páirc Uí Chaoimh. It was a lovely, sunny, fantastic day. We met a class Cork team. The full-forward line was Tomás Mulcahy, John Fitzgibbon, and Kevin Hennessy. One of my memories of that was a goal that we conceded, which should never have been allowed… Tomás Mulcahy fouled the ball on his way to flicking it into the back of the net.

But, you know, you didn't have VAR or Hawk Eye at that stage to prove that it shouldn't have happened. It was a turning point in that game. It goes back to my point, that was a good Limerick team, but maybe a bit of bad luck cost us and we were out of the championship after that.

It is a bonus for Seán to be involved.

Me being a Limerick man and being involved in the GAA and Limerick GAA all my life, the fact Limerick are winning and continue to win is key. Seán being there nearly brings more pressure when it comes to going to matches.

In 2021, the way I was feeling wasn't down to a genuine belief that Cork were going to come back. As Seán said, that game was won after 30 minutes, but it was just a hang-up of what happened to us in 1994.

I never in a million years expected a Limerick team to be doing what this team is doing now.

I didn't even see it when I was watching Seán play with that under-14, 15s, and 16s team, with the likes of Cian Lynch involved. Going back and looking at history, Limerick won three under-21 All-Irelands at the start of the new millennium in 2000, 2001, and 2002, and there was great expectation that they would come good. To some degree they did, in that a lot of that team were on the 2007 All-Ireland final team.

In 2007, Limerick met a Kilkenny team that effectively reflects the present Limerick team, so no matter how good you were… you were meeting one of the best teams of all time, maybe, to some degree. Even getting out of Munster at that time was very difficult.

Limerick's current success kind of came all of a sudden, so it didn't feel like the false dawns of the past. If you look at it, we qualified as the third team in Munster in 2018, we beat Kilkenny by two points and were maybe lucky to do it because we were under the cosh in the last few minutes – and against Cork in the semi-final Nickie Quaid's miraculous save was the turning point so, to some degree, we scraped through in 2018.

It wasn't anything that was expected, it was totally unexpected, but the rest has happened and they have proven themselves to be a great team.

I started my hurling career playing with Bruff, until I was 15, then as a family we moved into the parish of South Liberties to Donoughmore. I played with South Liberties then from the age of 15 until I was 24. I moved back to Bruff again, and finished my playing career there.

At one stage with South Liberties, we had Pat Hartigan, Joe McKenna and Éamonn Grimes over our senior team… three All Stars. No management team in the country would have had the quality that we had.

I've been involved at all levels in Bruff, and all levels with Limerick. I was involved in the Limerick academy, and I could see with the academy that things were progressing well.

I look back at my time playing with Limerick with huge pride. When you play on a county team it bestows a certain status and a certain sense of pride. I am thrilled that I was involved from 1986 onwards as a senior player. I played two years as a minor in 1982 and '83, and three years at under-21 level from 1984. We were the first team that won Munster under-21 for Limerick.

A lot of those players did come through into the 1994 and '96 team that got to the two All-Ireland finals… Ger Hegarty, Anthony Carmody, Ciarán Carey, Pa Carey… all those lads that I played underage with. I played with some great players, some real legends of the game. My time starting off with Limerick coincided with the ending of the likes Éamonn Cregan, Liam O'Donoghue, and Joe McKenna. I played with those guys. They are legends in their own right.

How I looked up to those guys is similar, I'd imagine, to how young lads are looking up to Seán and his pals at the moment.

99

MARK FOLEY

LIMERICK 4-7 TIPPERARY 0-16
Munster SHC Final Replay
Páirc Uí Chaoimh
JULY 14, 1996

Mark Foley escapes the clutches of John Carroll and Seamus Butler of Tipperary

★ **LIMERICK:** J Quaid; S McDonagh, M Nash, D Nash; D Clarke, C Carey (capt) (0-1), **M Foley**; M Houlihan, S O'Neill, F Carroll (1-1), G Kirby (0-1), M Galligan, O O'Neill (2-0), D Quigley (0-2), TJ Ryan (1-1). **Subs:** B Foley (0-1) for Galligan, P Tobin for Carroll.

★ **TIPPERARY:** B Cummins; G Frend, P Shelly, M Ryan; R Ryan, Colm Bonnar, P Delaney; B O'Meara, Conal Bonnar; M Cleary (0-6), L McGrath (0-1), J Leahy, L Cahill (0-1), D Ryan (0-4), N English (0-3). **Subs:** A Ryan for Leahy, K Tuckey (0-1) for B O'Meara, P Fox for L McGrath.

★ GAME OF MY LIFE ★

THE ACTION

AS LIMERICK CAPTAIN Ciarán Carey collected the coveted provincial trophy, many in the crowd in Páirc Uí Chaoimh remarked that Tom Ryan's men had just won the greatest of all Munster Championships. Sentenced to a Himalayan route by the draw, Ryan's men brushed aside the doubters. Cork away, All-Ireland champions Clare, and now Tipp were cast aside by a team on a mission to put to bed the demons of 1994. Although only scoring six points from play in this Munster final replay, four goals and a solid defensive display were enough to win the day.

After both sides played out an epic 0-19 to 1-16 draw in front of 43,525 at the Gaelic Grounds a week previously, Tipp, who at one stage held a 10-point lead, did not want to toss to decide the venue, and the replay was played on the banks of Lee.

First-half goals from Frankie Carroll and Owen O'Neill had Limerick 2-3 to 0-9 at the break, before a TJ Ryan goal and a second raising of the green flag from O'Neill secured Limerick's eighteenth Munster SHC title. And the goals came at vital times. It was the four-minute period after the restart, during which Limerick scored 1-2, that really sealed the deal for the Treaty men. By the time O'Neill booted the sliotar to the net, giving Brendan Cummins no chance, Limerick were in the driving seat.

★★★★★

> 66

THE 1996 MUNSTER final replay!

That is most memorable in a lot of ways. When you are looking back, it is almost from another time in comparison to the way things are for players today.

That game was at the very start of my playing time with Limerick and it was very memorable because obviously you are successful number one, but number two, just looking back, things were just so much simpler. At the end of the day, it was all about getting the result. There are various things that stick out in my mind.

I remember we were fortunate enough to get out of Limerick with a draw in the first game, because we were nine or 10 points down at one stage. We managed to claw Tipperary back and reel them in in the second-half.

There were a number of different things that happened then; Gary Kirby was injured. He'd been in hospital the week of the game – he got a bang on his head. He played IN the replay alright, but probably wasn't himself to be fair. Gary would have been a huge part of the team at the time. Going down to the match, the one thing I remember about it was we all used to travel in cars at the time, which is unheard of now. That would be very, very old school. I remember being stopped in Buttevant. There was a tailback about four miles outside Buttevant, nearly all the way to Ballyhea. We got an escort. We drove on the right-hand side of the road all the way through Buttevant… and on to Cork for the match.

Everything is so structured now, and down to the last nth degree in terms of timing and in terms of what you do before games in terms of nutrition, and in terms of fluid intake and all that type of stuff.

In fairness to Dave Mahedy, he was ahead of his time. He made huge improvements in terms of the physical preparation – we were always very, very fit, and a lot of that was down to Dave and the training regime we had at the time. In relation to other teams at the time, we were probably a little bit ahead in terms of preparation. We trained very, very hard, but it was very structured as well and I think Dave Mahedy did a fantastic job while he was with Limerick.

One of the things the current players are missing out on is the fact that they don't realise or don't appreciate what was involved when we were playing – we had a lot of fun, a lot of banter, and great craic. That's kind of gone out of it now, but having said that if you spoke to a current player, they will say they really enjoy it.

But it is certainly a lot more serious now. You have a situation now where – and obviously there is no debate on the issue, because it is great that everyone is wearing helmets now for safety – the public don't recognise a lot of the big hurlers, and I think that is kind of regrettable. A lot of them are walking around and they could pass young lads on the street, and they wouldn't even know them.

It has completely changed, but it has also changed for the better. It is a better game, and it is more skilful. There are different attributes now… athleticism is huge, and the skill level has gone through the roof. Though, there is maybe not the same question of toughness in the modern game as there once was. I'm sure a lot of lads playing at the moment wouldn't have made it in our time, but there are certainly loads of lads from our time who wouldn't make it today. The game is continuing to evolve and that's brilliant as well.

I played underage with Limerick, minor and under-21, and we hadn't even won a match so things were at a very low ebb at that stage. We got a lot of hammerings at underage so the prospects wouldn't have been that great when I was coming through. Having said that, there was a very good senior team there at the time, and I was fortunate enough to get on the panel and win something with them in 1994. To actually win something with Limerick was huge, not only for myself personally, but because Limerick hadn't won a Munster Championship since back in 1981.

To win in dramatic circumstances as well against Tipp then in '96 having come back the week before from the dead, and manage to win it the week after was gold. On a personal level, it was great just to win the game. It was a very warm day for the replay in 1996. We struggled a lot in the first-half. Tipp were well on top… I can remember really struggling, I think we all kind of struggled, but Frankie Carroll got a goal, more or less against the run of play, and that set us on our way. We were very comfortable in the second-half.

Even though we weren't fantastic, and some cracks appeared that maybe manifested themselves down the line in the All-Ireland, we got over the line by scoring goals. It wasn't a great performance… but it was a great day for Limerick.

Tipperary were very strong at the time. They had a lot of players who would go on to win an All-Ireland afterwards in 2001, and then they had the tail-end of that great team from the 80s and the early 90s… Nicky English was still there, Declan Ryan was still there. They timed their run really, really well that year and came into the Munster final playing very well and kind of blew us away in the first-half. When you look back on it, it was the last ever straight knockout championship, so when you lost you were gone… no second chance. From a Limerick perspective, to beat Cork and Tipp to win a Munster Championship, but also to beat the All-Ireland champions Clare in the semi-final… that had never been done before! The big thing about 1994 was the great campaign we had in Munster. We tapered off a bit after that. To be fair, we probably played our best hurling earlier in the year. Even though Cork weren't great at the time, we were very impressive against them.

To do that was hugely satisfying. It was a really, really fantastic campaign. It is one that will live long in the memory because Clare had their best team they ever had, and to beat Cork down in Cork, which Limerick had never done before, was huge. And to finally get over Tipp in the Munster… it was a great campaign, one that rubber-stamped that Limerick team as a decent team. It just a pity we didn't cap it off and win an All-Ireland.

The biggest regret about 1996 is not ultimately the result in the All-Ireland final. Wexford were the better team on the day, they fully deserved their win. There are no qualms on Limerick's behalf or anything like that, but the one regret is that we didn't really perform to any kind of a level in the final.

Any final you play in, you want to give it your best and give a decent performance that you hang your hat on and say, 'Right, look, that's what I am capable of… that's my best!' But we didn't on the day, and it was very, very disappointing.

Looking back, you just look back very fondly on very simple things… the big matches we won, and the great campaigns we had. You look back at the camaraderie… the dressing-room after training, or being at training on a Friday in the Gaelic Grounds with the sun setting and you could smell the Chinese takeaway from over the wall. We've all heard the stories about Kilkenny training matches, when they had that great team in the 00s… but we used to have legendary 15-a-side matches in training too.

My first experience coming into the panel was after the '94 Munster final; they wanted to make up numbers in training – I was just out of minor at the time. I was called in by Tom Ryan. I was very happy to be called in. We were playing

15-a-side matches at the time. Mike Quaid was the referee, and he used to bring in his umpires. It was very official and it was all above board. It wasn't like Tom Ryan had the whistle or anything like that.

Some of the matches we had were really... really legendary... epic stuff in training. I remember Seán O'Neill and Mike Houlihan marking each other. It was real... real hard stuff, and true championship stuff inside in training.

Some of those matches, you'd stand back and you'd think, *Jesus, this is unbelievable, to be involved in this!* Some of those days, you'd really miss and not so much the championship days. Obviously, there is a lot of talk and razzmatazz about the championship, and rightly so because it is a big event, but it's the simpler things you really miss... being in training and witnessing those kind of matches... being able to improve month-on-month, year-on-year. Just being part of that journey was very satisfying.

We were up in the Red Cow Hotel – Tom Moran is a great supporter of Limerick and was sponsor for a few years. We had some sort of a function there in the winter of 1994. At the time, we had these green blazers, beige pants, and a shirt and tie. We all went up to Dublin to the function and that was the gear we wore as a team going up. And that was fine!

But there was a nightclub next door to the Red Cow. The function ended at about 11pm. After the function anyway, myself and Davy Clarke decided to go in next door and have a few drinks. It was good auld craic. We'd still the gear on... and the Australian rugby team were playing Ireland in an international in the old Lansdowne Road the day after.

And, of course, there we were with the green blazers and the beigy pants, and Davy Clarke decided to put on an Australian accent, telling people he'd pulled a hamstring and he was out of the match the next day. We ended up having this crowd of about 25 or 30 people around us and they followed us hook, line, and sinker.

I was able to tell them I was the bagman, that I'd no part in the team, but the fact that Davy was after pulling his hamstring meant I was allowed to go out, but I had to mind him to make sure he didn't get into any trouble.

Looking back, it's great to have won the two All Stars, it's some kind of recognition, but at the time it didn't mean a whole lot because you were more into the team than yourself. In some of those following years, we used to get beaten early... we used to get some right beatings in the championship, so to be nominated for an award was something. Looking back, it was great, but at the time other people probably got more enjoyment out of me winning them than I did myself, because we were so driven as a team in trying to succeed and trying to get back up there with Limerick.

A quarter of a century later, you take a bit of pride in winning them alright! Though, there were other lads that I played with who were probably just as much deserving, if not even more deserving, than me of the awards.

It is very difficult to build something when it is straight knockout, because you can gather no momentum. The ultimate test is championship, and we were only getting one or two games every summer. It is one thing the present players will never experience, especially players who never play in an All-Ireland final. Every day for us was an... All-Ireland final.

There was no difference between the first round going down to Cork, or going up to play an All-Ireland final. The only difference was that for an All-Ireland final most of the country was tuned into the fact it was an All-Ireland final... whereas, for the first round, it would really only be the hurling people and people in your own county who would be really attuned to what was going on.

It was straight knockout, and if you were gone... you were gone.

It is good that they get more games nowadays. It is a fairer system and it definitely reflects the preparation that is being put in. It is not fair to be asking guys to be putting their lives on hold and to only get one chance, but at the same time, in our day it was real championship, and in real championship... you cannot recreate that. All the systems that are in place at the moment are fantastic, and it is a very good championship, but the cut and throat nature is not there until you get to the knockout stages.

It is a positive and a negative; but certainly, the dog-eat-dog championship that was there at that time, is not there now until teams get into Croke Park.

It was definitely unfair that we were training for six months and could be gone after one day...

Different times!

"

TJ RYAN

GARRYSPILLANE 1-14 KILMALLOCK 1-10
Limerick SHC Semi-Final
Bruff
SEPTEMBER 6, 1997

TJ Ryan beats Colm Kehoe of Wexford for the ball in the 1996 All-Ireland hurling final

★ **GARRYSPILLANE:** C O'Connor; I Mansell, E Stapleton, W Burke; G McGrath, **TJ Ryan (0-1)**, D Ryan; M O'Brien, J Murnane; M O'Dea (0-1), F Carroll (1-4), R English (0-3); D Ryan (0-3), P Tobin, J O'Keeffe (0-1).

★ **KILMALLOCK:** T Hennessy; D Barry, D O'Shaughnessy, G Houlihan; M Lyons, D Clarke, J Fitzgerald; J Connery, M Houlihan (0-3); M Cronin (0-2), M Nelligan (0-1), P Connery; L Neenan (0-4), S O'Grady, P Dowling. **Sub:** P Tobin (1-0) for P Connery.

THE ACTION

HISTORY WAS MADE as Garryspillane reached their first ever Limerick SHC final, beating hotly tipped Kilmallock – All-Ireland club finalists just three years previously – to set up a mouth-watering championship final against Patrickswell.

Just 13km separate these two great clubs, but in the end four points was the gap as the proud people of Knocklong and surrounding areas no doubt shed a tear when Mick O'Sullivan blew the final whistle. Garryspillane, just crowned Intermediate champions 12 months previously, were in bonus territory and played hurling with a freedom that could only take place in a team risen to such heights in such a short period of time.

Once Frankie Carroll found the net with an 18th minute penalty, after Donie Ryan was pulled down inside the square, Garryspillane opened up a comfortable 1-7 to 0-5 lead at the break.

Mike Houlihan had opened the scoring from the throw-in but that was the only occasion the men in green and white were in front. Once Donie Ryan rounded Donal Barry to level and Garryspillane led from the second minute, the show was on the road and the Bouncers never looked back.

On September 21, 1997, Patrickswell won the championship after a 1–12 to 0–9 defeat of Garryspillane in the final – securing a famous three in-a-row. The championship journey paved the way for Garryspillane to win their first senior county title eight years later.

★★★★★

>

IT IS A club game for me!

It is the 1997 County semi-final when we beat Kilmallock to get the club to its first-ever final. That's the game!

The history of it is…

I come from Garryspillane.

Garryspillane up to the 1990s was always a junior club. It was a very small rural club. It was only formed in 1952 and its history was all around junior. In 1990, we won the Intermediate Championship for the first time, but I was 16 and I was only playing in goals.

For whatever reason, it was agreed that after winning the county that we wouldn't join the senior ranks. I'm not fully sure of the reasons… different people had different opinions within the club, but the bottom line was, we didn't go senior.

I'd probably put it down to maybe a lack of ambition, or else they honestly didn't believe the team was good enough.

Roll forward to 1996… Frankie Carroll was playing, my brothers Donie and Davy had arrived on the scene… we had a nice team playing and we won the 1996 Intermediate Championship.

And this time – because of a group of ambitious young lads, and maybe some bravado – we were saying, 'We are going senior!'

I am sure people would have thought, *Yeah let them off!*…

We had just won the Intermediate Championship, we had just managed to get over the line, we were young, and we had won the final after a replay. So, then roll forward to 1997. We got off to a good start in the Senior Championship. We were up there with the big boys, we had a couple of games won, and we had a great win over Ballybrown in the quarter-finals after a replay. On to a semi-final of a senior championship… and NOW we're facing Kilmallock!

And I'm sure people would have said, *This is the end of the road now*. Kilmallock were a senior team over the road, a neighbouring club… these boys had done it all before. Brilliant history! Great club! And we beat them in the semi-final by four points.

I was captain of the team at the time… and we got Garryspillane to a first ever county final at senior level. We lost the final afterwards, but why does that game against Kilmallock stand out? I felt that particular day that Garryspillane was rejuvenated. We had arrived at the top table and announced 'We are here!'

For me, that game stood out because it showed that we had both talent and ambition, the club acknowledged this and improved the all-round set up. For me, the club was just reinvigorated and were now one of the key players in the Limerick Senior Championship. We had a great time at senior level even though we only won one title.

That game, when we beat Kilmallock… the atmosphere was unreal! It really was the dawning of an era. And today, the club is alive, the facilities have improved no end, we were a senior club up until 2023, and it is just brilliant.

There is a large number of that team involved in the club now at underage, management and administrative levels. You get one chance at this and my belief is when you are finished playing, you should get involved with your club. You are a product of your community and I feel there is a duty to give something back.

I've been chairman of Bord na nÓg now in Garryspillane since the end of 2010 and it's a very enjoyable time. Frankie Carroll, who was part of the set up with me, is now chairman of the senior board.

We now have another great group of young lads. There is ambition there, it is being recognised, and we're having a go. We may not always be successful but we are giving them every opportunity that's possible. There needs to be hope, and hope has the ability to see the impossible and to see it happening.

Back then we had a chairman, Jim Dooley, who supported us. Maybe deep down he thought we were mad, but he supported us and he got us to somewhere that was unbelievable. I truly believe that everything good that came after that day was because of that game!

I won't say that I suffered from an inferiority complex or anything before that game, but it definitely gave me a lift and it certainly took away the 'small club' syndrome.

I've been fortunate to play in THE best of games… Munster finals, we came from 10 points down against Tipp in the Gaelic Grounds in 1996 and drew, which was electric – obviously lost two All-Ireland finals, and we won a National League title. I went on to win a county senior title for Garryspillane in 2005 which was amazing, but the one game continuously comes back to me… that semi-final against Kilmallock.

I was centre-back that day, and would probably have been playing my best hurling. I remember it was one of my better games for sure. Maybe that helps your memory because GAA people have a great ability to let the good games and the victories paper over an awful lot of not so good days. It is a trait of GAA people.

My two brothers were playing – Davy and Donie – and it was the dawning of a new era. It was a really exciting time. We had Brendan Bonnar from Cashel training us. We used to refer to him as the most famous of the Bonnars, even though he actually didn't play with Tipperary. He is the brother of Cormac, Colm and Conal… and Brendan gave us great confidence and belief.

That game was actually postponed by a week. When we arrived the first day to play them the heavens just opened. There was a load of water on the pitch. We would have arrived there nervous, as we were effectively playing one of the big powers of Limerick…. and it was put back by a week!

When the following week came around, we got our opportunity and we won by four points. It was a very tight, tough, tense game. We rocked on then to play Patrickswell in the county final. If someone had said in the two, three, four… five years previous that Garryspillane would go on to play senior you'd be kind of saying… 'Okay?'

But to go and play in a county senior final, and go on eventually to win it in 2005… it is just massive!

It was MASSIVE.

At that time, those teams playing senior just seemed so far away, it was like they were playing on a different planet to us.

I have some great memories!

I was just fortunate to have been around at a good time… the 90s. My first year in the Limerick panel was the 1994 season and playing with guys that were there… Davy Clarke, Mike Houlihan, Ciarán Carey, Ger Hegarty, and Gary Kirby. It was a massive team to be involved with.

Super characters! I learned hugely from them, and it just took off from there.

I was just fortunate to have been around to win Munster titles. We got to two All-Irelands. Yeah, there is a little bit of disappointment that we didn't take our opportunities in 1994 and in '96… especially in 1996, when we had been there before. You definitely look back, even now 25 years on, and say, 'That was the game that got away, that shouldn't have got away from us'.

I don't have an excuse for that game. I don't think anybody has. You just have to say fair play to Wexford on the day, they were the better side, there is no doubt about that!

To be fair to the current Limerick crew, they've put to bed all the stuff that's gone on in the past, and all the disappointment. Everybody is living the dream in Limerick at the moment. It is just phenomenal to be around a fantastically well managed side.

John Kiely was with Galbally at the time. They weren't playing with us, but after that time in 1996 and '97, John Kiely decided to transfer to Garryspillane.

Obviously, that particular game and that time had an influence on him as well because afterwards he transferred to our club and he went on to win a county senior title with us in 2005. It just all goes back to that game.

Everything I've done with Limerick, I've enjoyed it. I don't have any hang-ups about it. I don't have regrets. I am one of those guys who believes that, most of the time, regrets are about stuff you didn't do… whereas I got to do all this stuff and I don't have any regrets about it, even though it didn't turn out how I wanted.

We had a reunion recently for the 1996 Limerick team. We met in the Gaelic Grounds and had a few beers afterwards. It was great to meet all those guys because there would be fierce respect among that group for each other. That team in the 90s was a very, very good Limerick team – we just don't have the All-Ireland medals to prove it. But we had everything else. We had the craic, we had the parties, we had the holidays… we just didn't have the medals.

I'd be fairly good at letting things go.

There is disappointment that we didn't win an All-Ireland medal. You can look back at the game and say we had opportunities, but if you roll the clock all the way back to sometime in the 1980s and you said to me, 'This is what is ahead of you, you'll get to play in an All-Ireland final'… I'd have taken the hand, and everything off you, just to get to do that.

I just wouldn't have thought it was physically possible!

After we won the county title in 2005, the craic around Garryspillane was just unbelievable! It was also an unbelievable sense of achievement. We had Tony Considine managing the team in 2004 and '05. We had lost the final in 2004 by one point to Ahane. It was a team that had never won a county before and we had just lost, but that gave us that drive and that hunger to get over the line.

And in fairness to Tony Considine, he was a massive character at the time, he was brilliant in the dressing-room for us. We got first-hand experience of trying to do something that hadn't been done before.

Even though we were exceptionally well prepared and we were better than Kilmallock on the day in 2005, when you are heading for that winning post, when the winning post is in sight… when your movement gets slower, your stride gets slower, and when you are just trying to get over the line… it is just unbelievable when you do!

I had some great days with Limerick too.

I treasure that day in 1996 in the Munster final against Tipp. It was an unbelievable second-half – I scored four points from play. We came back and got a draw.

That was MAGIC!! It was an atmosphere that was buzzing, it was the old Gaelic Grounds where it was terrace… people were wedged into it. It was just electric.

A lot of great memories from great games, but that game for Garryspillane in 1997, that was THE game!

"

MARK KEANE

LIMERICK 3-14   TIPPERARY 2-16
Munster Under-21 Hurling Championship Final
Gaelic Grounds, Limerick
AUGUST 2, 2001

Mark Keane is tackled by Galway's Brian Mahoney during the All-Ireland under-21 final in 2001

★ **LIMERICK:** T Houlihan (capt); D Reale, B Carroll, K Bermingham; M O'Riordan, B Geary, W Walsh; S Lucey (0-1) P Lawlor; E Foley (0-1), S O'Connor (0-1), K Tobin (0-2); C Fitzgerald (1-2), N Moran, **M Keane (2-7)**. **Subs:** M O'Brien for Walsh, P Tobin for Fitzgerald.

★ **TIPPERARY:** D Rabbitte; C Everard, J Devane, C Morrissey; D McGrath, P Curran, B Dunne; K Mulryan, E Brislane; D Shelley (0-1), D Gleeson, E Kelly (2-9); S Butler (0-3), L Corbett (0-2), P McGrath. **Subs:** T King for D McGrath, C Houlihan (0-1) for P McGrath, S Mason for Mulryan.

★ GAME OF MY LIFE ★

THE ACTION

LIMERICK, THE DEFENDING Munster and All-Ireland champions, came into this Munster final on home soil on the back of five championship wins in-a-row having defeated Clare, Cork, Antrim, and Galway in 2000, and Cork thus far in the 2001 Munster under-21 semi-final.

It was a late Mark Keane free that proved to be the winner as almost 20,000 people crammed into the Ennis Road venue on what a beautiful Thursday summer evening on Shannonside.

Tipperary had scored first when Eoin Kelly pointed after just 35 seconds. Limerick responded well and enjoyed a slice of good fortune when a long clearance by Brian Geary which had dropped into the Tipp goalmouth but looked to be going wide kindly bounced into the path of South Liberties man Mark Keane, who volleyed into the back of the net.

Just as he did in the semi-final against Cork, Keane played a crucial role for Limerick, and boosted by his early goal, the 20-year-old corner-forward chalked up an awe-inspiring tally of 2-7.

After trailing by 10 points at half-time – 2-11 to 0-7 – Tipperary, and Kelly, who almost single-handedly pulled his side back from the brink of extinction, managed to level two minutes from time, but when Keane pointed that late free to give the home side the lead and ultimate victory, referee Ger Harrington wasn't long blowing the full-time whistle.

Man of the Match Keane finished the championship top scorer with an impressive 3-29, an average of almost 10 points a game as Limerick went on to defeat Galway and Wexford to be crowned All-Ireland champions.

★★★★★

>

FIRST OF ALL, personally I had a huge game in terms of scoring, but what probably stood out for me more was the fact I was after breaking my ankle in the first minute and I didn't know it.

I went in and chased a dead-end ball, and myself and the goalkeeper, Darragh Rabbitte collided... and I wound up getting the goal. I got up off the ground and I knew I'd done damage, but I didn't know the significance of the damage.

I went in at half-time and I remember Dave Boylan saying to me, 'Don't take off your boot because if you take off your boot it will swell and you won't get it back on'.

And I still genuinely didn't think it was as bad as it was! So, to then go on afterwards... I wound up that night with 2-7... 2-3 from play! And then to realise afterwards that I'd done it with a broken ankle... is probably why that would stand out as more memorable as well!

And then there was the last minute free that Tipperary gave away... that's why that game sticks so much in my mind!

I look back at that time now with huge pride!

When you are in the middle of it and when you are in the middle of something great – just like the present Limerick team who are in the middle of something great – you don't realise how important it actually is to people.

But when I look back now and see photographs of it... the crowds that were there for mid-week matches. It is amazing thinking back, especially when you consider what happened to the Limerick seniors... I know it was unfortunate that they won an All-Ireland in 2020 with no one there. When we were under-21, there were 25,000 or 26,000 in the Gaelic Grounds on a Thursday... same with Thurles or Páirc Uí Chaoimh, or wherever we played in that scenario. And we have to be very realistic in the fact that to start it all off we went down to play Clare below in Ennis in 2000 and Clare were the All-Ireland minor champions in 1997. They would have been fancied to beat us with a great John Reddan team. It was a poor enough game against Clare but we got through it, and that started us off on a 15-game unbeaten run after which we wound up winning three All-Irelands.

It was an amazing time! I don't know whether it coincided with the start of the 'big boom' where there was lots of money around and people were going to the matches, but there was never an issue that there wouldn't be an atmosphere at a match. Even coming up to finals, be it Munster finals or All-Ireland finals, the last training session beforehand would have been a media session that would have been open to the public… those nights, there used to be huge crowds at them.

In 2000 we beat Cork in the Munster final, and in 2001 we beat Tipperary in the Munster final… you are beating the elite there. But then we have to be very realistic. A lot of those Tipperary lads went on to win a senior medal, something we never went on to realise… that was huge, to think of where they went and where we went afterwards. And that was all for different reasons.

I do remember that game against Tipperary was a lovely, bright evening.

I was marking a fella called Colm Everard. Tipp were strong. They had John Devane, Eoin Kelly, and Lar Corbett, who got an equaliser in the last couple of seconds, before Tipperary gave away the free.

Kelly and myself had a shootout that night. That free is very significant in the fact that… whatever about taking the free, we raced off into a good lead and Tipp clawed back seven or eight points, so all the momentum was with them going into the last couple of minutes… and then Corbett got the equaliser. A puckout then came down the field. The ball broke and Paul Curran fouled the ball on the ground. In fairness to Ger Harrington, he saw it and he gave us a free in.

I took the free.

Eoin Brislane, John Devane, and Paul Curran created a pyramid. The boys lifted each other in front of the free. I don't know if it has been done before or after in any hurling match, but looking back now I can probably take that as being one of the highest compliments paid in the fact that, with the form I was in they knew they had to do their best to put me off to stop the score going over.

When you are in a zone, it makes no difference at that stage… it was going over! We won the game by a point then.

They had Eoin Kelly doing the same on the other side. He wound up scoring 2-9, I wound up scoring 2-7. Because of that, we couldn't give away a free inside the '65', and they couldn't give away a free inside the '65'.

You can go back as far as the 1996 team, when Ciarán Carey got one of the most iconic points ever, but you have to respect Gary Kirby's involvement in that score, the fact Clare knew they couldn't foul Ciarán because they Gary was going to put it over anyway. In terms of free-taking and how important it is; the way I explain it is, for a good free-taker you obviously need to have your routine that you can't waiver from. It is all about repetition, repetition... *repetition*.

Whether you are down in South Liberties on your own, or whether you are in Croke Park in front of 80,000, you still have the same routine. You still pick the same spot behind the goals, and you still go through the same thing in your brain – you get your set-up right. The most important thing after that then is, you get the ball off the ground to where you want to strike it. Obviously, direction is huge, but if you fail to hit the ball right you are chasing after it.

In terms of confidence, you need ice in your veins when you are taking frees like that because you are always going to miss frees. There is no greater certainty than you are going to miss frees. You can't let it affect your general play then.

I played with, and played against, some of the most fabulous free-takers, and if they scored the first one, you know you are in trouble all day. But if they miss the first one, physiologically they could be caught once or twice.

That evening was unbelievable in terms of the weather. The elements were perfect. There was no real wind against us. There was a bit of sun alright, but that evening was perfect. But other nights then… you could have an evening where the wind is coming across the field so you have to take that into account as well, so you have to be very aware of your surroundings.

Even to this day, if I am going out to Thurles to watch a match, going into the town end, the wind always comes across the Ardán Ó Riáin. You just have to be aware of that. I was down there with a county minor team two years ago and I was saying, 'Always hit for the left post'… and they were asking me, 'Why?'

It's because the wind always comes across from that stand. You have to be aware of those things. You are not going into the Gaelic Grounds and just standing up over a ball and hitting it over the bar. You are going in and you are seeing where the wind is coming from, you are seeing what way the flags are blowing, and you are seeing what way the grass is blowing when you throw it into the air. You want to know whether the flags over the scoreboard are going down the field, across the field… behind the field?

★ GAME OF MY LIFE ★

Adrenaline 100 percent got me through that game against Tipperary in 2001.

I remember coming into the dressing-room after the match. I actually came in with a different ailment. I said to the doctor, Dave Boylan… and to Barry Heffernan, who was the physio at the time, that I was after getting a belt somewhere else.

They both looked at me and said, 'Look, you might think about getting an X-Ray'. I said, 'Sure if I get an X-Ray, it could potentially put me out of an All-Ireland semi-final against Galway'.

I went in, got the X-Ray… and it turned out there was nothing there for the first injury. But then they turned around and said, 'You are limping'.

They added, 'While you are here, we might as well X-Ray that'. And sure, didn't they turn around to me then and tell me that my ankle was broken. I didn't expect it, obviously. Back then, there were none of these boots they have these days, so I was put into a plaster. I was so sheepish after it, thinking that I was going to miss an All-Ireland semi-final against Galway.

It was a race against time effectively. I think we had three or four weeks until the semi-final. For about three weeks then I had the cast on, and probably against better judgement I took the cast off and I tried to get back training.

But sure, I wasn't moving any way right.

I'll never forget it… below in Ennis against Galway, I remember my name being called out over the loudspeaker that I was playing and sure the whole crowd erupted. That gave me more adrenaline, even though physically I was nowhere near being right. That gave me the confidence to go on and score 1-4 that day against a good corner-back in Brian O'Mahony.

We went on to beat Wexford in that year's final.

I don't think I was technically given the all-clear by the medical staff. I still have issues to this day during cold weather with the ankle I broke. I don't doubt for any second that it wasn't stemming back to then. I think it was just the nature of the beast that was in me; I didn't want to miss out. Was I right?

Looking back on results, I probably was right! But looking back on health implications, I probably wasn't right!

Looking back then, on the other side of it, I don't know if I was being overly fair to my teammates, especially when I take into account what Cian Lynch did in 2022, when he sacrificed himself for the All-Ireland final knowing that he wasn't going to play. That's very selfless.

So, was I thinking about myself at the time? I don't know. You could be keeping someone who is 100 percent fit out of the team.

There was HUGE expectation after we won those three under-21 All-Irelands in-a-row. There was no huge pressure from the public themselves, but there was a huge sense of excitement because of the fact that this team was after doing so much, and it was potentially a chance of doing something at senior. But as we know now, there is no guarantee of it.

Obviously, there is huge disappointment. We were given every opportunity.

With progress, everything gets better. Would I love to train in today's regime? Of course, I would. I'd love to test myself out in today's regime. But, would I be any good in today's regime is another side of it! There is definitely a sense of and a tinge of disappointment; there were definitely regrets of not going on to fulfil our potential.

It is a boyhood dream of us all to go on and win an All-Ireland senior medal.

The whole three panels we had with the under-21s… the reason we were so successful, it is very clichéd to say we were friends and that we were tight, but there was an absolutely unbelievable bond amongst that team and that management team to succeed.

You often hear John Kiely talk about honesty and resilience, and that was certainly there with that group. It was driven into us, and it just happened naturally. We didn't have a Caroline Currid to tell us how to think. I think she is an amazing woman for what she's done for Limerick hurling, but we didn't have that avenue there at the time for us.

"

OLLIE MORAN

LIMERICK 1-24 TIPPERARY 2-21 (AET)
Munster SHC Semi-Final 1st Replay
Semple Stadium, Thurles
JUNE 16, 2007

Ollie Moran races past Eamonn Corcoran of Tipperary before setting up teammate Pat Tobin to score one of the decisive goals in the epic trilogy against Tipperary in the 2007 Munster Championship

★ **LIMERICK:** B Murray; D Reale (capt), S Lucey, S Hickey; M O'Riordan, B Geary (0-2), M Foley (0-1); P Lawlor, D O'Grady; N Moran (0-3), **O Moran (0-5)**, M O'Brien; P Tobin, A O'Shaughnessy (0-6), B Foley. **Subs:** B Begley for Lawlor, M Fitzgerald (1-3) for B Foley, D Ryan for P Tobin, K Tobin (0-2) for N Moran, J O'Brien (0-2) for Mike O'Brien, Maurice O'Brien for Reale, N Moran for O'Grady, P Tobin for Ryan.

★ **TIPPERARY:** G Kennedy; E Buckley, D Fanning, D Fitzgerald; E Corcoran (0-1), C O'Mahony, H Maloney; S McGrath, J Woodlock (0-1); J Carroll, B Dunne (capt) (0-2), D Egan (1-2); S Butler (1-3), E Kelly (0-9), L Corbett (0-3). **Subs:** P Bourke for Corbett, T Stapleton for Corcoran, D O'Hanlon for Woodlock, R O'Dwyer for Bourke, Corbett for McGrath, W Ryan for Butler.

THE ACTION

LIMERICK HAD WELCOMED Tipperary to the Ennis Road venue the previous Sunday in search of a first Munster Championship victory since defeat of Cork in 2001. The replay brought as much excitement, if not more as the first game. In Thurles, Tipperary looked the better side for the majority of the game and with only six minutes of normal time remaining, the home side held a seven-point advantage. A Seamus Butler goal after 21 minutes had boosted them into a 10-point lead at the interval, 1-12 to 0-5.

However, after James Woodlock pointed in the 62nd minute, incredibly Tipperary would not add to their 1-19, their exact same tally as in the opening drawn game, in the remaining eight minutes of normal time – while Limerick, led by the inspirational Ollie Moran, would bring the game all square in the dying moments courtesy of an Andrew O'Shaughnessy free.

It looked like Tipp had finally got over the line in extra-time when 'Babs' Keating's men edged ahead once more, thanks to an early Darragh Egan goal, but a never-say-die Richie Bennis-managed Limerick side fought back with a spirit not witnessed by the Treaty County faithful in previous years. When O'Shaughnessy slotted over a late '65' the Kilmallock star brought the game to a second replay, this time back in Limerick.

★★★★★

★ GAME OF MY LIFE ★

"

I WILL ALWAYS remember the trilogy against Tipperary in 2007.

We were on a fairly bad run with Limerick for a good number of years, but we were kind of threatening. We got to a League final in 2006. We had got a bit of momentum going in 2004 aswell, but we just couldn't break the duck in terms of winning Munster Championship matches. But you've got to remember too that Munster was very, very competitive, as it always is, but we were just falling that little bit short all the time. Tipperary were turning into our arch-nemesis. Just when we thought we were getting going in 2006, Tipp turned around and gave us a fair beating in Thurles after we got to a league final.

We were going into 2007, and there was a change in manager. Richie Bennis was after coming in. It was yet another Limerick management team and everybody pretty much expected the same thing. I remember Richie came in with a load of energy… he was old school in the sense of he wouldn't be all that au fait with modern tactics or modern training techniques. But what he had was unbelievable passion, and fellas absolutely loved him. He had a great sense of fun, but he knew how to talk to fellas in a way that was going to resonate with them.

We went away early on that year to Breaffy House up in Castlebar.

I was coming out of there thinking… *This year is going to be a good year…* because there was a lot of soul searching going on, and a lot of fellas came out and said where they were at.

We were scheduled to play Tipperary in the Munster semi-final on the 10th of June. It was a belter hot day. Damien Reale was sent off relatively early in the match, and we were always playing catch up… but we eventually squeezed out a draw. It was a great game… 1-19 to 1-19 in the Gaelic Grounds.

As far as we were concerned, that was a win, or a moral victory of sorts, because we weren't out. Tipp had their own little bit of disarray going on at the time. There was talk of in-fighting, but the way Tipp are, they were always going to come out all-guns blazing. We got a draw after going down to 14 men against Tipp.

The game that is most memorable for me is the first replay, but not because the game itself was fantastic… it wasn't a particularly good game. We had played Tipp in the first game on the Sunday, and the replay was on the following Saturday night. We were playing them in Thurles and we felt we'd have the measure of

Tipp. In the game itself starting off, we just couldn't get any momentum going early on. Tipp then started to take control, and got a couple of goals.

Tipp were hitting us for goals, and they were hitting us for sucker punches. They just got a head of wind up. They were 10 points up at half-time. We just hadn't played at all. Tipp were way ahead and they were bossing us all over the field. The first day I'd marked Benny Dunne, but I got a run going on him and I played well the first day. The second day, I was marking Conor O'Mahony – a very tough, uncompromising centre-back – and I just could not get away from him.

It was just one of those days. Every time he went to make a move, he was one step ahead all of the time. We were kind of negating one another, but I kind of felt myself that I wasn't really getting into the game. Second-half rocked on, and we were far more competitive. We had stopped the rot, but the problem was, we still weren't putting up enough scores at the other end. Fast forward to the 64th or 65th minute, we were still seven or eight points down… and you could see up in the crowd that people were starting to leave their seats. It was like as if the white flag was nearly being raised at that stage. But, forever whatever reason, and by virtue of the fact we dug in, we got a bit of a kick going.

There were a couple of incidents that just got us going. I remember Brian Geary winning a great ball at one stage and throwing the ball out to Mark Foley. The ball was hit down towards me then and I remember finally getting rid of Conor O'Mahony. Conor was relatively inexperienced at the time, and, to be fair, I think Tipp at that stage felt they were over the line. It was the first time in the game that I'd broken free from him, got a point, and I said, *Great, the game isn't over yet*. At that stage it was down to about six points.

There were about eight or nine minutes left, but everyone thought that the only way of getting back at that stage of the game was by scoring a goal. Ironically enough, what happened afterwards was that we were just chipping away. You could see Tipperary visibly wilting and you could see Limerick getting stronger. Then we just started rolling off point, after point, after point… and it came down to a situation then where people that were leaving started to stay.

It was gas actually… you could see that all the exits in the stands were clogged up. Obviously, what had happened was that people who had gone had done a U-turn. I subsequently heard afterwards that there was an amount of people out on the road home that had actually stopped their car and ran back into Thurles, because they were hearing what was going on. From that point of view, it was very, very unique.

It was the first time in a couple of years that we'd got a proper championship performance, but we were poor for probably 80 percent of the match the second day. Tipp actually, ironically, if you watch back the seven or eight minutes, had opportunities for goals, but I think they were mentally drained at that stage.

One thing we knew was that we had an amount of work done.

EVENTUALLY, IT CAME down to... I remember Andrew O'Shaughnessy winning an unbelievable ball. At this stage, there was about three or four minutes of injury time gone.

What happened was, we brought on some subs... James O'Brien scored a great point. Kevin Tobin scored a great point. It was just one point after another, and eventually O'Shaughnessy won the ball. He had been very good the first day too, but he was well shackled as well. It was the first time in the game that he really sprung to life. It was like everyone was just feeding off one another, and there was a freedom in the way we were playing that we hadn't been able to do up to that point.

O'Shaughnessy caught a great ball then. He was marking Diarmaid Fitzgerald. Shaughs, because he was so strong, and his centre of gravity was so low... there was nothing Fitzgerald could do but foul him. He fouled him literally in front of the posts. We were a point down. The clock was up. O'Shaughnessy got that point to draw the game. That was unbelievable! It was like we had won the game. The crowd were absolutely off the charts at that stage. The emotions were really, really high. We went into an extra-time situation then. We thought we'd have all the momentum. The opposite happened. Tipp had all the momentum.

Tipp rattled over points. But one guy who really stood up to the plate in extra-time was Brian Geary. Brian and Mark Foley were phenomenal in extra-time. It was like a carbon copy of the game itself in that we were all the time chasing the game. We were never in a position where we could get a killer blow. They were landing the punches all the time, but we just couldn't land enough punches.

We were three points down at half-time in extra-time that night. I remember Geary scoring an unbelievable point, and Shaughs was getting his frees. It came down then to... we were a point down with a minute gone in added time and a ball landed on the end line. There was a skirmish. There were a few of us involved… myself and Conor O'Mahony anyway. It was just one of those tussles. Brian Gavin was refereeing the same night. The ball went out over the line. If I was to put my hand on my heart, I'd say it touched me last. I can say that now 16 years later!

It was very difficult to see who touched it last. We knew it was our last chance because at that stage Tipp were leaking nothing, and Shaughs was just getting his frees. I went up to Brian Gavin and I basically made the argument that it couldn't have been me that hit the ball out over the line because of the way my body was shaped or contorted at the time. I went up to the umpire and said the same.

To be fair, it was such a dramatic game you didn't want there to be a loser. If anything, it was a very marginal call. The benefit of hindsight and the benefit of a little bit more clarity 16 years later, you could probably argue it should have been a wide, not a '65'.

We got the '65', and I remember Shaughs standing over it. He was just dead-eyed the same night. He was a phenomenal free taker. The pressure… the crowd… everything hinged on that one '65'. He had the composure, the peace of mind, and the cool edge to just slot it straight between the posts. No sooner had the ball gone over the ball and the game was blown up.

It was like we had won the All-Ireland with the pitch evasion. It was reflective too of where we were at as a county that we were craving any kind of success, or any kind of victory, so much that it felt like a massive victory. There was so much backdrop to it too. It was not like this was a great victory. There was no cup at the end of it. All you were doing was getting a second replay and trying to earn the right to qualify for a Munster final.

When you are in the middle of it, you don't realise how big a deal it is.

It is like the current players… they are in the bubble. And you are in that bubble because that's all you know when you are at that stage of your life. Sixteen years later, I am well past that stage, but when you are in that stage, your whole life is consumed by matches, and it affects your mood, your demeanour, and how you relate to others.

Some people are very outgoing and some people are very private, but you have to keep yourself afar in a sense. It is great now to be able to dip back into it, because now I have a much better perspective. That trilogy against Tipp was just phenomenal. Everybody can relate back to that time in their life.

I see my son now. He is starting off on his journey. It is a great journey, and I hope it takes him as far as he can go. That happened in my lifetime, and I think to myself, *How lucky were you to experience that?*

We got some high off that replay going into the second replay.

Richie was a free spirit like that. There was no science to it. There was no kind of coming down off it. He was a realist. We had been catapulted from hopefuls and also-rans to now there being a lot of hype. All of a sudden, Limerick hurling was front and centre.

Richie was one of those guys who understood the team dynamic. Players trusted him and they liked him because he was a very likeable guy. What he did was he understood that he needed to see what we were seeing on the field.

When the dust had settled on that game, I think Richie realised we got a lot of stuff wrong. Emotion probably kept us in the game, but we need to change something up. He had the peace of mind to say, 'Okay, I need ye to tell me what ye are seeing'. He used that then to formulate a game plan. It wasn't as scientific as what game plans are now, but at the time there were just a couple of tweaks.

Going into the last game then, the third game against Tipp back in Limerick, there were just a couple of curveballs thrown out. Kevin Tobin was picked at 15. He wouldn't have been on many people's radar, but for the first 20 minutes that day we actually blew Tipp off the ground.

That gave us a platform that eventually helped us get over the line. I often credit Richie and Gary Kirby with that, the fact that they just understood players and built up a trust. It was probably one of the few times during my time playing with Limerick that we really loved management. Fellas knew Richie was Limerick to the core. He had that telepathy. I don't think we played particularly well in the Munster final that year. Again, there were a couple of things at critical times that didn't go our way. As a collective, we didn't play well, but we knew there was way more in us. We went on then and played Clare in an All-Ireland quarter-final. We did what we had to do in Croke Park. That pitched us then with Waterford again.

There was such a sense of determination at that stage. For the first time in my Limerick career there was a real unity there. There was a togetherness, and there was a determination that you were going to try and achieve something, because we were so annoyed at ourselves for underachieving, and falling short.

I always felt in Limerick that we were lagging behind other teams, because we would be catching up on what other teams did two years previously. They always seemed to be ahead of the curve. In 2007, it was the first time we really had the level of guidance that there should have been.

Joe McKenna was there the year before, and Joe had brought in a level of professionalism that we needed. We needed to be kicked and dragged into that. There was definitely a foundation there in terms of getting dietitians on board, getting psychologists, and whatnot, to come in on an ad hoc basis. But I don't think there was the same level of buy-in as there should have been. We were at a relatively early stage of what you see now, because now it is at a whole new level altogether.

It is different now. I often get the impression that fellas' priorities nowadays are different… it is still an amateur sport, yet for fellas now it is all about getting your recovery drinks, getting your ice baths, or getting straight into the pool afterwards. I get the sense that they don't have that bond that we had in our day.

Obviously, the current Limerick team are phenomenal, and people allude to how tight they are as a group, but it was different for us. I just think there was a little bit more of a Bohemian mentality about it, and there was a bit of freedom, but all the teams were the same.

We still ate our pasta and chicken two hours before the match, so it wasn't like it was from the dark ages, but the likes of the Cork team and the Waterford team had really pushed that out and took it to a whole new level. They were well ahead of a lot of teams in terms of their preparation.

That sea change was starting to really take place at that time.

That game in 2007 was coming at the back end of my career. I was on the Limerick panel for about 10 years at that stage. I'd missed out on the success and euphoria of 1994 and '96. I had just come in in 1997.

That's why I needed to make things happen quick, because if I didn't… you were just going to be another fella to play with Limerick with nothing to show for it.

99

NIALL MORAN

LIMERICK 0-22 TIPPERARY 2-13
Munster SHC semi-final 2nd replay (AET)
Gaelic Grounds, Limerick
JUNE 24, 2007

Niall Moran and the Limerick team that thrilled the country, and won back the love of their own supporters, in the long summer of 2007

★ **LIMERICK:** B Murray; D Reale (capt), S Lucey, S Hickey; M O'Riordan, B Geary (0-3), M Foley; M O'Brien, D O'Grady (0-1); **N Moran (0-5)**, O Moran (0-3), M Fitzgerald (0-2); A O'Shaughnessy (0-6), B Begley, K Tobin (0-2). **Subs:** Peter Lawlor for D Reale, J O'Brien for B Begley, P Tobin for K Tobin, B Foley for Fitzgerald, H Flavin for P Tobin.

★ **TIPPERARY:** G Kennedy; E Buckley, D Fanning, D Fitzgerald; E Corcoran, C O'Mahony, H Maloney; S McGrath (0-1), J Woodlock; J Carroll, D Egan (1-0), B Dunne (capt); S Butler (0-2), E Kelly, (0-9) L Corbett. **Subs:** T Stapleton for S McGrath, P Bourke (0-1) for J Carroll, W Ryan (1-0) for B Dunne.

THE ACTION

THE SUMMER OF the trilogy. With 50,000 packed into a sold-out Gaelic Grounds to witness the final game of this epic three-game battle, this second Munster semi-final replay brought over the passion and excitement from the previous two encounters.

The unstoppable Andrew O'Shaughnessy, who got another six points, finished the championship that summer with a dazzling 2-46, and Limerick were helped along to victory by an impressive tally of five points from play by Niall Moran.

The sides traded scores throughout, and with only five minutes remaining they were yet again deadlocked. A third replay beckoned, but the Moran brothers from Ahane inspired Limerick to a three-point lead to seal the deal. After Niall Moran's long-range point all but secured victory, the Limerick supporters could not contain themselves as they entered the field when they incorrectly thought the final whistle had sounded.

Moments later, the whistle did sound for an end to an epic 250 minutes of hurling at its finest, and as Limerick earned a famous victory, the Treaty County finally found themselves in their first Munster final since 2001.

It was level at half-time, 1-6 to 0-9, before Tipp opened up a two-point lead four minutes into the second-half. However, 'Babs' Keating's men wouldn't score again for another 21 minutes, albeit during a period that Limerick landed just another three points. Seamus Butler slotted over a stoppage time point to force extra-time.

It was Limerick, however, who outscored their battling neighbours by seven points to a goal and a point to end a marathon tie and claim their first championship win over Tipperary since the Munster final replay in 1996.

★★★★★

>

NO DIFFERENT TO any child growing up, it had always been my ambition and my dream to play with Limerick.

For us in Castleconnell, we came from a house where both our parents were Tipperary people. We would have grown up in the late 1980s going to all the Tipperary games… the end of the Munster 'famine' in 1987, and then the All-Ireland wins in 1989 and '91. My father was a cousin of 'Babs' Keating, so we would have always had that interest.

But my mother, she was a Maher from Mullinahone; and she would be an aunt to Eoin and Paul Kelly, who were both playing on that Tipperary team in 2007. Myself and Ollie were on the Limerick team, and prior to that our brother James had been on it.

As we were all coming up along the age ranks, we always had that kind of link with Tipperary. Every time we used to play them underage – for example in minor – we had to have a little bit of success against them. At under-21 level… in the famous Munster finals in 2001 and '02 we had beaten Tipp.

There always had been that natural competitive element in our own house, as well as that affiliation. We always wanted to beat Tipperary more than everybody else.

Going into that first game on June 10, given where Limerick are at now, people will find it hard to see why there was such a furore about winning a Munster Championship match, but in the six years previous, since 2001, Limerick hadn't won a game in Munster. Framed within that, Limerick had experienced a three in-a-row of All-Ireland under 21s from 2000 to '02 and with that came huge expectation at senior level.

However, it didn't quite go to plan. Between 2002 to '07, we went through five managers in six years. Huge expectation in Limerick was met then by huge disappointment and huge underachievement, riddled with stories of ill-discipline, and a lack of commitment… most of which was hugely, and grossly untrue. The nature of the environment in Limerick at the time was that Munster Rugby had won a Heineken European Cup in 2006 and were to go on to win one in '08. Rugby was really king of the castle at that time.

One standout memory from early in the season was a meeting we had with Richie Bennis.

For anyone who knows Richie, he is one of the most passionate people about Limerick hurling you could ever meet, one of the most knowledgeable, and above all else one of the most charismatic.

He is somebody that you would just automatically die for!

In Richie's words, he was a very pragmatic guy. I remember him saying in a meeting in late December or early January that there was one date in our heads and that was going to be June 10 when Tipperary came to town… 'JUNE 10'. Everything else along the way was going to be a stepping-stone to it.

The expectation from outside the group wasn't massive going into that game on June 10, but from within the group… we knew this was our be-all and end-all.

That game on June 10 was 1-19 apiece. I think we might have been level nine times in the game. What is most famous about that game is that Pat Tobin got an absolute screamer of a goal right on the death of the game to gather us a draw. In the years prior to it, we had lost a lot of those tight games by a point, so to get that draw in Limerick gave us an awful lot of belief going to Tipperary the following Saturday.

Even with all that belief, with six minutes left in normal time that day, we were seven points down. Andrew O'Shaughnessy got a great score to draw it, but the same evening Ollie was in inspired form. It was definitely the peak era of his career. That particular evening, along with O'Shaughnessy, he dragged us into extra time.

I think for a lot of Limerick supporters, they started to fall in love with that Limerick team again that night in Thurles.

Roll on June 24.

The Gaelic Grounds was sold out. It was one of the early days of the new, redeveloped Gaelic Grounds. It had taken on a life of its own. This was now becoming a trilogy, no different to a Hollywood blockbuster; people had framed it as that.

Going into that game… I just remember, even in the week coming up to it, at that point in time the professional standards wouldn't be as tight as they are now – lads still had a few pints on the Saturday night after the second game. But in terms of recovery, we spent day after day inside in Clare Glens in the falls; there were ice baths everywhere.

It was probably at that point that we were getting to a level of professionalism, because it was three weeks in-a-row of major championship games, which for a lot of us, was different! In our early days as inter-county players, usually we played one championship game and maybe a qualifier, and you were close on finished there.

Going into that game, the atmosphere in Limerick was ridiculous. It felt like something more than a Munster Championship match. I remember warming up, and the noise coming from the crowd was unbelievable. It had been a lovely day… and then the rain started to fall.

In terms of selection, Eoin Kelly hadn't started the first game, and he was now back in the Tipperary starting line-up.

The same day for us, Kevin Tobin started for us in a kind of redeployed role as a third midfielder. He was just magnificent in the early parts of that game. After about 20 minutes we had Tipp blown away. We wouldn't have used major tactics, as most teams wouldn't have at the time, so Kevin as a third midfielder really threw Tipperary… and after 20 minutes we were seven points to one up.

With that then, Tipperary got a grip of the game and by half-time they had actually gone 1-6 to 0-7 up. They got a soft goal, and maybe with the Limerick team at that time there was that little bit of us being unpredictable; when we'd go ahead, we'd let in soft goals. It always seemed we were making things harder than what they were.

We were level five times during the game, and it finished up 0-15 to 1-12. Tipp got a goal early on in the first-half of extra-time and went 2-13 to 0-17 points up. Again, the rain was starting to teem down. 'Rashers' – Mark Foley – came out twice in the second-half and won two unbelievable frees. He came out with one ball and I remember he broke the tackle, was fouled, and the fist went up… serious inspiration! And, of course, the crowd responded to him!

Tipperary came out with a ball straight out afterwards and 'Rashers' turned them over… that was vintage 'Rashers'. I remember Andrew O'Shaughnessy… when you think of personalities in that team, he was really our superstar underage coming through those under-21 teams. He was our Cian Lynch of those days. No different to a lot of us, his inter-county career up until 2007 had been frustrating through injuries, losses, and otherwise.

Maybe coming into that year Limerick supporters were down on him a little bit, but I remember in those games, and especially in the final game, he was just magnificent! He took a leadership role. That same day, Brian Geary really announced himself as a centre-back of top quality. Stephen Lucey… brilliant at full-back. Damien Reale… one of the top corner backs in the country at the time.

All of a sudden, we found ourselves a point up. Ollie got a ball. Barry Foley had held on to possession and Ollie broke onto it. We went two up. The crowd… the noise! It was just about trying to bottle the atmosphere. It was just an outpouring of emotion.

There are three times that I can epitomise a real outpouring of emotion; that game in 2007, the Munster final of 2013, and the 2018 All-Ireland final. It was just that sheer passion.

We were two points up, and we were still holding on for dear life. Prior to this, Eoin Kelly had a free to go level. He actually mis-hit it and the ball was hanging in around the edge of the square. Seamus Hickey nearly decapitated Darragh Egan. The referee never gave a free. Then we were two points up and Gerry Kennedy pucked out the ball. It was one of the last puck outs of the game.

There were two guys under it. I was never the greatest in the air, but one thing I always had was, I was always able to take a ball down in the air. The momentum was behind us at the time. I remember taking the ball down – I was nearly inside in my own '65' – and just letting rip. I didn't care if it went to hell or high water, I just wanted the ball to go dead. God was on our side that day, even with that ball. The ball went over and the outpouring of emotion was there again.

We looked to the stand. There were people hugging, there were people standing on seats… jumping. I remember Richie looking back into the crowd, like a child that was after getting his favourite ice cream. I think one of the most memorable scenes came after that point. Gerry Kennedy pucked out the ball.

The whistle was blown. The referee was taking a note. The crowd had gathered at that point for a pitch invasion. The supporters felt that that whistle had signalled the end of the game. Straightaway from the town… they just erupted onto the pitch.

They were on the '65' line by the time the referee was trying to say, 'Lads, this game ain't over!' Anthony O'Riordan, our selector, was trying to usher people off… and Richie was on the pitch. They were afraid of their lives that, after all this, the game could have been abandoned.

A part of the reason that day stands out, is the supporters. I know every county says they've great supporters, but that day the supporters really willed us on to win.

It felt like the dawning of a new era. It felt like this was *finally* it, these glorious under-21s are now going to come in and they will be seniors, and this was now going to be the start of that era. You had Richie at the helm. The year took a knock straight afterwards, but we got to an All-Ireland final so people felt it was the *dawning* of a new era. I'll never forget the bus afterwards. Marty Morrissey was on commentary and David Punch from Patrickswell was doing his statistics, as he still does to this day.

Dave and Marty are great friends, and Dave would have been a selector with those Limerick under-21 teams, as well as being a great Limerick player in his time. We got the bus back with them. The 50-seater definitely had 100 to 110 people on it.

Marty was in the back seat with us. There were bottles going. A few of the boys would smoke a fag at the time. The fags were going.

Everyone and anyone was either in the dressing-room or on the bus. Richie was in absolutely pantomime form. Even that night, I remember Peter Clohessy's place, The Sin Bin, was crawling outside of it. You had Tony O'Donoghue from RTÉ… every lad and any lad, everyone wanted to be a part of it.

Again, in context, it wasn't an All-Ireland final. It was a Munster semi-final. It was just the characters and the great times that we had that make it stand out… the carefree fun. Every other Sunday evening you were running for cover, and every Monday morning you hated getting up out of bed because of what was coming at you… the criticism, and the frustration.

That day was all about the fun, the laugh… and the craic. For us as players, and for the supporters, we could finally stand with our chest out, and our head high.

"

ANDREW O'SHAUGHNESSY
(BRIAN BEGLEY & STEPHEN LUCEY)

LIMERICK 5-11 WATERFORD 2-15
All-Ireland SHC Semi-Final
Croke Park
SEPTEMBER 12, 2007

Ollie Moran, Andrew O'Shaughnessy and Brian Murray with their All Star awards at the end of a brilliant 2007 championship

★ **LIMERICK:** B Murray; D Reale, **S Lucey**, S Hickey; P Lawlor, B Geary, M Foley; D O'Grady, M O'Brien (0-1); M Fitzgerald, O Moran (0-2), S O'Connor; **A O'Shaughnessy (2-7)**, **B Begley (1-0)**, D Ryan (2-0) **Subs:** N Moran for Fitzgerald, M O'Riordain for Foley, J O'Brien (0-1) for O'Connor, K Tobin for Ryan, P Tobin for O'Grady.

★ **WATERFORD:** C Hennessy, E Murphy, D Prendergast, B Phelan, T Browne (0-1), K McGrath (0-1), A Kearney, M Walsh, E Kelly (0-3), S Molumphy (1-0), S Prendergast (0-1), P Flynn (0-4), J Kennedy (0-1), D Shanahan (0-4), J Mullane. **Subs:** E McGrath (1-00) for Kennedy, S O'Sullivan for Mullane, S Walsh for P Flynn.

★ GAME OF MY LIFE ★

THE ACTION

ANDREW O'SHAUGHNESSY STOLE the show as Limerick returned to the All-Ireland final for the first time in 11 years, setting up a highly-anticipated showdown with All-Ireland champions Kilkenny.

The Treatymen got off to a scintillating start and led by 2-9 to 1-8 after a manic first-half which saw Donie Ryan and O'Shaughnessy net for the winners, and Stephen Molumphy pull one back for the Déise. Another three goals from Richie Bennis' charges, who outscored their south-east counterparts by 3-2 to 1-7 in the second-half – with O'Shaughnessy and Ryan adding to their first half goals tally, after Brian Begley raised the green flag – ensured the Limerick tasted a sweet victory.

The overwhelming underdogs, following their 3-17 to 1-14 loss to Waterford in the Munster final four weeks' previously, Limerick got off to a perfect start when Donal O'Grady's ball into Brian Begley broke for Ryan to open the scoring with an emphatic drive to the net with just five minutes on the clock.

In a shock start to the game, the men in green and white were eight points ahead by the 15th minute, when the unplayable O'Shaughnessy turned his marker, Aidan Kearney, 30 metres from goal before racing clear and hammering the sliotar to the net to put his side 2-4 to 0-2 ahead. When Molumphy found the net eight minutes before half-time, Limerick were still double scores in front – 2-8 to 1-4 – a lead cut short to just four at the interval, 2-9 to 1-8.

Despite an Eoin McGrath goal on 57 minutes, which had reduced Limerick's advantage to just three points, Richie Bennis' men finished strongest. An O'Shaughnessy penalty and a Begley goal at the death ensured Limerick were worthy winners.

★★★★★

> 66

AS A TEAM, we hadn't won an All-Ireland semi-final before. It was a match we weren't expected to win, especially after losing the Munster final to them. We went out with all the odds against us in everyone's opinion. Those are the kind of games you remember that little bit more.

We showed a lot of promise, but I will always say it… we lost the Munster final that year, and we went on and lost the All-Ireland final. We lost the National League final the year before, in 2006, but it was still good to show that you could actually compete at that standard and at that level. Though, it was disappointing that we didn't have anything to show for it at the end of the year.

I was Man of the Match that day against Waterford too, so I reckon I played okay. I got 2-7 which makes it seem like I was heavily involved, but I was hitting frees. I wasn't involved in too much of the game, but once or twice the few hits I made, I was happy enough with them, which made the difference, I suppose.

Waterford were favourites… raging favourites… absolutely no question! They had beaten Kilkenny in the National League final that year, so this was *their* year! Any match you go out and play… you always have to believe you can win.

The whole combination of Richie Bennis and the backroom team… they were superb at judging that group. They were excellent. But the players did it as well. We were really focused and knew what we wanted to do, and just went out and implemented it. After the match, Waterford were obviously dejected, but we were elated. You take the plaudits for the few days afterwards, and you look back on the good win for a few hours, and maybe a few days, but then you have to focus on the final.

My focus turned very fast… I'd be like that, I always just go onto the next task and the next drill, or whatever you need to do. It was ecstatic and it was enjoyable, but it was short-lived.

In hindsight, Kilkenny were at a different level in the final. They hadn't won the four in-a-row at this stage. This was only their second year. It turned out that they were a fantastic team, but that's not to say we didn't have a chance that day. If we won, it wouldn't really have been seen as an upset. But that is easier said nowadays with time.

Of all the finals you'd want to be in as a senior hurler, we were in them in the space of a year. In 2006 and 2007, we were in a National League final, a Munster final, and an All-Ireland final, but without winning any of them which is obviously disappointing. I don't look back and think, *What if you did this and what if you did that?*

Life is too short to be worried about the past. You just have to focus on your present, your now… and what you can do in the future.

I am happy. I have a wife. I have kids. I have a happy home. I have a good work environment. The older you get, the more those things become important in life.

When you are growing up, all you want to do is play inter-county hurling, or play rugby with Munster, Leinster or Ireland, or play soccer… whatever your focus is. That goes with time once you pass your sporting peak.

Playing hurling was always on the radar growing up.

Kilmallock have won the county championship 12 times. We are a strong sporting community, predominantly hurling, but there is a lot of soccer and there is a rugby club in Bruff, which is very dominant underage. The sporting environment was ingrained in me from a very young age, not from my parents or anything, but just from my natural habitat and the environment and the community I was in.

I went to school in Fermoy, in St Colman's, another hurling stronghold that shaped me towards the game. It was always something that I took to naturally. When you are underage you take to things naturally that you enjoy, and I loved it. I still love it.

I never said I wanted to play inter-county… I just wanted to be the best I could be. I won three Harty Cups with St Colman's. Unfortunately, they haven't won one since, but hopefully they will be back soon enough.

When you play at that level in school, you know you have a chance of going on to play with Limerick, especially when I went down to Fermoy when there was Mike O'Brien, Richie Murphy, and Paddy Kirby, and a few more from Limerick. And you'd the likes of Stephen Molumphy and Aidan Kearney, and a few from Waterford. You are mixing different hurling theories and different styles of hurling, and it is great to develop that.

It was a nice sense of pride to get that All Star in 2007. Of course, it was, but I'd have taken a medal over an award any day of the week. It is nice now, I appreciate it now, more so than at the time.

We are fortunate enough to have six All Star awards in our club. Paddy Kelly is the first All Star we had in our club in 1984, then Dave Clarke… Mike Houlihan won two, and we've Graeme Mulcahy now as well as myself.

It is great that we have a good tradition. Every generation seems to produce hurlers for the top level, which is a good reflection on the club.

In that All-Ireland final in 2007, we lost to a better team on the day. Kilkenny had a good start. We were a bit naive at times. We allowed them two goals in the first five-to-10 minutes. After that, we actually hurled superbly for the rest of the game, but we just couldn't claw it back.

We had decent success at club level.

I was involved in the senior team from when I was about 16, but it was nine years before we won the county championship in 2010. We were always getting to the semi-finals and finals, but just couldn't get over the line.

We had a great underage structure. My minor team won three county titles in their day. The team that came three years after me won three or four in-a-row. That's seven or eight minor championships, before we won the senior championship in 2010.

We were fortunate we won three county championships then in quick concession. But, again, it moves on, and after we won the county and Munster in 2014, we went another seven years without winning a county championship.

I am just supporting these days.

Every person wants to play for as long as they can and, ideally wants to retire on their own terms after winning the All-Ireland, or winning something big. They want to retire on their own terms, but that is the ideal situation; it is rarely the case.

It is often luck if you win something, if you come into an era where there is a good team… or have a special group of players coming together at the right time or have the infrastructure in place, the right management in place… have the support systems in place.

I watched the Waterford semi-final from 2007 a couple of months ago, and I'll admit it was a horrible watch. It was an atrocious match. It was littered with mistakes, and no one passed the ball. It was all heart and determination in that era, but it has come on.

The game is totally different now, and it is for the better!

Limerick have brought it to a whole new level now, after trying to catch up with the likes of Kilkenny, Galway and Tipperary. You need to try and emulate what teams have been doing well. Every team is trying to reach perfection. Perfection is never reached, but you are trying to get there and reach it, and get close enough to be able to get over the finish line.

It comes down to your own self-belief too.

I went up to Croke Park in 2007 thinking that we were going to win, but that necessarily wasn't the case for everyone.

Psychology wasn't as prominent back then as it is now, but it played a massive part in every game. If you can't grasp or have control of that part of the game, you are putting yourself at a huge disadvantage.

Social media wasn't as prominent as it is now, either, but you had newspapers. I stayed away from them, and I know other players knew they had to stay away from them as well, because there is no point reading things. Whether it is a newspaper article, an online forum, or an online article, they are all about giving an opinion in order to generate talking points… to sell newspapers, to make profit for an organisation.

Some of it is accurate and true, but players going into games – like our game against Waterford in 2007 – have to think for themselves. You would be aware of general opinions, because you'd hear about things when you were walking down the street to go down to the shop. Even though you might not want to talk about hurling, people would talk to you about the game.

'They are the favourites… this is going to be a tough game'.

But that is all part of the GAA community and the spirit of people within the association. If you don't have that, what is the point of the GAA… because the GAA should be for everyone, not just the elite.

99

BRIAN BEGLEY

Brian Begley celebrates hitting the net against Waterford in the 2007 Munster final

"

THAT WHOLE YEAR… there was an awful lot going on. I'd an awful lot going on in my own life personally as well! I got married, and I moved jobs. I was a garda based in Tralee and I moved back to Limerick. We were building a house at the time as well.

I remember our wedding was in February, so we were honeymooning just as the start of the league was happening. We were over in New York but we were delayed due to a snowstorm, and I was on to Richie Bennis telling him we were trying to get flights out.

But we got delayed a full week… we just couldn't get out of there.

When I came back then, I found it hard to settle back into the league games and training. The training was going okay, but I found it difficult to *settle*. My form wasn't great. We had the trilogy against Tipperary which was just a super couple of weeks of hurling, and then we were into the Munster final against Waterford… they beat us fairly well in that.

Everyone had us written off for that second game against Waterford. All the talk was about Waterford. They won a lot of Munster Championships. They had a really, really good team with a lot of good players and the one win they were missing was the All-Ireland.

All the talk was about them going into that game!

I remember the morning of it… we came into it nice and quiet. They beat us by nine points in the Munster final that year so there was absolutely no pressure on us whatsoever. We were completely going in under the radar.

We went up the night before. The next morning, we were getting ready for the game and people were checking out. Myself and one or two of the lads were coming down and there were about six or seven people inside in the lift in the hotel… when the lift got stuck. We ended up being about half an hour or three quarters of an hour inside in the lift, waiting to come out… and ringing the boys. We didn't delay the bus or anything like that but we just couldn't get down. It was after breakfast, I remember. We came out finally, and we were soaking wet.

Our tops were soaking wet because people were starting to panic inside in the lift.

Waterford had won a couple of Munsters. They had a high-quality team that time. They probably deserved an All-Ireland, but they just weren't able to get it there. And the fact they had beaten us by nine points in the Munster final was mentioned during training sessions or the odd time in the dressing-room. There was no pressure on us on the day because we weren't expected to win it.

But we knew we had the players to do it.

It was all about the goals on the day. The five goals made a huge difference. The game was up and down, and score for score for a lot of it, but we were able to get the couple of goals then which made the difference.

Andrew O'Shaughnessy was on fire that day.

I was fouled for a penalty and Shaughs took the penalty. He must have been a centimetre or two off the crossbar. Just the angle there… he couldn't have got it anymore into the corner if he tried with the way he struck it.

I got a ball on the end line and Donie Ryan was coming around the edge of the square. I hand-passed it off to Donie… and he let fly. Somebody asked him about it afterwards and I remember him saying, 'Ah yeah I used to play with a tennis racket back home once upon a time'… he just let fly with it and he scored.

The backs were solid that day.

If you go down through that Waterford team there were a lot of household names. Dan Shanahan got Man of the Match in the Munster final, and you'd the famous quote from Richie Bennis then after the semi-final… 'We got five and Dan the Man got none'.

The goal I got then… there were only a couple points in it at that stage with a couple of minutes to go. The game was still in the melting pot. A high ball came in… I just slipped in behind Declan Prendergast. I was able to come out in front of him. I was going away from goal then because there was someone coming back against me, trying to stop me, but I was just able to slip inside him and bury it into the back of the net. The relief, the emotion, and the roar from the crowd at that stage sealed it for us. It was blown up after that.

The scenes were like we were after winning an All-Ireland final. I remember the lads – management and players – came in from the sideline. I remember at that stage not even being able to take in the fact that we were in a final… we were written off completely… and we were after winning.

Everything was high profile after the trilogy against Tipperary. There was a lot of talk and a lot of hype. When we were beaten in the Munster final things settled down a small bit. The support is always there in Limerick and they were just crying out for something to get behind.

There was a huge build up to the final. We were signing autographs in the Gaelic Grounds under the stand before training. There was a specific night set aside for that and the crowds that came in to get their jerseys signed… was incredible.

You can see it there now, that the support for the Limerick hurling team is massive, and it was back then. It was great to get into that final… and to be there and to be in with a chance of winning it.

Myself, Stephen Lucey, Brian Geary and a few more of the lads had grown up together and played together over the years. You had the likes of Ollie Moran and

Mark Foley a couple years ahead of myself then.

There was a great closeness in the team. There was a great bond. That trilogy against Tipperary really galvanised us. We had to come out of some very difficult places in those games, and the fact that we came through that was huge! We were able to build that little bit of momentum as well.

Richie was after coming in and training had been going well… there was just a great set-up.

I remember the night of the semi-final we went back to Limerick and it was a super night back there. It is important to enjoy those occasions when they come around because we had a lot of long days with Limerick as well over the years when we were beaten by narrow margins, and just couldn't get over the line.

Richie Bennis was really down to earth. He was a real players' man. Richie is a legend in Limerick… and still is. He was just really, *really* passionate about what he was doing, and I think that rubbed off on all the players. Richie just wanted players to give their best. The way he went about things… he'd put his arm around fellas! Or if you needed a bit of a bollocking, you'd get that as well. He was very fair.

It was a great experience to get to play in that All-Ireland final against Kilkenny.

But we didn't get off to a good start… 2-3 to 0-1 down after about 10 minutes. Kilkenny really blitzed us. It was hard to come back after that. When we settled down after the 10 or 15 minutes, we started to hurl away… we were able to get a couple of scores, and it was over and back with Kilkenny after that.

That was an awesome Kilkenny team and the start that they got knocked us back a good bit… and it was very hard to recover after that.

I came on the scene in late 1999, and I hurled until 2003. I picked up an injury on my ankle then which kept me out for a couple of years. I only got back then for the 2006 and '07 season. Joe McKenna was there in 2006 and he helped me out a lot in relation to getting my injury right and getting to see the right people.

After the All-Ireland final in 2007, I had another operation on my knee. I was hoping to be able to come back from that, but I came back training in 2008 and I remember myself and Barry Heffernan, the physio, were doing a lot of work together… trying to get back jogging on the pitch, but I just couldn't. My knee just kept swelling up during training, and I wasn't able to get back in with the bigger group.

I had to pull out then… that was the end of my inter-county career. I hurled away with the club for a good bit after that, and it was great to be able to do that, but I just wasn't able to train at the time to get up to the level required at inter-county.

In 2000, we were beaten by Tyrone in the All-Ireland under-21 football final in Mullingar…and in that same year we beat Galway in Thurles in the under-21 hurling, having won Munster in both.

I played in the All-Ireland football and hurling final in the same year. We were young lads and there were a good few of us that played both codes for Limerick… Conor Fitzgerald, myself, Mark O'Riordan, Brian Geary and Stephen Lucey.

We were on the road for that year. The memories I have from around that time are of the big games and winning… but we used to have some great times coming back on the buses as well.

A lot of the lads that I played with at under-21 level are still good friends of mine today. A lot of really good bonds and friendships were created over that time… between the players themselves, and the girlfriends also got to know one another as well. When we were meeting up for the seniors as well, they were able to keep their relationships going. That was a brilliant time… really, *really* enjoyable… and the fact that we were able to get that bit of success as well was *massive*!

I grew up in Raheen… up in Meadow Lawn, close to University Hospital Limerick (UHL).

Even though Mungret had a massive pick at that time, it was still the same core group of players that was there over the few years. You'd a couple of families there… maybe two brothers playing from a couple of different families…. you'd the Tobins and the Giltenanes, and you'd myself and my brother Patrick as well.

Despite having a big pick from the area, the group of hurlers we had was tight enough. But when you see the way it has gone now… the underage work that is being done in the club is superb, as are the new developments in the club. There is fantastic work being done there, and it bodes very well for the future.

I wouldn't really see it as a city club. You are extended far enough out of the city. You have Kildimo, Ballybrown, and Patrickswell around you there as well, so I would still see Mungret as a country club in that sense.

I look back on my time playing with Limerick with huge pride.

I enjoyed that part of my life. We were very unlucky with the footballers in 2003 and '04 not to beat Kerry in the Munster final, which would have been massive for the football because there was huge work being put in by Liam Kearns at the time, and a very good team came together.

When I first got involved, our championship could have been one game… if you were beaten, you were out. When the backdoor came in, you had more games and you were getting more experience.

I would love to have had more days out in Croke Park, especially after experiencing the All-Ireland in 2007. After getting that under your belt, you would have loved to have got back there again, and you'd be hoping to have had that experience and to maybe draw on that a bit more… because All-Ireland final day is massive… the build up to it, and everything. It's a huge day!

The relationships you build over the years stand out for me. When you look back, it is a long time ago now. It is 23 years since we were on that under-21 team together. It is a lifetime ago really… and just to see what has gone past… fellas have moved on to different jobs and different careers. It is interesting to see where fellas are now, but the relationships that I've made and that I still have today, that is the one thing that sticks with me. It is brilliant!

"

STEPHEN LUCEY

Stephen Lucey beats Paul Flynn to the ball in the 2007 All-Ireland semi-final against Waterford

> "

RATHER THAN ONE game, the whole season in 2007, especially the trilogy against Tipperary, stands out. And the Waterford All-Ireland semi-final was just crazy.

It was bedlam! The sun was splitting the rocks, it was a roasting warm... a real summer's day... and the match itself was chaotic. It was helter-skelter.

At the start of 2007 we had a training camp in Breaffy House. What we did in that weekend really stood to us. Dave Moriarty, the coach, and Richie Bennis, Gary Kirby, Bernie Hartigan and Anthony O'Riordan, did a kind of a review. They brought us into a room and there were loads of newspaper cuttings and things printed up on the wall, just about the stick we were getting.

Newspaper cuttings of how things weren't going great. We addressed that, and we sat down and we spoke about it, and we did some goal-settings. We were in small groups. That weekend then, we went for a night out and that was good craic. Dave 'D'Arcy' Moriarty then ran the s**t out of us… which was good. That mentally toughened us.

We set our goals, that we were going to do things differently. We said that in the first round of the league we had Tipp and we wanted to beat Tipp, and we said we had Tipp in the first round of the championship and we wanted to beat Tipp again. Two huge targets… our third target was to get to an All-Ireland semi-final.

We reached all of our targets that year. The fact that we played Tipp three times, we were absolutely exhausted…. knackered, mentally! We had to come back and play Waterford in the Munster final and I don't think we gave it the same focus as we had the Tipp games, because it wasn't one of our goals initially. Things kind of took over when we played those three matches.

Waterford beat us well, but we weren't at our best. That brought us then to Clare and we regrouped and we beat Clare in the All-Ireland quarter-final. Then we were back playing Waterford again… in the All-Ireland semi-final.

Waterford had two tough games against Cork, so maybe they were a bit tired in that match, but either way we played out of our skins. In fairness, they came back and they brought it back to a point at 64 minutes.

Brian Begley got the last goal after that, and we pulled away again.

2000 was my first year with Limerick… we lost to Cork. There was no backdoor… we were gone!

In 2001, we got to the quarter-final after beating Cork and Waterford, and losing to Tipp in the Munster final. Then we lost to Wexford in Croke Park in the All-Ireland quarter-final. They got four goals that day… two penalties. That was a game that got away from us.

In 2002 then, we lost to Tipp… and we lost to Cork, so not great. 2003 wasn't great under Dave Keane. 2004 was the year there was hassle with dual players, so I wasn't involved that year. 2005 was kind of hit and miss.

A career can move fast.

Waterford had one the greatest teams of their generation. And Kilkenny were Kilkenny back in those days. That was their greatest team, and people say they are one of the greatest teams to ever play the game. Cork had a very good team as well, and Tipp were good. They won a couple of All-Irelands.

We kept getting beaten by teams that were very, very good. We had our own issues then as well, switching managers all the time, and other stuff going on in the background, so not a lot was expected of us.

That's why 2007 was the one bright spark… because 2008 wasn't a good one either. All those things in the background make it even better that we got to an All-Ireland final in 2007.

But we didn't win anything.

In hindsight, it is not so much the medals that you win. At the time, that is what you want, but often the things that stay with you longer are the memories and the friendships. They are very important. But you only really appreciate that later.

There was a great buzz, and there was great colour ahead of that All-Ireland semi-final against Waterford in 2007.

The three Tipp matches had the whole county really excited. There was lots of talk, and there were lots of flags and bunting up. There was a real buzz going to training and preparing, and everybody was on to you, talking about it.

In the build up to it, I met Mark Foley down in the Corner Flag bar and we said, 'Look, is there anything else we can do or suggest, that can help us?' And we came up with a strategy that we hadn't done fully before, and we said it to the management.

It was where we brought our wing forwards back to the half-back position, under the opposition's puckouts, to allow our wing-backs to take a step back so they weren't fielding… they were covering behind. Our midfielders came back as well. Everybody dropped back. Basically, it is a tactic that is now often used, and easily done… where everybody drops back one.

Waterford didn't see that before, because we hadn't done it before and it actually stood to us. We were able to hoover up the breaks, and close down their space. That was one thing that definitely helped… but sure, goals win games and we got five of them.

Andrew O'Shaughnessy brought it up a whole new level that day. That was one of his greatest days, and he had a lot of great days. If you look back on his

Laochra Gael show… that match and those scores are on there. That particular year 'Shaughs' was laser focused and the two words I'd use are determination and aggression.

If you saw his face that day, his eyes were searing. When he got the ball, he absolutely turned and went for the throat… he just ran through and just *buried* it!

He absolutely buried a '21' as well. Thank God he stuck those goals… and Donie stuck two, and Begley got his one.

Limerick have incredible supporters and great colour, and have been starved of success, but as soon as things get going everybody is out. The colour was unbelievable, as was the noise and the celebration after we won that match.

We probably celebrated too much, but we had never been in an All-Ireland final, any of us, at senior level. There was no control over it in the aftermath, between the semi-final and the final. There was too much stuff going on, there were too many distractions, and that definitely negatively impacted our preparation and our performance.

The Limerick team in 2018 were forewarned before their All-Ireland not to repeat the mistakes that were made in the build-up to the previous All-Ireland in 2007. Everybody was able to talk about it and everybody knew it. I had something like 50 tickets to distribute the week leading up to the match.

I was driving around and texting people, because I wanted to get rid of them. I was the one ringing them to get them to come and take the tickets, or going to meet them. There is no way in the world I should have been doing any of that in the lead up to the match, and that's just one example.

There were businesses ringing us up directly, or people that we know, asking, 'Would you mind standing in for a photo… say a few words and do an interview'.

That stuff was going on and while it seems fine… everybody was doing it left, right, and centre. It just took off a bit too much. A bit of it is fine, but ideally, you'd like to have been left to focus solely and have tunnel-vision on the final. If we had the experience of another final before us, and that had happened to us, maybe we'd have been a bit different. But we were where we were… and what happened, *happened*.

There were ups and downs in the football and hurling.

We never won the Munster football final, which was something we wanted to do and we came awful close. We kept getting beaten by the All-Ireland champions or finalists. In 2009, we lost to Cork, and then they lost to Kerry who won the All-Ireland final. Then in 2010 we lost to Kerry, who had beaten Cork, before Cork won the All-Ireland. They were all very close.

In 2003 and '04, we lost to Kerry in the Munster final… and they won the All-Ireland in '04. We boxed above our weight and we went toe-to-toe, but we didn't get over the line so that's disappointing. The football career was good, but in the hurling, we didn't go so well a lot of the time which is disappointing.

It is what it is though, you can't look back with regrets. You'd drive yourself mad if you did that.

I had a lot of influences.

My mother and my father were big influences on my career. They were driving me all over the place… and I mean ALL over the place! When I was in Roscrea in school, and then when I was in tutorial in Limerick and UCD, they'd take me here, there, and everywhere… and collect me and bring me to training and all this stuff.

In Croom there were a number of coaches… Seamus Cregan for a long number of years. In Roscrea, Hugh McDonnell was our hurling coach. We got to the All-Ireland Colleges 'B' final with Roscrea. Paddy O'Brien and John O'Brien from Toomevara were playing with me on that team… All-Ireland winners with Tipperary.

Another huge influence was Davy Billings in UCD. They were some of the biggest influences on my career, as well as all the other coaches and mentors. Richie Bennis, however, was a massive influence in 2007.

At the time, I called him Richie 'Benítez'. There were these green t-shirts being sold in Penny's. I remember passing one day, and I bought one actually because I thought it was hilarious. They were green t-shirts with a picture of Richie printed on the front… and it said, 'Richie says relax' underneath it.

Richie was infectious. He was the right man at the right time. Richie and Gary Kirby came in… and the passion, enthusiasm, and charisma they had for Limerick was just unbelievable.

And we just followed them. We would have followed Richie anywhere. Anyone that meets him meets him with a smile on his face. He is a rogue. He is great craic. He'd always be slagging you off. He would be very quick-witted as well, so he could slag you off and take you down a peg or two very quickly. We always enjoyed that. I am delighted, lucky, and privileged to have been managed by him.

He was very intelligent. He united us, and he gave us that drive and passion… and that definitely is what we needed to get over the line against Tipp in the trilogy, and to fight back all that time. We were 10 points down in two of those matches at different times against Tipp, and we came back and we persevered.

Watching the Waterford game unfold from full-back, there was definitely a point when I thought we might *have* this here. I can't remember exactly the point in the game, but I remember thinking, *We are going very well… we're scoring!*

Then Waterford started coming back, and I thought, *Oh Jesus*! You are trying your best and you are marking tight. I actually fractured my wrist in the match. In the second-half, I was running out for a ball and I was out ahead of Dan Shanahan. The ball was coming in low from the right half-forward position. I ran out and my man pulled from behind me to try and flick the ball, but he actually hit my wrist which was on the top of the hurley.

I finished out the game and that was grand, but I couldn't train between the semi-final and the final because of it. Diarmuid O'Farrell had to inject my wrist with a local anaesthetic and a steroid in the dressing-room before the Kilkenny match started.

"

DAMIEN REALE

HOSPITAL-HERBERTSTOWN 1-12   BALLYBROWN 0-13
Limerick IHC Semi-Final
Bruff
SEPTEMBER 18, 2010

Damien Reale takes the field at Thurles to face Waterford in the 2009 Munster Championship

★ **HOSPITAL-HERBERTSTOWN:** A Murphy; E Dooley, P Reale, C Barry; M Fitzgerald, **Damien Reale**, J Fogarty; Donal Reale (0-2), M Deegan (0-5); S Deegan, B Ryan, B O'Donoghue (0-1); C Wallace (1-0), K O'Loughlin, J Fitzgerald (0-4). **Subs:** K O'Connor for S Deegan.

★ **BALLYBROWN:** D Lyons; R Quinn, D Kenny, J Hall; S O'Reilly, B Quinn, M Sheehan; L Loftus (0-1), I Burke; R Kenny (0-1), B Hartigan, R Burke; M Kiely (0-1), A O'Connor (0-9), S Kenny. **Subs:** P McCarthy for R Burke, S Foster for I Burke, P Hartigan (0-1) for B Hartigan.

THE ACTION

HOSPITAL-HERBERTSTOWN MADE A dramatic return to the top flight of Limerick club hurling when they overcame massive favourites Ballybrown with two points to spare, and four weeks later defeated neighbours Dromin/Athlacca.

Not only were Ballybrown favourites for this semi-final clash in Bruff, they were tipped to win the entire Intermediate Championship, so when the men in white and green drew level with nine minutes to play (0-11 to 1-8) hearts were in the mouths of the Hospital-Herbertstown faithful.

Hospital-Herbertstown, who had a 20th minute Conor Wallace goal under their belt, finished strongly, however, with four points from play and the lively corner-forward's raising of the green flag proved decisive. When Wallace crashed the ball into the net with a first time pull, the men in maroon and black went 1-3 to 0-3 ahead and never trailed Ballybrown for the remainder of the game.

Mike Fitzgerald, Damien Reale and Joe Fogarty were dominating in the half-back line and the determined Declan O'Grady trained side took a well-deserved five-point lead into the break.

A resurgent Ballybrown came to life after the restart, and reduced the deficit to just two, thanks to three points – a Richie Kenny effort and two O'Connor frees – as Hospital-Herbertstown managed just one point in the opening 18 minutes of the final half hour. With the momentum now with Ballybrown, the pre-match predictions seemed inevitable for many when the men from Clarina levelled with nine minutes to play.

However, when Mark Deegan fired over his fifth point of the afternoon a minute later to regain the lead, Hospital-Herbertstown got a new-found sense of belief. Three late points from impressive corner-forward John Fitzgerald sealed the historic win for the south Limerick men.

★★★★★

> 66

THAT GAME WAS one of the best club games to be involved in, because at the initial stages of the competition we were hitting hot and cold.

Ballybrown had a flaking team at the time. They were number one favourites for the intermediate title that year… and we weren't given much of a chance in the semi-final. It was an unbelievable game! We just hit a purple patch right through. What we heard afterwards was that Ballybrown had booked a recovery session for the following morning.

It was just one of those games that we didn't think we'd win, but we hurled so well… and nothing went past us. Everyone played well and we got over the line by two points, and then went on and won the county.

At the start of the year in 2010, nothing was really going our way… and then you also had the whole furore of all the players pulling out of the Limerick senior team that year, so my focus was back with the club. Ballymartle beat us in the Munster semi-final that year, and went on to win the All-Ireland.

It was tough on the day against Ballybrown… there was nothing easy given. They pushed us right to the finish, but they just couldn't close it out. We got ahead of them, and stayed ahead of them.

We went into the county final and our tails were up. At the time, Dromin-Athlacca had been in an awful lot of county finals. They were good. They were always there or thereabouts, so there was nothing easy in that final either, but we came out of that as well on the day.

I was playing centre-back that day against Ballybrown. Paudie Reale was playing full-back, and Joe Fogarty was on one wing. Paudie was playing well, and then we'd Edward Dooley inside in the corner. Edward was on fire that day as well.

All six of the backs had to be on top form. We just seemed to get out in front of our men, and blocked them down and hooked them. It was all about our work-rate on that given day… anything to keep them out.

Winning the intermediate title in 2010 was great, because it was the exact same bunch of players nearly from 2005 to 2010. At the time we got promoted, I would have had experience of playing senior – I played in the senior championship with Emmets for a good few years.

We went fairly well one of the years. We got to the semi-final… Na Piarsaigh beat us that year.

I don't think the senior teams were too happy with the Emmets playing, as it allowed all the intermediate teams to come together to play in the senior championship.

Jimmy Carroll was looking after the Emmets team in 2010. I ended up pulling out of the Emmets that year. I remember Darren Moynihan from Athlacca called to my house wondering would I come back playing with them? I said, 'No', and told him that I was going to focus on the club.

The senior and the intermediate ran at the same time. You could be playing with your club on a Friday, and you would be out with Emmets on the Sunday. That's the way it worked. Emmets would have been playing the city or East teams, and whoever came out of that would be playing in the county championship. It was busy enough at the time.

It worked well for a while, but it seemed to kind of filter out. There was a bit of a kick-back on it, especially from the clubs at the lower end of the senior championship. And to be fair to them, you had the likes of Knockainey, who were at the lower end at the time, up against the pick of the intermediate teams in South Limerick. It probably wasn't fair on them, but the intermediate teams didn't care because it gave their players a chance to play senior hurling.

We were supposed to play Ballymartle down in the club's home field in the Munster semi-final, and it was absolutely lashing out of the heavens for the whole week.

I remember the lads down in the club had hoovers trying to get the water off the pitch. Pat Fitzgerald from Doon – he was with the Munster Council at the time – came out to inspect the field and told them, 'No, can't play it here'.

We had to go back to Castletown Ballyagran. They were a good team, but we would have had them in a tight enough pitch down here in Hospital. There would have been a massive crowd at it. We had to go back to Ballyagran and it took the shine off it.

But any time you win a county here, it is a huge thing because they are rare. For two small parishes, you'd be thinking there is a big pick, but there isn't really. When you look at it, you still only have a panel of 22 or 23 players.

After any of the big wins, we used to always go to Herbertstown first. We'd be below in Wrights in Herbertstown, and the craic would be unreal. And then you'd come to Hospital, and sure, at that time, there were eight or nine pubs in the town… and we'd be in every single one of them. We'd be in the small pubs, like Mrs Carmody's at the bottom of the town…a small little pub and the sing-songs would be going.

In 2000, I remember Donnie Carroll had a Massey 35 tractor and a transport box, and he was bringing boys up the town on the back of the transport box.

Seeing what it meant to people locally at the time definitely made all the hard work and training worthwhile. That year, in 2010, it was really only after the Newcastle West game – the quarter-final – that we got on a roll. Then it was like, *Jesus, we could actually win a county title here!*

It was just pure momentum. It was also funny that year. No one really believed we could win it. In the early stages it was just pure… *Sure look, let's see what happens!* But sure, once the Newcastle West game came, and we won it, we were like, *We've a right chance here!*

We were up against Ballybrown. We weren't expected to win it. I think we were maybe four-to-one to win it. They were dead sure they were going to win it. That was a massive scalp for us.

Things kind of just flew in the final against Athlacca. We were never under pressure that day. It is a great feeling when you are winning with the boys you are training with all of the time, and fellas you grew up with. It doesn't matter what parish you are from, it is a great occasion. It isn't just a one day thing… it is two or three days!

When I was in with Limerick, after the run with the under-21s, Richie Bennis used to be saying to us, 'Ye drank ye'r way through three All-Irelands'.

And do you know what? He was probably right…

But that seemed to bond us. In that whole under-21 set-up, we would have played with each other from under-14 up. It was like an academy. Brother Philip Ryan, Sean Finn's father Brian Finn, Joe McKenna, and Pat Hartigan… they were all inside in the initial Limerick academy.

The likes of myself, Brian Geary, Brian Begley and Stephen Lucey all came up through that academy. They would have been a year ahead of me… my group was

Peter Lawlor, Conor Fitzgerald, Kevin Tobin and Eugene Mulcahy.

My most memorable game out of that was in 2002 when we played Tipp in the Munster final. Tipp had the likes of Eoin Kelly and Donal Shelley... a very good team. They had the better of us that day in 2002. I remember Mickey Cahill gave an unbelievable display on Eoin Kelly. He was playing a No 4, I was at 2, and Eugene Mulcahy was 3. Cahill didn't give Kelly a sniff.

We were under pressure. We were three points down coming into the final stages, and we got a penalty. Eoin Foley had a great belt of the ball. Foley went down and he stuck the ball in the back of the net, and it went to a replay. The first day was wet, the second day was hot. There was 18,000 or 20,000 at it. It was packed. It was unbelievable.

It was hell for leather then the whole way that day against Tipp. Point for point. Over and back. I remember Tipp went four points up and people were starting to leave. We always had this mentality that we were never going to lose. Dave Keane instilled that in us.

We won it 2000, and we won it in 2001 – we went nine games unbeaten in those two years – so that mentality was there. They went four points, and there was only about five minutes left.

Timmy Houlihan pucked the ball out. The ball went up and 'Shaughs' stuck the ball in the back of the net. He kicked it in... a point in it. I'll always remember thinking to myself, *We are going to have to win this puckout.* I was playing cornerback but it just so happened that I was up in a more wing back position for the puckout. I remember saying to myself, *I have to win this ball, I have to win this ball!*

The ball came down, and I wouldn't be a man for catching too many balls in the sky but I caught the ball, and the game developed. The ball went over to the far side of the field where the old stand is in Thurles. The ball went out for a sideline. Eoin Foley – another super man for sideline cuts – took the cut. Kevin Tobin blocked it. He shimmied left to right, and stuck the ball over the bar.

Drawn match. It was going to extra-time. There were Limerick people going home at this stage, thinking we'd been beaten. We went back into the dressing-room. Dave Keane calmed us all down again, and we went back out... and we blitzed Tipp.

It was another half an hour – 15 minutes a side – and they just couldn't hold us. Conor Fitzgerald was outstanding the same night, as was Peter Lawlor. We'd some great players. 'Shaughs', of course, was there, and so was Mossy O'Brien.

That was my favourite under-21 match of the whole lot… and we'd some good battles! That was the one game we looked beaten – in any of the other matches we never looked like being beaten. In this one, we were beaten.

I think the whole thing was poorly managed at the time. From those three under-21 All-Ireland wins, there were something like 56 players that came through it. You had a lot of talent, and, I suppose, managing that talent is a hard thing to do. I think the talent was there to win an All-Ireland, but it just went… year by year filtered away.

That time with the under-21s were special years though. We'd serious players all over the field. You'd a lot of characters in there as well. We went out after every single match, no matter where we were. I remember we went out in Cork one year and we ended up staying below in CIT, and we got the bus home the following day. But of course, we were all college age… there were none of us working.

It was just a pure family.

I look back at that time and have fond memories.

I made friends for life. We went on holidays every year, but you are talking about a different era. You are talking about a drinking culture and stuff like that. Did we drink and enjoy ourselves? Jesus, we did! Did we have too much craic? We probably did.

But at the time no one minded, because we were winning.

That was something that probably wasn't managed very well when we went to senior. You were back in that era where there was kind of a drinking culture in a lot of senior inter-county teams too.

I spent 11 years playing inter-county and the only thing I have is three under-21 Munsters and All-Irelands, and a Waterford Crystal Cup medal…that was it. Limerick won Munster in 2013, but that whole players strike scenario in 2010 put an end to it for me.

Do I have regrets? Yeah, possibly.

But at the time, Justin McCarthy was doing his own thing. I still think that if Justin had picked the phone up to some of those fellas and said, 'Look, you are not on the panel. This is the reason'… sure what could they say? All they could do is accept it, but he didn't do that.

A lot of people would see it that you refused to play for Limerick, but I didn't refuse to play for Limerick. I stood by the boys that were not being allowed to play and weren't picked. It wasn't even the fact they weren't being picked; it was just the way it was dealt with.

That was a low point.

We played Waterford in the first round of the Championship in 2011. I was marking a young Brian O'Sullivan. Brian was lively that day. I couldn't get out to him. I was thinking, *It's maybe time to hang up the boots.* When we came back in 2011, Dónal O'Grady was over us. He left then, and John Allen came in.

Joe Hannon – Declan Hannon's father – was the liaison officer then. I was saying to Joe that I possibly wouldn't go back. John Allen rang and said, 'Look, it's up to yourself'.

I kind of had my decision made then. It was a fairly low time then because from under-14 up… I was involved with a county set-up. Fourteen years of age all the way until I was 31… then overnight, GONE!

You had been meeting these same fellas four or five times a week since you were 14. Overnight then, it was all completely gone. I missed the buzz. I missed it an awful lot… what I missed most was meeting the lads and the social side of it. I found it difficult. I didn't know what to do with myself.

It is the very same as if a tap just turned off overnight… and I was there like, *What do I do now?* It took me a long time to readjust to not being involved. I got involved with the Limerick academy then after that. I was in the academy for about five years. I went from the under-14s all the way to minor. It was good to be back involved, and getting involved with teams. That kept me going. But definitely, around that time I pulled out, it was like, *What do I do with myself now?*

It takes a few years but you get on with your life then.

99

DAMIEN QUIGLEY

NA PIARSAIGH 2-18 AHANE 0-13
Limerick SHC final
Gaelic Grounds, Limerick
OCTOBER 2, 2011

Damien Quigley in action against Cork in the 1996 Munster Championship, 15 years before the greatest day of his career when he helped Na Piarsaigh make the breakthrough at provincial level

★ **NA PIARSAIGH:** P Kennedy; A Hennessy, K Breen, K Bermingham; A Dempsey, J O'Brien, B Hartnett; C King, P Gleeson (0-2); R Sheehan, D Breen (0-2), S O'Neill (0-1); S Dowling (1-10), K Downes (1-1), K Ryan. **Subs:** A Breen (0-2) for Sheehan, D Lynch for Dempsey, **D Quigley** for Ryan, K Kennedy for Gleeson.

★ **AHANE:** T Flynn; A Doherty, D Madden, J Doheny; C O'Reilly, M Carr, P Treacy; N Moran (0-5); F Ahern (0-1); D Morrissey (0-1), J Meskell (0-2), D Laing; B Healy, O Moran (0-1), R Ryan. **Subs:** S Madden (0-2) for Healy, M Foley for D Madden, P O'Connor (0-1) for Meskell, S O'Connor for Laing, C Ryan for Doheny.

THE ACTION

'THE FAMINE IS over, let the feast begin,' rejoiced team captain, Kieran Bermingham from the podium after his fledgling northside city Limerick club, only set up in 1968, won its first county senior hurling title with a comprehensive 11-point victory over Ahane at the Gaelic Grounds.

Motivated by the bad memory of a heavy defeat at the hands of Adare in their first final two years previously, the youthful and skilful men in blue and white were determined not to let this one go. After John Meskall and Niall Moran slotted over two Ahane points within the opening four minutes, it was the men from nearby Caherdavin who opened up a comfortable nine-point lead midway through the first-half. By the time referee Shane Hourigan from Rathkeale sounded the half-time whistle, Na Piarsaigh were in a very comfortable position, 1-11 to 0-7.

After Na Piarsaigh went nine ahead just seven minutes after the restart, the John Daly Cup looked like it was on its way the very short distance to Elm Drive, but then Ahane scored four without reply to cut the deficit to five. However, up the field went Sean Stack's charges and when Cathal O'Reilly brought down David Breen, the flawless Dowling made no mistake and Na Piarsaigh's eight-point lead was restored 12 minutes from time to ensure the famous victory was beyond doubt.

It was par for the course after that. Na Piarsaigh ran in Damien Quigley, an All Star from 17 years earlier, to join his Limerick colleague from the 90s, Shane O'Neill, for the emotional scenes at the end. Despite the fact of a fortuitous goal in the 10th minute, Na Piarsaigh firmly shut the door on a potential Ahane recovery at the three-quarters stage with that second goal from Dowling and their excellence throughout their overall display made them deserved winners.

★★★★★

❝

FROM MY PERSPECTIVE, the most significant game was the county final in 2011 when Na Piarsaigh won their first county championship. Now, it might not be a game I was heavily involved in… I was a sub; Seán Stack was the manager and he brought me on for the last couple of minutes of the match as kind of a token gesture. I had done my cruciate a couple of years earlier.

If somebody was to ask me to relive a period of my GAA world, that would be it… because when I first started playing championship, the club was junior. My first adult game was in 1988 and that was the first time the club fielded an under-21 team.

We were a very young club; we couldn't even field an under-21 team before 1988 and we won a 'B' Championship that year, the first time we had an under-21 team. We won the 'A' competition the following year, and then we won the Junior Championship in 1990…. and 21 years later, to go on and win the big one, having won the intermediate in 1994, was the culmination of an incredible journey for the entire club!

There were a couple of soldiers who had been hurling for 20 years at adult level, who'd hurled for the club all through that period, and then you'd all the work that everyone had done at underage for all the years… so to finally get over the line in 2011 is something I'll never forget! Afterwards, we won Munster club titles, and we won an All-Ireland club title, but that day in 2011… THAT WAS THE DAY!

Two years before that, in 2009, we reached our first senior final. We overachieved by getting to the final, and Adare beat us by 17 points – 1-17 to three points… and we got our first point from play in the 52nd minute. Two years later then, you are top of the pile and you go on and win Munster, which was lovely.

It is hard to put words on what it meant to people. If you talk to the young people now in the club, they wouldn't grasp what it meant back then, with the success in the club since.

Limerick won the under-21 Munster Championship in 2011. John Kiely was the coach at the time. There were seven Na Piarsaigh lads on that team; a wave of fellas came at the one time, young lads who drove it.

If you ask them, they probably wouldn't have as much emphasis on the first county championship because some of them have gone on to win four, five, or six afterwards, along with Munster club titles and an All-Ireland.

The young lads in the club now couldn't possibly fully grasp what 2011 meant to the club and where it came from.

In 2011, you'd that crew that came into the team – the seven that were involved with the Limerick squad – and in 2013 then, you'd another wave of players. Mike Casey, William O'Donoghue, David Dempsey, and a couple more with them, they came along... those fellas' ambitions were far above the ambitions the likes of myself and Shane O'Neill had when we first started playing. It is certainly a long way to even think about winning a senior championship when you are playing junior hurling.

Those boys' ambitions and horizons would have been far bigger. Some of those lads' ambitions now are to win All-Ireland club titles. When I first started playing, we'd watch those club games on the telly. You'd go to the local pub on Paddy's Day and watch the match, and almost be in awe of those fellas getting to play above in Croke Park.

That win in 2011 broke down huge ceilings; it broke down barriers.

The team that went on and won the All-Ireland afterwards would have hammered the 2011 team! Even the 2013 team was a much better team than the 2011 team, but the 2011 team went off and won Munster, and were beaten in extra-time by Loughgiel Shamrocks, who won the All-Ireland club final handy.

The momentum opened a lot of people's eyes that the club All-Ireland wasn't that far away because, afterwards, after the semi-final against Loughgiel went extra-time, people started saying, 'Hang on a second here!' Before that, Limerick clubs in Munster were abysmal... really bad.

Adare won five County titles in the 00s, but only contested one Munster final. Kilmallock had been the last Limerick team to win a Munster club title, way back in 1994, so when we won in 2011 not alone did it break ceilings for us, it probably broke ceilings for other clubs as well because the following year Kilmallock beat us in the semi-final in a fantastic match, and they went on and won the Munster club title in 2014... and then the year after, we won the Munster club again.

I think clubs were kind of saying, 'If they can do it, we can do it!'

I'm not saying that Na Piarsaigh were even remotely responsible for what happened with Limerick, but once one of your neighbouring clubs does something, all of a sudden it becomes tenable and it is not the unreachable thing anymore.

You are watching Ballyhale Shamrocks and Kilkenny win All-Irelands and, then, all of a sudden, a club down the road win an All-Ireland club, and that brings its own reality to it... it becomes achievable. Obviously, the standard in Limerick would have been raised by Na Piarsaigh because, to be fair, the other clubs had to catch up. If they wanted to win the county championship they had to improve.

2011 itself was the end of a marathon for the club. It was just incredible for all the people who'd been involved in the underage, and even for the volunteers and for people who had passed on. Noel Dromgoole, the founding chairman, was a huge influence – he passed away in 1995. He didn't even get to see us win it, but for the older men and women like him, who gave huge time to the club, to finally get over the line for everyone was just dream stuff. It is surreal to see how far the club has come since I first started playing. It is bonkers really!

Before we had won one county title, we got to one county final in 2009 and we got hammered. We had never been in a senior county final before that. We had a couple of near misses in semi-finals. You look then and you roll the clock forward and say the club have won four Munster club championships and you are second in the roll of honour behind Blackrock... ourselves, Ballygunner and St Finbarr's have four. If someone had said to me 10 years ago, I would have bitten their hand off.

It's incredible. No other Limerick have won the All-Ireland club.

You have guys at the club now who are recognised at national level, and respected; more importantly at national level for their dignity and for how they have behaved themselves.

The club has exploded since we first won that county title back in 2011. We always had a good pitch and a nice clubhouse, but there has been massive work done by the membership.

We went from having one full pitch and one small pitch, to having three full pitches and extended clubhouse and facilities, all of which was done in the past 10 to 12 years.

I am not suggesting that it is on the back of winning the county championship, it was necessary because the facilities weren't enough to cater for the growing membership, but it just shows that the club has turned into a huge club now.

I gave it up for a couple of years when I was in my early 30s. I stopped playing for a couple of years. My first game back after a few years away was a relegation play-off. The fact of the matter is, if we lost the game, we were back down to intermediate. It is not as if we were knocking around as contenders back in the 00s; we weren't, nobody new was coming in and we had the same players, as often happens in clubs… and here we were facing a relegation play-off in my first game back after a couple of years. I came back because I couldn't contemplate the fact we could be getting relegated. That couldn't fit in at all after everything everyone had done for the club.

The 00s were a trying enough time. The underage had been neglected a bit. A second wave of ferocious underage players then started to come through.

That was all achieved during the 00s when Munster Rugby at the time was absolutely flying… to a stage where Munster won a Heineken Cup. Thomond Park is only less than two miles up the road. We would have lost a good few really talented players to Munster. Hurling in the city was not the first sport. Junior soccer is also very strong in the town.

At that time there was only one senior hurling club team in the town, and for a city the size of Limerick, that's not enough.

There was real competition for players.

There was a bit of validation there then for all the hard work that was going on in the club. It was a huge achievement as a city team making the breakthrough, something which hasn't really happened too often in counties. That breakthrough happened, and it acted as a springboard for what happened afterwards. What happened afterwards was backboned by a huge number of young players that came through. You had a pool of ferociously talented lads coming just at the time when the team had just broken the glass ceiling.

Seán Stack was a huge part of it in 2011. Sean was the difference between us winning the county championship or not with that team. We were going to win one afterwards with what came, obviously because the players were so good, but that 2011 team was before that second influx of players.

Shane Dowling had a storming game that day against Ahane in 2011. He was only 18 at the time. Ahane had a phenomenal team; their history speaks for itself. We had beaten Patrickswell in the semi-final who were another team who have had ferocious levels of success over the last number of years.

The most enjoyable day out I ever had was the first round we played in the Munster club that year, the semi-final against Ballygunner. We travelled down to Waterford. It was unseen stuff. It was an absolute novelty for me. I travelled on the bus and the craic and the fun going down, and the craic in the clubhouse beforehand, was just brilliant. Stack, in fairness to him, said to us to go and enjoy it. He was right. You just go off and play. We went out for a day out, for the novelty, and the freedom… it was just fabulous, a fantastic day out. We'd great craic on the way down and we'd great fun on the way back, but then we realised here we were on this Munster club journey. It was quite odd.

I really enjoyed that period of 2009, '10, and '11, even though I was only able to train for about six weeks before the county final because of my knee. I had a few complications after my surgery. Despite that, I really enjoyed that time… and 2012 and 2013 were ferocious. For me… I was playing away and it was a total freebee, it was bonus territory.

After doing my cruciate, I couldn't wait to get back. I got back, and I was getting to know a whole generation of new players. I was in my forties at that stage and I was getting to know all these young fellas who were 17, 18, 19, 20, who I'd never have gotten to know otherwise. I'd coached a few at under-21 level, but that's a certain type of relationship. When you are sharing a dressing-room with them it is very different; you are peers, you are a player, you are not a mentor.

I got to go on and play in the 2013 campaign, when we were beaten by Portumna in the 2013-14 All-Ireland club semi-final. I was marking Mike Casey every week in training. Mike was 17 at the time. Shane Dowling was playing that campaign. Some of these guys weren't even born when I first started playing with Limerick, yet I got to know them really well.

I was lucky enough to hang around long enough to get to know the next generation of Na Piarsaigh players. It was a pure privilege. It is not about the medals; it is about the people and the experiences you've had with them. The GAA is wonderful that way.

99

GRAEME MULCAHY

KILMALLOCK 3-22   SARSFIELDS 3-20 (AET)
Munster Club SHC Semi-Final
Fitzgerald Park, Kilmallock
NOVEMBER 9, 2014

Graeme Mulcahy (top) celebrates with Robbie Egan and Jake Mulcahy after victory over Cratloe in the Munster Club Championship final

★ **KILMALLOCK:** B Hennessy; L Hurley, M O'Loughlin, A Costello; P O'Brien (0-1), P O'Loughlin (1-1), K Donnelly; J Mulcahy (0-1), B O'Sullivan (0-1); R Hanley; G O'Mahony (1-0), R Egan (0-3); **G Mulcahy (capt) (0-4)**, K Kennelly (1-2), E Ryan (0-7). **Subs:** P O'Loughlin (1-1) for Egan, C Barry (0-2) for Kennelly.

★ **SARSFIELDS:** A Kennedy; W Kearney, C Leahy, C O'Sullivan; D Roche, R Ryan, E Martin; D. Kearney (0-3), E Quigley (1-0); R Murphy, M Cussen (1-2); C McCarthy (0-12); E O'Sullivan (0-2), K Murphy (1-0), T Óg Murphy (capt.). **Subs:** Gavin O'Loughlin for R Murphy, R O'Driscoll for E O'Sullivan, C Duggan for T Óg Murphy, R Duggan for Quigley, E O' Sullivan for Martin.

THE ACTION

KILMALLOCK MADE IT to a third Munster final when late points from Paddy O'Loughlin and captain Graeme Mulcahy stopped an enthralling game of hurling from going to a replay.

With the game deadlocked late in extra-time, minor star O'Loughlin, a 49th minute substitute, sent the vast majority of the sold-out crowd wild with the match-winning point, before senior inter-county star Mulcahy sealed the famous win against the much-fancied Cork champions.

Victory was made even sweeter by the fact Kilmallock had trailed by a point – 1-6 to 2-4 – at half-time, despite having the strong breeze behind their backs in the opening half hour. Star man Kieran Kennelly, who finished with 1-2, had opened the scoring for Kilmallock when the Balbec full-forward somehow managed to bundle the sliotar into the net from a crowded goalmouth.

Kilmallock were up against it however when Eoin Quigley and Michael Cussen responded with two quick-fire goals to give the Cork champions the lead midway through the opening half. Kilmallock knew they had to raise their game in the second half, and that they certainly did. When Bryan O'Sullivan found the net with a long delivery, the winners found themselves two points ahead, a lead extended to six with eight minutes to go.

Sarsfields, boosted by a Kieran Murphy goal five minutes from time, fought back however and forced extra-time. The thrilling encounter set up a Munster final against Cratloe two weeks' later – a game that saw the Balbec also require extra-time to get over the line against the Clare champions. A classy Ballyhale Shamrocks got the better of the south Limerick men in the subsequent St Patrick's Day All-Ireland final in Croke Park.

★★★★★

>

THE GAME ITSELF was in November but it was a perfect day for hurling. It was a nice crisp winter's day. It was on in Kilmallock as well, in our home field… its massive to get to play a Munster club game in your home field.

Anyone who knows Kilmallock knows there is a stand going down both sides of the field, and you've a hill and a complex to the back of one goal, and a field behind the other. Once the stand is full you can really have an intimidating atmosphere because the crowd are almost be on top of the field. That day the stand was absolutely jam-packed.

I have played in front of big crowds in Croke Park and the Gaelic Grounds, and I remember it being just as intimidating a crowd as any of those stadiums.

Our full-forward, Kieran Kennelly would scare the living daylights out of any full-back. He was Man of the Match; he got a goal and a couple of points. He was a guy that had been around the club for the bones of 15 years at senior level, carrying a lot of injuries, but he really dug it out that year. He travelled up and down from Cork.

The physicality of that game, however, was something else. I got hit with a shoulder late on by Conor O'Sullivan, who played corner-back for Cork for a few years. Michael Cussen, another huge man, buried Paudie O'Brien with another shoulder.

Paddy O'Loughlin, a Limerick minor, came off the bench and he got a very important goal late on for us. We were six points up coming into the last 10 minutes and Sars managed to pull that gap back to level it, and take it to extra-time.

In extra-time, we had to dig deep and level it with a couple of minutes to go, before we got two late points. Paddy got a point… and I got an insurance point then at the very end.

It was a special day out for everyone in the club. A lot of us would have grown up watching Kilmallock in the 90s and they would have played some Munster club games in 1992 and '94 on our home pitch. I certainly remember watching videos down the years when I was younger, with my brother Jake, of Kilmallock against the likes of Toomevara and Sarsfields of Galway.

My own personal performance on the day was probably average. I scored three or four points. It was more about the day that was in it with the home crowd and the manner the game took on in terms of it ebbed and flowed for pretty much the 60 minutes.

You are coming into the winter period when things can get quiet, so it definitely gave the town a lift. The atmosphere around the town on that day and the days leading up to it was absolutely phenomenal.

We went on to win Munster against Cratloe. It was a toss-up between which game stood out in my memory more – the Sars game or the Cratloe game in the final, because that was another game that actually went to extra-time. We went down to 14 men in that final. Gavin O'Mahony got sent off… he would have been one of our key players.

I remember in the Sars game, Gavin was playing centre-back and Daniel Kearney was well on top in midfield. They moved Gavin out and that gave us the foothold, so for him to get sent off was a big blow for us in the final. We really had to knuckle down and put the shoulder to the wheel, and take the game to extra-time. We got it back to fifteen on fifteen in extra-time.

They were two massive games in the space of two weeks and they are great memories to have.

It was a fantastic feeling to win the county and Munster with a group of friends I grew up with and went to school with. Jake was playing, and then I'd my cousins playing in Bryan O'Sullivan and Conor Barry, who came on, and I had a couple of other cousins scattered around the panel.

Philip O'Loughlin had two brothers, Mark and Paddy, playing. Then you had the likes of Gavin O'Mahony there, and his brother, Kevin would have been there on the panel. You'd have cousins then with the likes of Robbie Hanley, who was playing, and Eoin Ryan who was a big player for ourselves.

It was a big family affair really.

It was a bittersweet ending to that journey though, the fact we were well beaten by Ballyhale Shamrocks in the All-Ireland final that year.

That was a super Ballyhale team with the likes of Henry Shefflin, TJ Reid, Colin Fennelly, Michael Fennelly, and James 'Cha' Fitzpatrick – a couple of Hurlers of Year dotted in there. Their experience of Croke Park on All-Ireland final days stood to them.

The journey overall was fantastic. We played Portaferry from Down in the semi-final up in Mullingar. That was another good day out. It was a fantastic year with great memories with the club.

At the time, a Limerick club hadn't won an All-Ireland so to get to the final really gave the town a lift and it gave the people in Limerick a lift too. I know we weren't successful, but we kind of set the benchmark for Na Piarsaigh to go and try to do one better... and thank God they did because they got that monkey off the back for Limerick.

It is tough on the body when you have success in the county with your club and you proceed onto the Munster club and then the All-Ireland. You are kind of riding the crest of a wave and when that is over then, you tend to settle down and your body does get tired, and mentally you are tired. It is hard to transition back to inter-county at that stage.

Limerick traditionally found it difficult over the last ten years, especially with Na Piarsaigh being so successful at club level, then guys have to come back into us in March and April. They are after having such a long campaign, and it is difficult for us, but that's the joys of being successful.

My family are steeped in the tradition of the club.

My uncle, Donal played for Limerick in the 80s and 90s. We would either have watched him or watched the club, which was very successful in the 90s as well with the likes of Dave Clake and Mike Houlihan, and the likes of Paddy Kelly then who was involved at underage level.

They all instilled that love for the game in the youth growing up in Kilmallock. That tradition has been carried forward by this generation that are playing at the moment.

There are a few coaches who certainly influenced me growing up. When I started off at underage first, there was the likes of Jimmy Moloney and Mick Cain, who has passed away since. Those two guys would have been the first I would have been coached by at under-6s.

Then there was the likes of Paddy Kelly, who would have taken the summer camps. He was subsequently involved in a lot of the underage teams. Then you had Bernie Savage who was a great supporter of the club and still remains to be.

Another huge influence would have been Donie Hayes. He was actually my coach and manager of my soccer team in Kilmallock. As much as you learn the skills of hurling off your coaches in the GAA, he would have not only taught me a lot of soccer skills but a lot of leadership skills and management skills. I'd be very thankful to him as well.

Playing other sports growing up definitely helps you. I played gaelic football as well at underage, and I dabbled with a bit of rugby, but not too much. Other fellas in the club, the likes of Paudie O'Brien and these guys, played a lot of rugby. The skills are always transferable, and I think you can pick up new skills that you can bring to the game that benefit you.

The more sports you play at a young age, the more it benefits you. It does get to a point when you are 16 or 17 and you have to make a call, and you choose the one that you really want to focus on. I think it is important to try everything, however.

I don't do a lot of looking back. It is only when you are retired that you might start looking back, but I am more focussed on what is ahead of me now. You can look back, though, and be proud of what you've achieved and have no regrets.

In 2014, we were successful and there were great celebrations, but it is actually more the training sessions we used to have, and the meeting up, that stands out.

For a period on a Wednesday night, we'd meet up there in the 41 Bar, a number of us, and we'd just play cards. It was the small things like that that really brought us together as a team.

We used to have days out as well, where we'd go and do something completely different. They are the memories that I have that are different from the memories on the field, but they are just special in their way.

The medals are neither here nor there really, at the end of the day; it is all about people and the friends you make, friends you'll hopefully have for the rest of your life.

There are people that were on that 2014 team that are no longer playing anymore, the likes of Liam Hurley and Kieran Kennelly… great guys. They are guys you can pick up the phone to tomorrow and if you need something they'll do it for you. Those friendships are very important.

I am living in Cork city and there a number of Kilmallock lads down here. Philip and Mark O'Loughlin, and Gavin O'Sullivan, who I won a county championship with in 2010. Kieran Kennelly, who was full-forward in that Sars game in 2014 and Man of the Match, lives in Cork city as well.

Up to 2018, you would have thought success was never going to happen with Limerick.

Luckily, it has. We had a bad year in 2017… the fact we were beaten in both championship games, by Clare in Munster and then by Kilkenny in the qualifiers. We were looking at 2018 trying to build some bit of momentum, and try and get some championship wins under our belts. We got the monkey off our backs in terms of beating Kilkenny in the quarter-final, and from there… we just didn't look back. I was kind of lucky with the way it came because I would have questioned if it was ever going to happen for us.

It is a great feeling, and hopefully it continues. It is not going to be easy. There is just so much competition out there in the championship. There are seven or eight up there and any of them could win the All-Ireland each year.

It was a bit surreal on the pitch in Croke Park in 2018 after winning the All-Ireland with Limerick, no one really believed that we had achieved it. That time on the field, with everyone after the final whistle, was special… with The Cranberries playing out over the speakers.

"

MIKE CASEY

NA PIARSAIGH 2-25   RUAIRÍ ÓG, CUSHENDALL 2-14
All-Ireland Club SHC Final
Croke Park
MARCH 17, 2016

Mike Casey and the Na Piarsaigh team celebrate being crowned champions of Ireland

★ **NA PIARSAIGH:** P Kennedy; **M Casey**, K Breen, K Kennedy; M Foley, C King, R Lynch (0-1); A Dempsey (0-4), W O'Donoghue (0-1); S Dowling (0-7), D Breen (0-2), D Dempsey; K Downes (1-2), A Breen (1-4), P Casey (0-3) **Subs:** K Ryan for D Breen, P Gleeson (0-1) for O'Donoghue.

★ **RUAIRÍ ÓG CUSHENDALL:** E Gillan; A Graffin, M Burke, R McCambridge; D Kearney, E Campbell (0-1), S Delargy; S McNaughton (0-4), A Delargy (0-1); C Carson (0-1), N McManus (1-7), D McNaughton; C McNaughton, S McAfee, P McGill **Subs:** P Burke for S Delargy, K McKeegan (1-0) for D McNaughton, A McNaughton for C McNaughton, E McKillop for Graffin.

★ GAME OF MY LIFE ★

THE ACTION

NA PIARSAIGH MADE history to become the first Limerick club to win an All-Ireland senior title, beating Ulster champions Ruairí Óg in a one-sided game in Croke Park.

Winning the coveted title with 11 points to spare, the Shane O'Neill managed Caherdavin side had the famous Tommy Moore Cup in the bag long before Diarmuid Kirwan sounded the final whistle. In truth, the game was a blow-out and over as a spectacle by the third quarter. But Na Piarsaigh, who had only won their first senior county title four years previously, didn't care. This was all about the result.

The Limerick champions overwhelmed their Antrim counterparts, striking a goal in the first minute as Adrian Breen settled any nerves the modern kingpins of hurling on Shannonside may have had, all while putting serious doubts into the heads of their opponents.

Thereafter, Na Piarsaigh spent much of the hour nursing a double-digit lead, and if it wasn't for an impressive tally of 1-7 from Antrim star Neil McManus, who scored half of Cushendall's return of 2-14, the scoreboard would have made for far worse reading.

Na Piarsaigh had opened up a five-point lead (1-4 to 0-2) inside 10 minutes. Four points without reply put clear daylight between the sides, before a coolly taken Kevin Downes' goal made it 2-10 to 0-3.

Na Piarsaigh held a 12-point lead at half-time. By the time the gap opened up to a whopping 15 points five minutes after the restart, the dream quickly became a reality for those in sky blue and white scattered throughout Croke Park. Not bad for a club founded just 48 years previously.

★★★★★

>

THE GAME FOR me… the All-Ireland Club final in 2016 is one that is definitely up there.

I hadn't really played with Limerick seniors yet, and that game definitely propelled me to putting my name on the door.

I don't massively look back at the 2018 All-Ireland final with fond memories, having been taken off injured. I know it is an unbelievable achievement, but on a personal level I wouldn't have been massively satisfied having been brought off so early.

I'd actually hold the 2022 All-Ireland win with Limerick a bit higher up, having come back after the last couple of years and being able to do what I did there. That would be up there more so than 2018, if I am being totally honest.

Looking back on it, that All-Ireland club final in 2016 is definitely one that stands out. Being able to look back at the past few years and having the heartache then two years later against Cuala, we kind of maybe took for granted the glory days that we had… the Munster club runs that we had, and seeing how Covid came in the way of another Munster club campaign in 2020. And then, a year later, injuries for myself and Peter came in the way of us trying to progress out of Limerick.

Because of that, the All-Ireland club final is definitely one that you look back on as one of your fondest days!

It was definitely the start of a golden era for the club.

We had two main groups of players at the club; you had the likes Kieran Breen and Dave Breen, and then you had the younger fellas… myself, David Dempsey and William O'Donoghue, all lads that were the same kind of age.

We had two different golden generations, perhaps. You had the first golden generation that won the first ever county championship for Na Piarsaigh, and then you had us coming through. At the time, it was about seeing if we could break through and do what the 2011 team had done in bringing the club forward… and we have definitely done that.

The game itself… it was a beautiful day in Croke Park. We actually got to go up to Croke Park two weeks before, and puck around on the field. That is definitely my fondest memory ever on a hurling field because it was the only time I've gone to Croke Park and I haven't been nervous… or we haven't had a semi-final or a final to play. We got to go up and have what was literally a training session for 45 minutes in probably one of the greatest stadiums in the world, which was just unbelievable.

It was such a surreal couple of years for the club. The club won its first Limerick Senior Hurling Championship in 2011 and here, less than five years later, we were heading to Croke Park for an All-Ireland senior club final.

It was such a quick turnaround. We didn't have the history that the likes of Kilmallock and Patrickswell had, but we knew the type of team that we were, that if we could get out of the county, we could cause major upsets. That was shown the very first year they got out in 2011 when they won Munster, before coming up against Loughgiel Shamrocks, who had massive experience. It was all learning curves at that stage.

At the time, it was very much the case of living in the moment, and producing performances that would write us into the history books. I didn't think of what went on in the past. It definitely took years for the club to get to that stage. A culture was starting to be created in the club.

Even in 2009, we lost our first senior county championship final. We lost every final that year. We were in everything from under-21s to minors… under-16s, and under-14s… so we knew the work was being done underage.

That is a big thing to keep the club ticking over. We know that now. We may have slacked off for a couple of years, and we could see some of our teams not performing at underage as they should have been in years gone by. That underage structure has definitely been put in place over the last couple of years and we can see that we are starting to reap the awards there again, contesting finals and winning finals, and getting underage players ready for that senior programme.

It is not a coincidence that so many great players came through at Na Piarsaigh around the same time. The Harty Cup success that was there, and the coaching that was done in Ardscoil Rís… the likes of Liam Kennedy from Na Piarsaigh putting in huge effort in Ardscoil Rís. It is all about your underage coaching, and making sure that you are coaching kids for the future. The fact that they are in our area means that we have access to some of the best coaches at schools' level, and that definitely helps bring on a club like Na Piarsaigh.

It was surreal to win a club All-Ireland at such a young age. I was only 20 at the time. You are kind of naive in a sense.

I think there was a sense of nativity there and a sense of fearlessness, especially when you are at that age and you are playing with everyone around you… when you've a really young side and you don't fear anything put out in front of you.

The last couple of years gives perspective and it means that you don't take things for granted anymore. From that moment on, you knew you should be challenging every year whether that is with Limerick or with Na Piarsaigh, because you know the quality that is in the county. It is just about tapping into that.

You go back to the Limerick circle… and you know the work that has gone in at underage level, and that's what it is all about.

Bringing the All-Ireland trophy back into the clubhouse, and the place being absolutely packed with your friends and your family, was just absolutely incredible. It genuinely feels that everybody in the club is part of your family. People say it is such a big club, but there is a small cohort of people that are there week-in, week-out, and training kids.

Some of those who trained you up along the way are the mothers and fathers of people you are after winning an All-Ireland club with… and bringing that cup back was definitely a moment I'll never forget. Cathal King had the cup up in his arms and the place erupted as we came in. That's definitely a moment that will always stick out.

It was my first year involved with the Limerick seniors, so we were back a week afterwards. We had done a small bit of pre-season work with Limerick, and with the All-Ireland run we were allowed back to the club. We played Dublin in a league quarter-final about two weeks later so the celebrations for the couple of days were incredible, but you don't be too long getting back to the grind after that.

To get to go on that run and play in an All-Ireland club final at such a young age is a huge learning curve. It was only the second time I played in Croke Park, and it is such a big occasion. We had the hurt of losing an All-Ireland semi-final to Loughgiel Shamrocks so we weren't taking anything for granted… you never do.

The early goal that Adrian Breen got after only a couple of seconds definitely settled us into the game. In the game itself, it is very hard to take things in and it is very rare you can think, *Yeah, this game is won*… especially in an All-Ireland final.

But, definitely, with four or five minutes to go when we had that nice cushion of being nine, 10, 11 points up, that was a moment when you realise you're after winning an All-Ireland club and you can take in the stadium… the beautiful day it was, and the emotion of it all.

Hurling in the city is continuing to grow as a result of the success. The city has such untapped talent.

You even see the likes of Gearóid Hegarty, someone from the city coming from a club like St Patrick's and he is getting Man of the Match awards, Hurler of the Year awards, and All Stars… that can only bring it on. The kids in the area, instead of having the soccer ball in the estate… they've now got their hurls and ball, which is just incredible.

To think that you are playing a part in that and you are a role model for kids around Limerick city is just unbelievable. Saying that, when you are in the middle of it all you don't really appreciate it, it is only afterwards that I think we will appreciate it.

When we were growing up in the city, we were competing with soccer, rugby, and all these other sports, more so than they are in county Limerick. It is difficult at times, but there has definitely been a shift in direction, especially with the numbers of kids that have started to come down to the club to play gaelic football and hurling.

You'd be very proud, that you've played a part in that.

When you are playing in All-Ireland finals, semi-finals, and Munster finals with Limerick and Na Piarsaigh you are definitely going to influence the kids that are nine, 10, 11 years of age, because at the time we were growing up rugby was so big. Munster had been going so well in 2006 and '08, but there is definitely a shift now. More kids around the place have hurleys and balls in their hands, especially around the city, which is excellent… and hopefully it will continue.

With Kilmallock getting to the All-Ireland final the year before, in 2014-15, it just showed with the club hurling scene that the players were there in Limerick, and we could go to Croke Park, and we could compete on these days against clubs from real traditional counties.

It meant that we knew that the talent was there, and it was about then trying to get over the line with a Limerick side in Croke Park, something which hadn't been done since 1973. It definitely gave other rising clubs the ambition to go and replicate that because when you were playing every year with the club, and playing against these lads who have done it… *Then why can't we?*

That definitely brings on players. Players know they are competing at the top level and whoever comes out of Limerick can compete. In 2021, Kilmallock lost in the Munster final to the eventual All-Ireland winners so you can see that the players are definitely there and it does stem from one club getting over the line to show that the talent is there in the county and we're not seventh or eighth down the line, like we had been for a long time.

Breaking into that Na Piarsaigh team, it was hard to imagine what would follow and what we'd go on to do with Limerick. Once we got over that line in 2018, then it becomes a habit. I know what has to be done now… and I know I need to improve on that again. It is kind of like the success we had with Na Piarsaigh, that when you get the belief from getting over the line, you are able to crack on from there.

The split season has been great. Last year was the first time we had a couple of weeks off. We had three or four weeks off in the middle of the club campaign, and you could go away and do things.

The emphasis has really been put back on the club… and it's not something that just has to be gotten out of the way. You can now really put a lot of time, effort, and commitment into it. That's our sole focus at the moment. It has never been anything but brilliant going back to the club, but we are really able to focus on it now with the split season.

I know from talking to players that it is something that has worked really, really well and a lot of people are definitely enjoying it. You are not going to suit everybody, you are not going to have the perfect blend. Some people say the All-Ireland finals are too early in the year, but from a players' point of view, you now have a little break. Before, you'd be rolling on from one year to another… to another.

When we were going well with Na Piarsaigh it was genuinely continuous there for a couple of years, where it would just roll on to another year… and then roll on to another year with no real break at all.

"

DAN MORRISSEY

LIMERICK 3-16 GALWAY 2-18
All-Ireland SHC Final
Croke Park
AUGUST 19, 2018

Tom and Dan Morrissey left the Liam MacCarthy Cup high into the air in 2018

★ **LIMERICK:** N Quaid; S Finn, M Casey, R English; D Byrnes (0-1), D Hannon (capt) (0-2), **D Morrissey**; D O'Donovan (0-1), C Lynch (0-1); G Hegarty, K Hayes (0-4), T Morrissey (1-1); A Gillane (0-3), S Flanagan (0-1), G Mulcahy (1-2). **Subs:** R McCarthy for M Casey, S Dowling (1-0) for Hegarty, P Casey for Flanagan, W O'Donoghue for O'Donovan, T Condon for English.

★ **GALWAY:** J Skehill; A Tuohy, D Burke (0-3), J Hanbury; P Mannion (0-1), G McInerney; A Harte; J Coen, D Burke (capt.); J Cooney (0-3), J Canning (1-10), J Glynn; C Whelan (1-0), C Cooney, C Mannion. **Subs:** N Burke (0-1) for C Mannion, P Killeen for Hanbury, J Flynn for C Cooney, S Loftus for Coen, F Flannery for Skehill.

THE ACTION

FORTY-FIVE YEARS OF heartbreak… officially over! Limerick survived a valiant comeback from Galway to banish the ghosts of five final defeats and win their first All-Ireland hurling title since 1973.

John Kiely's side were sharper from the get-go and led 1-10 to 0-9 at half-time, thanks to a goal from Graeme Mulcahy that somehow managed to scramble over the Galway goal-line.

By the time Tom Morrissey dispossessed Gearóid McInerney, before raising the green flag for Limerick's second goal in the 54th minute, the Treatymen were nine clear. Limerick eyes were smiling.

Galway had clawed Limerick's lead back to six with minutes to go, but when Peter Casey set up fellow substitute and Na Piarsaigh clubmate, Shane Dowling for Limerick's third goal, there was again eight between the sides with just two minutes of regular time to play. There were however gasps from the capacity crowd when eight minutes of stoppage time were announced, and Limerick stomachs began to somersault when Conor Whelan promptly rippled the net to make his first real impact on the game.

Just a five-point lead now and still over five minutes to play. Sound familiar? Those of a 1994 vintage certainly felt so. When Nickie Quaid stopped Joseph Cooney's goal-bound effort with his hand, Galway had a 20metres free that they had to go for. Canning stepped up and lashed it into the roof of the net. Just two points between them with three minutes to go.

Niall Burke cut the gap to one. Mulcahy popped up with his second point to give the Treaty men a crucial two-point cushion. Canning coolly slotted over a '65' but… a long free from the Portumna man with the last puck of the game fell short and Tom Condon cleared it to an outpouring of emotion not seen from a Limerick crowd in 45 years.

★★★★★

★ GAME OF MY LIFE ★

❝

I THOUGHT THAT day would never come!

I had been to every All-Ireland final since 1999. My dad brought me to my very first one... I was only six. Cork against Kilkenny. Every year since then I remember going up to Croke Park for the final and watching the teams in the parade. I was lucky enough to see Limerick there in 2007, but to be playing for your own county on All-Ireland final day was probably a far-off dream.

The build up to that game, and the whole summer was so unique that year. There was a new format. We had eight games in total. We nearly had a game every week or every second weekend. After winning the semi-final against Cork, we had a three week break to the final. The other semi-final went to a replay, so Galway only had two weeks. On a training camp two weeks before the All-Ireland final, we were watching the Galway and Clare game.

You don't know who you should be shouting for because you don't know who you'd rather want to play. Galway had been there before, so they were probably prepared for everything... getting your tickets, getting ready for the function that night, and just everybody talking about the game wanting to get a piece of you.

I was lucky enough in that I was studying for exams, so I was off work for those few weeks leading up to the final and I probably didn't have as many people talking to me about the game. Whereas, other lads working in offices, or out in public, were probably talking about the game 24/7, which probably wasn't ideal.

From the off – the Monday after the semi-final – we met up as a group and laid the plans for the next three weeks. We got all the small things out of the way in terms of what's going to happen, in terms of getting to the match – we were getting the train up that morning – and what's going to happen after the match in terms of where the function is on.

You get fitted for suits... and all that. That was all taken care of in those first couple of days after the semi-final. Then, in terms of tickets, everyone had to nominate someone from their family to look after the tickets, because the last thing the management wanted was players dealing with whatever amount of tickets we got and trying to distribute them to family members and friends.

Then, really for the two and half weeks before the All-Ireland final, all we had to concentrate on was training. Look, everyone is different. Some lads probably don't mind talking to someone for half an hour about an upcoming game, whereas others prefer to avoid any hurling talk. Everyone approached that final differently.

Personally, I really do like switching off when I am not training or playing matches. I don't want to be talking to every person about the match that just happened or an upcoming match, or how the other team are going, or what injuries the other team has, or what injuries our team has. I just personally like to try and avoid all that talk… you'd have your two or three lines rehearsed of what you are going to say and you are probably saying the same thing to every person you meet… not giving too much away and trying to change the subject as quickly as you can!

It was obviously huge for the club and for our family to have two members on the team.

Ahane is a proud club, going back into the 1930s with the Mackeys. I would have been playing with Tom the whole way up out the back when we were younger. But not in our wildest dreams did we think we'd be playing together on All-Ireland senior final day; especially when you are coming from Limerick and growing up you are just seeing the likes of Cork and Kilkenny being there on All-Ireland final day.

Seeing the crowds going up from Limerick on the day was just unbelievable. We got the train up from Limerick that morning. I think everybody preferred getting the train on the day, rather than going up the night before and staying in a hotel that you might not have stayed in before. It meant that we didn't have to put down a really long morning in Dublin; we got the train up in lovely comfort, and then a bus was there to pick us up and bring us to a hotel for the pre-match meal.

Literally, minute-by-minute, the schedule for the day was planned out for us. You knew when you were eating, and you knew you had a half an hour for relaxing when some lads might go for a 20-minute nap. Some lads might go for a rub down with a masseur or physio. Everyone had their different routines and we always aimed to be in the stadium one hour before throw-in. You then had 15 minutes to yourself… whether you wanted to go out and watch the minor game, or just listen to music in the dressing-room. I think routine is definitely one real important thing that was brought in.

Whether it is a league game, a championship game, an All-Ireland final, or a challenge game, you approach every game the same; you try and eat the same the day of the game at the same time in the same portions, and you try to get to bed at the same time. If you pack your bag the night before a game, you should do that consistently.

I think routine definitely added to the professionalism; just having everything there. You were never questioning why you were doing something, and you were never in need of something that wasn't there.

I think that discipline is something you develop from an early stage of life, because it is something that is very hard to just turn on all of a sudden. A majority of the team had played with the Limerick academy the whole way up from under-14s. There was always a sense of professionalism in those academies in terms of everything you do; preparation for games, and being on time.

I definitely think that when you are working full-time and training in between, it makes it easier compared to when you are at college, because you have more of a structure when you are working your 9am to half-five job. Whereas, those that are in college have summers off, and they might only have half-days in college and they are probably left without consistency and a routine.

When you look at all counties, whether it is hurling or football, they all put in the same amount of effort; and they nearly all train the same amount, so it is a lot easier for lads who know they have a chance of winning silverware. Whereas, I always admire lads from so-called weaker counties who train five or six days a week and maybe aren't getting the same reward.

I remember my first couple of years with Limerick… we were getting knocked out early. I was often questioning going back the following season for pre-season…Was it worth it?

Was it worth going back training in November for nine or 10 months of the year, and your chances of winning a Munster or an All-Ireland were quite slim?

But the last few years, when you know you have a great chance of winning… it makes the decision to go back the following year a lot easier.

My personal journey was purely down to hard work and believing in myself.

Everyone comes through different pathways from underage. A lot of players would have been on academies, but some lads wouldn't have been in academies and would have gone straight into a Limerick under-21 set-up. And you would have had lads who were on some very successful underage teams, whereas the underage teams I was on, although we had very good teams, we didn't win much silverware. I played two years minor and three years under-21, and we didn't get to any Munster final in any of those five years. Then I played a couple of years with the Limerick intermediate team as well. Through all those years, you are wondering is all the training really, really worth it?

I got the call into the senior panel in 2014, but there were times when you were wondering would you actually make it as a senior inter-county hurler. Even at the start of 2017, when John Kiely came in, you were wondering where you stood and where your career was going?

That day against Galway in 2018 was just a mad feeling!

I can remember the parade and trying to avoid looking into the crowd, and just focusing on the player walking in front of me. But when you see and hear the flags and the flares all around the stadium, and you look up into the stadium, it would be hard not to notice everything that is going on… and get a feeling of how big an occasion you are playing in.

The game itself went by very quickly. I know we were in a good position at half-time, and a few minutes to go when we got our third goal a part of your head was saying, *This is our day… we are going to win!* But Galway came back. When they brought it back to a point, people were thinking of the 1994 All-Ireland and was this another one that Limerick were going to throw away. That did cross my mind.

I was thinking, *We can't lose this.*

When that final whistle went it was just a mix of so many different emotions. You just really don't know what to do when the referee blows that whistle!

Even looking at videos today of the day after, when we came back to Limerick, still lifts the hair on the back of my neck, especially seeing the crowds and what it meant to everyone. I remember well getting the train down and getting back into Colbert Station, seeing the crowd there, and The Cranberries ringing over the loudspeakers. And then the bus tour around the city and over to the Gaelic Grounds… just amazing!

You had people who would have never really followed hurling or never followed Limerick… all out on the street. It really lifted the city.

When you see the buzz it gives everyone… even when they touch the Liam

MacCarthy Cup, and you can see how much it means to them. Forty-five years is such a long time to wait, given how big a hurling county Limerick is. Bringing the cup to all the primary schools and trying to inspire the next generation is what it is all about!

I remember in 1998/99, when Ahane won the county title, they brought the trophy back to the local primary schools. I was very young at the time, and I still remember it very well. Every single primary and secondary school had a chance to get the trophy in those four or five months after the All-Ireland in 2018, so it was definitely in big demand!

There are a few games that stick out in early 2018 that gave us belief!

The league game against Galway to win promotion up to Division 1A above in Salthill was a big one given that they were All-Ireland champions at the time. We were a good bit down at half-time and came back, and won by a point or two. That gave us huge belief because Limerick had been in the second division of the league for seven or eight years.

Our Munster campaign then was solid in terms of getting the wins. We beat Tipp and Waterford, and drew with Cork, but then our final game against Clare, where we got a heavy enough beating below in Ennis, that nearly put us back to square one. We were wondering where did we stand?

I think that quarter-final against Kilkenny really showed that we had taken a big step forward, that we were able to compete with the top sides; especially the way we got over the line to get a win after they got a late goal to come back… and outscore them by five points to one in the last few minutes.

Limerick hadn't beaten Kilkenny in Championship in 45 years. It really gave us belief that we were able to compete with the top sides! The second All-Ireland win then in 2020 really cemented us in the history books! It is not like any team can win an All-Ireland, but you really do want to get a second one for it to really prove that the first year was no fluke.

The last five years have been absolutely unreal for Limerick hurling, something not many supporters would have really thought possible! Even going back as far as the start of 2018, not many people would have had Limerick in the top six or seven teams in the country, so for us to be consistently competing for All-Irelands for the last five years has just been unreal!

There is so much of the celebrations in 2018 that you will always remember… whether it is JP McManus coming into the dressing-room and seeing how much it meant to him; that was huge for us because the McManus family have been so good to Limerick GAA down through the years without too much success on the field.

To be able to give that success, particularly in 2018, was just amazing.

I can remember the sing-song we had inside in the dressing-room that went on for probably the bones of two hours after the final. Those few hours are just really special… spending it with and enjoying the celebrations with everyone that was involved! It makes all those tough training sessions out in Rathkeale, and all those pre-season nights in the rain and cold, all worth it!

I've got to travel the world with hurling over the last five years. That's a real big bonus when you get these trips. It's great in terms of the memories. It is not always the memories that people think will be the memories, that you remember the most.

Growing up, it all starts with your parents! My parents were very good in terms of bringing me to training and to games. We would have gone to every Limerick game when I was growing up, supporting the Limerick hurlers… whether it was under-21 or senior.

And then my teachers in school, my principal in Lisnagry National School, Paul Kennedy had a big influence on me starting off. We played an awful lot of hurling in primary school.

And then your club… you are nothing without your club! We always had strong hurling people growing up in Ahane. It is always very good when your club has a representative on the Limerick senior hurling team that you can look up to, and thankfully in Ahane when we were growing up, we always had players on the Limerick team and they really inspired us.

And now, hopefully, we are inspiring some of the younger people in the parish!

99

SEÁN FINN

LIMERICK 3-32 CORK 1-22
All-Ireland SHC Final
Croke Park
AUGUST 22, 2021

Seán Finn in typical defiant pose against Cork in the 2021 All-Ireland final

★ **LIMERICK:** N Quaid; **S Finn**, D Morrissey, B Nash (0-1); D Byrnes (0-2), D Hannon (capt) (0-2), K Hayes; W O'Donoghue, D O'Donovan (0-1); G Hegarty (2-2), C Lynch (0-6); T Morrissey (0-3); A Gillane (1-6), S Flanagan (0-1), P Casey (0-5). **Subs:** C Coughlan for Hannon, G Mulcahy (0-1) for Casey, B Murphy for Mulcahy, D Reidy (0-1) for Hegarty, P Ryan (0-1) for T Morrissey.

★ **CORK:** P Collins; N O'Leary (0-1), R Downey, S O'Donoghue; T O'Mahony; M Coleman (0-1), E Cadogan; D Fitzgibbon, L Meade (0-1); C Cahalane, S Harnedy (0-4), R O'Flynn; J O'Connor (0-1), P Horgan (0-12), S Kingston (1-0). **Subs:** S O'Leary-Hayes for O'Leary, D Cahalane for C Cahalane, N Cashman for O'Donoghue, A Cadogan (0-1) for O'Connor, S Barrett (0-1) for Fitzgibbon, D Dalton for O'Flynn.

THE ACTION

LIMERICK OBLITERATED CORK in the first-half to win their third All-Ireland SHC title in four years, scoring a whopping 3-18 in the opening 35 minutes, a tally that would have been enough to win the majority of previous All-Ireland finals.

From 1990 to 2008, only one team scored more than 3-18 in an All-Ireland final. On August 22, 2018, Limerick scored that in one half in what was a sensational performance that truly was the stuff of legends.

Due to Covid-19 restrictions, the attendance was at 50%, albeit when Cian Lynch danced through the Cork defence before jinking away from Robert Downey to set up the incoming Gearóid Hegarty for Limerick's opening goal inside two minutes, those watching on might have imagined a sell-out, such was the noise from game-starved spectators.

Cork tails weren't down for too long, however, as Shane Kingston replied two minutes later with a goal for the Leesiders, cutting in from the left before shooting high to the net.

In the 15th minute, Aaron Gillane scored a second goal for Limerick with a low shot to the right corner after a pass from Seamus Flanagan to make it 2-5 to 1-5. By the time Hegarty had got his second and a third goal for the Shannonsiders on the verge of half-time, Limerick were ahead by 13 points.

Limerick continued to keep Cork at bay in the second-half and outscored their arch-rivals by 14 points to 11 in the final 35 minutes to win the game with 16 points to spare and retain the Liam MacCarthy Cup – their first time winning back-to-back All-Ireland titles.

★★★★★

>

IF I LOOK back on it now, in 2023, it was probably the most enjoyable summer that we've had in years. The weather was good, and myself, Gearóid Hegarty and David Reidy, and our girlfriends, were all living together as well… and just down the road in Castletroy, there were six other players living together, and every day we were meeting up for coffee.

Funnily enough, when we were meeting up there was no talk about hurling, but when we came back from training, before we'd go to bed, we'd have a cup of tea and we'd all be talking about who was going well and who wasn't going well.

I think we were playing some really good hurling during that championship as well, especially off the back of the 2020 campaign when there were no crowds at games. It was exciting to get crowds back.

We played Cork in Thurles the first day out in the Munster semi-final. We struggled that day… we barely got over the line, but as the games went on, we got better and better. The 2021 Munster final was in Páirc Uí Chaoimh against Tipperary. That led us then into the All-Ireland semi-final against Waterford. When I look back on the 2021 All-Ireland final, a lot of the talk coming up to the game was about how good Cork were. When it comes to Cork, you just don't want to lose to them. That was the biggest fear.

As for the game itself, as of now it could arguably be the best performance we've ever put in. You know you're going well going into a game. I remember saying to my father that we'll win by six or seven points, but you could never see us winning by the margin that we did… we nearly had it won by half-time.

We got a goal early on, and Cork responded with a goal. I thought, *This is going to be score for score here.* I could not believe the score we had put up by half-time… 3-18 in the first-half. You are sitting in the dressing-room and we were trying to tell ourselves that the game wasn't over, that we need to go out and do more in the second-half.

The Munster final against Tipp… we couldn't see ourselves losing that. Players often think about what they are going to do after the game. As much as you don't want to think about it, fellas are so excited to go out after the game because they might not have been out for a couple of months.

'Will we go here... will we go there?'

But then after 15 to 20 minutes, when Tipp got two goals in the first-half, you are like... *Did we talk about it too much?* ... even though we'd have been doing that for years. We went in at half-time 10 points down, albeit still playing alright. We just got punished badly on two particular incidents on their puckouts.

We all speak highly of Pat Ryan, and there was this great moment of him coming into the dressing-room and talking about just keep chopping at the tree.

'Keep chopping, chopping... and chopping, and these boys will fall'.

He was a sub at the time, so for him to come in and say that really powerful speech was excellent. Because Pat is a great speaker and thinks about the game differently. When he came in and spoke for five or six minutes, it really got fellas going. It wasn't that we were playing poorly... we were playing well, we just needed to continue to do what we were doing. Sure, in the first 15 minutes of that second-half, we pulled four points clear after being 10 points down.

The year sort of took off from that.

The build-up to the All-Ireland final that year was all about Cork.

It was just about how good they were, and all about their running game. I remember it quite clearly, before that game John Kiely spoke in the dressing-room and he was hyped up... and he was roaring at lads, like he would do. But he would pick and choose when he does those moments. He wouldn't be roaring at the team before every game.

A lot of the time he'd nearly have to calm the team down, and you'd be very calm going out. But this time, he'd heard the noise and they were talking about how well Cork can run the ball, and he says, 'Can we f***ing run the ball?'

'They are talking about Cork getting goals... we are going to be the ones to get the goals today,' he commanded. I remember so clearly him saying that, and then at half-time having three goals scored...it was very strange, but, obviously, we were quite delighted.

It was an unbelievable feeling to win it. You are going up to Croke Park and a lot of the time you'd be trying to convince yourself that you need to try and enjoy it. But it is very hard to enjoy an All-Ireland final, to just relax or chill out, because there is just so much pressure, especially after the couple of years we had.

Having been so far up in the game – and this is why I picked this moment in particular – you could actually enjoy the second-half for what it was. You could relax… you could look to be on the ball, and nearly take your time on the ball. It was that comfortable.

You could speak to any of the players now… we are as good a team to celebrate and enjoy ourselves as we are on the hurling field… it is encouraged quite a lot. The management understand the mental strain that is on lads and the pressure people are under, so it is important to just let loose for a couple of days, whether it be after a Munster final or an All-Ireland final.

Funnily enough, after the semi-final in 2021… we played on the Saturday night and Cork and Kilkenny were playing on the Sunday. Covid was around at the time. Typically, we'd drink cans on the way home on the train and we'd have a few drinks in the dressing-room. That is one of the most enjoyable times, when you have the music on, having a few drinks, and then you are going to the train and coming home.

The year that was in it, it was a public train we were on and they weren't keen on us having a few drinks together. So, they just said, 'Lads, go home tonight. If ye want to have a few bottles of beer at your own house do so, but there is a bar open in the Woodlands in Adare tomorrow for ye. Go out there and watch the other semi-final… and enjoy your afternoon. Have a few drinks and a bit of dinner'.

We went down on the train anyway, and we went back to the house I was living in with Gearóid and Dave. We might have had one or two bottles of beer, but we were tired at the time so we said we'd get up in the morning, do our recovery… and we'll go to the Woodlands for half two.

People talk about drink bans, but here we were two weeks out from an All-Ireland final. All the team went out to the Woodlands. We watched the semi-final… drinking away a few pints.

The minute the match finished, the TV was turned off. We didn't watch the celebrations. It was kind of a shifted focus as well, but we still went on to stay out.

We recovered for a few days after that and we went in training then on the Wednesday. In fairness, the management are great to allow us to do that. They understand the importance of relaxing and enjoying each other's company. To be allowed to do that, allows us to keep doing what we are doing as a team. The proof is in the pudding.

Sometimes, it can be hard because you are so focused on recovery, you are so focused on wanting to get ready for the next training session, that you spend so much time not switching off… and that's mentally draining. With the campaign being so long, and with us being on the road so long, we do need to come down off that high and relax. It is something we've learnt over the years. Some lads would be better at it than others, but I do think the longevity of the group has a lot got to do with being able to switch off and enjoy ourselves.

If you were a supporter coming onto the train going up to that All-Ireland final against Cork, you'd think we were a bunch of supporters going up as well… there was so much noise and energy going up on the train. There were board games going on; some lads were listening to music, and other lads were playing cards. There was a bit of slagging and a bit of craic on the way up.

Even an hour before the game, there was good craic, but people begin to focus 45 minutes out in the dressing-room. There would be a lot of nerves, especially when it was Cork. You just did not want to lose to them. Having to accept losing to Cork in that final, especially when we knew we were the better team and how well we were going, would have been tough. To leave it behind would be a huge regret because it would have been a missed opportunity.

Knowing that we were the better team put a lot of pressure on us.

The parade was enjoyable. I enjoyed the warm-up. The first five minutes were hectic. Shane Kingston got a goal quite early. Arguably, I could have done a bit better on it. But we responded. Peter Casey got a point within 20 seconds of that goal… and it just took off!

From the very first minute, we just weren't losing that game.

I couldn't believe the space Gearóid was getting that day against Cork, or even when the ball went across to Seámus Flanagan for the goal Aaron Gillane got. The ball went into the corner. Seámus Flanagan got the ball in 20 yards of space, gave it across to Aaron who was in 12 yards of space… and he just buried it from the '21'. That's unseen stuff!

That came from our own puckout. There were something like four passes before Aaron got the goal. I couldn't understand how there was so much space.

And then Gearóid, when he got the goal, how he ended up in that space on the '21'… you can see it unfolding. You'd be so proud of lads when they are producing big moments in games.

I am doing my job in the full-back line but I can see it all unfold in front of me. You'd just be so delighted for lads. Cian Lynch had an exceptional day that day.

You'd have a lot of conversations with Nickie in the goals about who is going well.

'Aaron is flying it, isn't he?'

You'd be doing it throughout the game, maybe to settle down and relax. You'd ask Nickie what he thought was working for us on puckouts. He has a great way of looking at the game. He never really gets too carried away either. He is very level-headed. He has stats coming in then at half-time from Seanie O'Donnell on puckout retention, where it is working, and whether to go short or long? He'd advise you whether you need to go short or wide… or if we need to play it through the lines.

The day before the game, myself and Gearóid were unusually anxious.

I'd often ask him, 'Will we win this game?' I'd know the answer myself, but I just wanted to get his thoughts.

He'd often say, 'No doubt about it!'

We said the same thing for Cork, but I didn't really hear the confidence in his voice when he was saying, 'Yeah, we'll bate them'. But, the morning of it, we were absolutely buzzing. We couldn't wait to get out the door. We had the train at half nine. We were up early, having a bit of breakfast, and we'd have the music blaring at half eight in the morning.

We would have briefly spoken about how great it would be to get a goal in an All-Ireland final, and what the buzz would be like… so just to see him doing it on the day was unbelievable. He is such a big-game player. Some days he doesn't play well but he produces big moments.

He actually didn't have a good game in the Munster final against Clare in 2022, but he got one of the goals of the championship. But the performance he put in against Kilkenny in the All-Ireland final that year was very good, as was his performance in the All-Ireland final in 2020.

He just produces big moments and special moments that will appear on reels for years to come, no different from Cian Lynch, Aaron Gillane, Diarmaid Byrnes, and Declan Hannon… all those lads produce big moments at particular times. If it is not Gearóid, it is going to be someone else like Diarmaid stepping up for a big moment for frees or catching puckouts.

When you do see those lads producing those moments, considering you are so close to them and when you know that they've spoken about these things, to see them do it is quite special.

We knew we were the best team in the country in 2021.

We were training so well. With the calibre of player we had, we knew we were the best. The fear of losing to a team that wasn't as good as us was the biggest pressure.

It is like any of the games we've been playing over the last number of years, if we perform to our ability, we win games. It is as simple as that. There is no other team that is able to deal with us, but there is always that concern that if we have an off day, like in 2019, you are going to be caught. The margins are very close.

The perception is that we are much better than others, and we're not! It is just when we perform, we tend to continually perform and that's the difference.

It is speculation to say that if we hadn't lost to Kilkenny in 2019, that we wouldn't have come back and done what we did in the years since. That game just passed every single one of us by. We had 22 wides the same day. We would never blame the last sideline incident. You don't deserve to win games when you have that many wides and that many missed chances. We never ever referred to it to be honest.

It was just a day that went by so quickly. I can't remember a moment of it other than being booked early on and I was under pressure for the rest of the game. Outside of that, I don't remember much of it.

The only other time that has happened to me before that was the All-Ireland minor final of 2014. The game just passed by… it is over before you know it. You learn from it too because oftentimes you'd be in a game and you'd think, *This is passing me by… and you can refer to those moments and say, I need to do something here.*

The team as a whole will acknowledge times like that.

Relax, we need to do something here.

We probably learned a lot more from the Kilkenny game, and arguably it was one of the most important lessons of the last five or six years, but it is speculation to say what happened afterwards was as a result of that loss.

I remember growing up, I was going to games across the county, going to training and my dad would have been coaching teams that I would have been training with, as well as going to camps. I always had a hurley in my hand, whether it was going up to the field, going around the town, or going to matches. I was always surrounded by it.

Was it something that I felt I needed to do? No. But I grew up with it, so naturally enough I went towards playing hurling. There were ups and downs when I was growing up. I was on 'B' teams and I was p****d off. I used to hate going back to Rathkeale every so often on a Tuesday and a Thursday. I wanted to spend time relaxing around home and chilling out the hurling field with the lads. That was much easier than going out to Rathkeale and training for two hours, but, in fairness, I remember dad packed my bag one day, collected me from the hurling field, and brought me to training.

I wasn't going to go. I didn't want to go.

Those were all important times as well. But once you were in that academy, inside in Limerick, you felt a part of something and it nearly becomes your identity. When you are under-16 you are looking forward to see if you can make the minor team, and when you are minor you are thinking, *Will I make the under-21 team?*

And then, when you are playing under-21s you are saying, *Will I get a call up to the senior team?* Next thing, you are in there. Once you are in there, you are always looking forward to seeing what's the next chapter… what you are going to do next. It has been some journey since 2018… unreal! John Kiely said it after 2018, 'Your lives are changed… 100 percent. No doubt about it'. With that comes responsibility as well. You have to behave in a manner that you'd be proud of. It has been unbelievable. We've been so lucky. The margins are so tight, yet there is such a difference between the teams that win and lose… and then the benefits for those who win. You get holidays, you get attention, and you get endorsements. The holidays are extraordinarily… and the memories that you make! And that only brings your team closer together as well. You get to travel the world for free through the GAA. I've got to go to some really special places. If you don't win an All-Ireland, you don't get those chances.

As you get older, you do acknowledge how significant this is and how lucky we are to be part of a special team. Teams don't have what we have internally as well, the bond we have and the craic we have. We are very, very fortunate. Credit has to go to the management for that as well, as well as the character of the players.

We are very lucky.

There is always a sense of relief when you win a final.

Even in 2018, there was a sense of relief. You are absolutely buzzing but there is always a sense of relief because you do put pressure on yourself.

As a player you are more relieved, but as a supporter you are absolutely buzzing – you are jumping around the place. But as players you are thinking, *Thank God that is over!* It is kind of hard to enjoy it.

The feeling in 2021 was satisfaction because the performance was so good. Okay, you were relieved, but you were so satisfied that you got the best performance, arguably, in an All-Ireland final on the biggest stage. That was the underlying feeling in 2021, how satisfactory it was to get that performance.

I remember just chilling out in the dressing-room afterwards with Westlife playing, and lads drinking and dancing. That hour and a half inside in the room is just so special when you know outside of those four walls there is absolutely mayhem going on down in Limerick. You know that inside in those four walls you are sheltered from that, but you know what is coming down the line. You know that the next week is going to be carnage. But for that hour and a half inside in the room, you're protected from all the noise, and it is just ourselves… and we can reflect on what we've done over the last two hours.

JP McManus coming in is always a great moment, because of the respect we have for him and what he has done and how proud he is of Limerick hurling. John Cregan opening a bottle of champagne and singing songs… that hour and a half is just something else.

It is something that, when it is over then, is always on the back of your mind… *Will I ever get that moment again? Will I ever feel that joy again? Will I ever be up in Croke Park playing in an All-Ireland final again… get to feel that feeling again?*

That keeps fellas going. The more you have it, the more you crave it.

I don't see it fading anytime soon.

"